The German Economy at War

by

ALAN S. MILWARD

UNIVERSITY OF LONDON
THE ATHLONE PRESS
1965

Published by

THE ATHLONE PRESS
UNIVERSITY OF LONDON
at 2 Gower Street, London WC1

Distributed by Constable & Co Ltd
12 Orange Street, London WC2

Canada
Oxford University Press
Toronto

U.S.A.
Oxford University Press Inc
New York

Printed in Great Britain by
WESTERN PRINTING SERVICES LTD
BRISTOL

PREFACE

MY INTENTION in writing this book was to make a study of the turning-points in Germany's economic strategy in the Second World War. I have also tried to give the beginnings of a history of German war production and its administration, and to set it in its strategic and political background. The book has drawn very heavily upon largely unexplored and unpublished material, in particular the records of the *Reichsministerium für Bewaffnung und Munition*, and those of the *Wirtschafts- und Rüstungsamt* of *Oberkommando der Wehrmacht*.

However, the book is not a comprehensive history of German war production to serve as a counterpart of the United Kingdom Official History of the Second World War, Civil Series. There are still too many serious gaps in our documentary knowledge of the German economy from 1939 to 1945 to attempt this. There is insufficient material on German naval production, and, for the earlier periods, on aircraft production. Many financial aspects of the German economy remain in considerable obscurity from 1940 onwards. Because of these gaps I have tried not to be too ambitious and to confine my subject to 'war production' except where it sometimes seemed reasonable to generalize about the economy as a whole. Since I have confined my subject in this way I have not included statistical material which can be found elsewhere, except where it was necessary to support my argument. If I have diverged too often into politics and personalities I beg the reader's forgiveness, but it seemed to me that the political framework in which the economy of National Socialist Germany operated was extremely important.

Without the kindness and co-operation of the Air Historical Branch of the Air Ministry, and in particular that of Mr L. Jackets, this book could, quite certainly, not have been written. I would like to thank the Air Ministry for permission to work in their archives. Apart from the mere permission, room to work in, and constant help in many small, but important, matters were all indispensable. Mr. Jackets's knowledge of the subject and his kindness have guided more people than myself in this field. Mr. P. K. Lickfold, Mr. G. Gately, and the late Mr. N. Low, never failed to provide help, even at the most inconvenient times, over a long period of research. To the whole Branch I would now like to record formally my gratitude.

The University of London provided me for two years with a research grant which enabled me to do the larger part of the research. The Edinburgh University Library has obtained books and documents for me, and for this I would like to thank the Librarian, Mr. E. R. S. Fifoot. I would also like to thank Mr. B. Melland, Mr. E. Robertson, and Mr. E. Williams.

But my greatest debt by far is to Professor W. N. Medlicott. No one could conceivably have given me better advice, nor been more patient, more kind, and more willing to help in every difficulty. Such thanks as I can record here are utterly inadequate to repay him. I am only sorry that this book, the faults of which are all my own, is not a better tribute to his initial encouragement and to his splendid help.

A.S.M.

CONTENTS

ABBREVIATIONS

'tons' is used throughout to mean 'metric tons'.

HWA	Heereswaffenamt
N.D.	Nürnberg Document
OKH	Oberkommando des Heeres
OKM	Oberkommando der Marine
OKW	Oberkommando der Wehrmacht
U.S.S.B.S.	United States Strategic Bombing Survey
WiRüAmt	Wirtschafts- und Rüstungsamt

CHAPTER I

The Concept of the Blitzkrieg

ALMOST all Germany's possible opponents before September 1939 supposed that Germany was fully prepared for war. More than this, they thought that since the seizure of power by the National Socialist Party the German economy had been consciously directed towards the purpose of waging war. Accordingly they also thought that at the outbreak of war in 1939 Germany had a considerable lead over other powers in the development of a full war economy.

It was on such assumptions about the enemy that, for instance, a great deal of Allied economic planning was undertaken. Convictions that the United Kingdom had a long way to go before she could catch up with Germany in war production probably played their part in the fortunate decision in 1939 to concentrate on future war potential, to bank on a long war and to gear the economy accordingly. Even as late as 1942 the Ministry of Economic Warfare believed that the peak of German armaments production had been reached in 1941, and that from 1939, at the latest, Germany had been fully committed to an all-out war.

Like an army in the later stages of a battle, Germany's economic resources are wholly mobilized and wholly engaged. They cannot be much further developed or differently employed until the strain on them has been relieved by victory or ended by defeat.[1]

Such was the opinion of the Ministry's half-yearly survey of the economic position of German Europe in June 1942. Nothing could have been further from the truth. But Germany's opponents had every justification for their belief in such myths.

In the first place almost every economist of any calibre had

---

[1] Quoted by W. N. Medlicott, *The Economic Blockade*, ii, 7.

been telling the world for years past that Germany's economy had ultimate military success as one of its main ends. This opinion was also held by many journalists and pamphleteers of all shades of political opinion, especially by political refugees from Germany itself. Germany was believed to have solved her domestic problems, due to international economic difficulties, by the development of a very nationalistic, inherently 'selfish', domestic economy. Unemployment, the curse of all the highly-developed capitalist countries from 1921 onwards, had been eliminated in the Third Reich by a widespread programme of public works, in particular road-building, and by an expanded programme of rearmament, allied to conscription.

It is undoubtedly true that the positive public policies of the National Socialist State went a long way towards eliminating unemployment. The direct control of investment and of foreign trade were very much more important in this way, however, than the creation of an armaments industry with a relatively high production capacity.

There were one or two writers, on a semi-popular level, who pointed out that the picture of Germany's economy as a war economy in peace-time was a false interpretation. Their common fate was to be ignored by the reading public. Sternberg,[1] for instance, pointed out that the German economy would suffice for a short war, that it was, indeed, prepared for a short war, but that its development from 1934 onwards indicated that Hitler, however much he might be looking for a short war, wished to avoid a properly planned war economy. But the public in France, the United Kingdom, and the United States preferred to believe in the picture of a monolithic, militaristic, highly-efficient, economic machine in Germany. And these beliefs were whole-heartedly shared by most of the statesmen they elected to office.

Such beliefs were lent great strength by the bellicose foreign policy which Hitler pursued. He appeared perfectly ready to risk war, even in 1936, over the occupation of the Rhineland. We are wiser after the event and know that in terms of military strength Hitler's reoccupation of the Rhineland was in many ways a clever diplomatic bluff. But the Anschluss with Austria,

---

[1] F. Sternberg, *Die Deutsche Kriegsstärke*.

the occupation of the Sudetenland, and then of Bohemia and Moravia all took on the appearance of overt military threats. It was the last of these aggressions that finally convinced the British government that its hopes of resistance could only be pinned on a long effort to catch up with German levels of armament. This apparent readiness on Hitler's part to risk war increased further the illusions about the nature of Germany's preparations for war.

Not only in his foreign policy did Hitler give the impression of being ready for war but in his domestic policy too. The public announcements surrounding the promulgation of the Four-Year-Plan on 9 September 1936 gave it the semblance of a plan for war. Göring was given the overall direction of the Plan and the memorandum to him by Hitler would seem to leave no doubt of Hitler's desire to open full-scale war at some point in the future. The German economy was apparently to be prepared for exactly this eventuality. In four years' time the German Army was to be ready to fight and the German economy to back it up. But as with most of the Führer's decrees, it is as well to examine what was done rather than what was said.

The Four-Year-Plan had two contrasting sets of objectives: one was military and economic, the other was political. In one aspect the plan was intended to lessen Germany's dependence on foreign countries for many of her raw materials, in particular iron ore, oil, and rubber. In any future war this was likely to be one of the most vulnerable spots in the German economy. From the other aspect the Four-Year-Plan was designed to strengthen the control of the National Socialist Party over German industry. These aspects were often incompatible. Both aspects were suitably crystallized in the most lasting monument of the Four-Year-Plan—the huge Hermann Göring works rambling across the Brunswick plain.

The Hermann Göring works were built to exploit the low-grade iron ores of the Salzgitter area. There had always been substantial reserves of unexploited iron ore, of about 30 per cent iron content, in the Hanover area. The motive to exploit such ores was much increased after the Treaty of Versailles when Germany was obliged to surrender the Lorraine ore fields to France. But it was less costly to manufacture steel from the higher-grade Swedish ores, and iron-ore imports from Sweden came, after 1918, to be one of the most important parts of Germany's foreign trade. To try to eliminate this strategic weakness Hitler decided to increase Germany's steel output by the exploitation of domestic ores, even though manufacture from such ores would require special plant. The money for this project was provided by the government and Göring owed some part of his personal fortune to the works at Salzgitter and Wattenstedt. Had the objectives of the Four-Year-Plan been purely military and strategic it might have paid better to overhaul existing steel plant by a deliberate capital investment policy spread throughout the industry. The leading steel firms had hoped this would happen. But the Hermann Göring works were a monument to the Third Reich. Dr. Walter Rohland, an official of the Ministry of Armaments, and a former director of a steel works, put the situation succinctly when interrogated after the war by the Allies.

With things as they are to-day, it can be said that the German steel industry could have produced more and better steel if the Hermann Göring works had never been founded.[1]

His conclusion was patently correct. Even during the war Germany still depended on Sweden for about ten million tons of iron ore a year. Germany suffered throughout the war from bottlenecks in the production of high-quality steel, bottlenecks which might have been widened if more capital had been put into the existing plant instead of into a completely new enterprise. Nevertheless, to observers from the outside the Four-Year-Plan gave the impression of being a conscious programme of public investment to equip the German economy for war. It was, at any rate, interpreted as such by all foreign economists.

Finally, German propaganda succeeded splendidly in reinforcing these illusions. The outward semblance of the German State, as, for instance, at the annual Party rally at Nürnberg, was highly militaristic. The small Air Force and Navy were constantly on public display. There was a proliferation of uniform-bearing para-military organizations, and Hitler himself wore

[1] Speer Report No. 98, 'replies by Dr. W. Rohland'.

Commander-in-Chief's uniform. Doubtless these factors go some way to explaining why Hitler's quite false statement that he had spent 90 billion reichsmarks on rearmament was believed so readily.[1] Faced, therefore, by a unanimity of popular and informed opinion, and by the observations of their own eyes, people came to an incorrect view of Germany's economic situation before the war.

The first steps towards grasping the truth about Germany's pre-war economy were taken by the United States Strategic Bombing Survey. This was a team of economists flown out from the United States and given every facility for investigating such archival materials on the German economy as had survived. They were also allowed to interrogate personnel who had been concerned with the administration of the German economy in war-time. Primarily the task of the Survey was to determine what effect the Strategic Air Offensive had had on the German economy. And it was to answering this question that their main efforts were directed. Consequently this led them to neglect many of the most interesting developments of the earlier periods of the war. As a study of the closing years of the National Socialist régime, however, the work of the United States Strategic Bombing Survey is unsurpassed in detail and depth. Many of its reports were at first classified as secret material, but much is now available to the public.[2]

Kaldor[3] and Klein[4] both published some of the Bombing Survey's information and conclusions shortly after the war. These conclusions, fortified by the evidence from interrogated German prisoners of ministerial rank, whose opinions were widely disseminated, especially by the War Crimes Tribunal, led to a thorough-going reappraisal of Germany's economic planning for war. In his book, *Germany's Economic Preparations for War*, Klein has published a fuller version of the information on

[1] Address by A. Hitler before the Reichstag, 1 September 1939, J. W. Gantenbein, *Documentary Background of World War II, 1931–41*, p. 713.

[2] In the European Theatre Nos. 4, 60, 64, 93, 95–99, 134B to 199 (except 138, 139 and 188) are classified as secret. In the Pacific Theatre Nos. 78, 91, 94, 95, 98–105, and 108 are classified.

[3] N. Kaldor, 'The German War Economy', *The Review of Economic Studies*, xiii (1945–46).

[4] B. H. Klein, 'Germany's Preparation for War, a Re-examination', *American Economic Review* (1948).

which this rethinking was based.[1] Klein was himself a member of the Strategic Bombing Survey.

The picture which these works present of the National Socialist economy is a much more realistic one. Germany, to use the phrase of the Bombing Survey, before the war was geared to 'armament in width' rather than to 'armament in depth'. She had organized her economy to maintain a relatively high level of ready armaments, but had not undertaken the basic investment and redevelopment necessary to produce the level of armaments sufficient to bring success in a war against the greater mass-productive powers. She had a high degree of armament readiness, but a low degree of armaments-producing potential. Her interest was in the production of ready armaments but not in increasing her armaments-producing plant and re-tooling her armaments-producing machinery. 'Guns *and* butter' was Hitler's aim.

Furthermore, once the United Kingdom, for instance, began to commit the whole of her resources, and even allowing for the fact that much of her investment was in potential armaments at three or four years' distance, she very quickly caught up with German levels of production. At the beginning of the war German and British aircraft production rates were running at about the same monthly level, and tanks were being produced in greater numbers by Britain.[2] Of course, Germany had a considerable lead since she had been pursuing a limited policy of rearmament for much longer. But in September 1939 Germany had not yet ventured on the basic reorganization of her economy which the war would eventually entail, whereas Britain had.

Therefore, the German economy, far from being at full stretch in 1941, as the Ministry of Economic Warfare, and Allied propaganda, so fondly supposed, was operating with a vast supply of as yet untapped reserves. Consequently the undeniable evidence of increasing armaments production by Germany in 1943 and 1944 ran counter to all Allied views of the German situation. This evidence came, in fact, as a very nasty shock to Allied opinion. Such increases of production were always open to Germany once she had decided to organize a full war

[1] Harvard University Press, Cambridge, Mass., 1959.
[2] B. H. Klein, op. cit., p. 6.

economy, and they were achieved with startling success. But such a reorganization was infinitely more difficult to achieve in the face of unceasing everyday demands of warfare on the economy than it would have been in peace time.

Why did Germany not organize her economy for a long war before 1939? What kind of war, if any, did Hitler envisage? No answer to these questions provided purely from economic sources can be conclusive. Indeed the answers could perhaps only be provided if we were given the insights into Hitler's mind which are not available to us. Much of the most valuable written evidence, even in the economic field, was destroyed in 1945. Klein's work has now been used to support the view that Hitler did not intend to fight a war at all.[1] But the pre-war German economy was a war economy, not in the sense in which that term was used in British planning, but in an equally meaningful way. Pre-war observers were correct in supposing that Germany had an economy geared to war. But they fundamentally misinterpreted the nature of the German war economy. In 1938, the last calendar year of peace, Germany spent on armaments—out of a total national income, calculated at market prices, of £7,260,000,000 sterling approximately—the equivalent of £1,710,000,000 sterling.[2] The United Kingdom spent £358,000,000 out of a national income of £5,242,000,000.[3] Although these are only very rough calculations, and not strictly comparable, the percentage difference is striking.

German strategic and economic thinking before the war revolved around the concept of the *Blitzkrieg*. This term, usually translated into English as 'lightning war', has been frequently misunderstood. Too often it has been used merely in its tactical sense of a quick knock-out blow delivered against the enemy's forces from a position of strength. But the concept was strategical as well as tactical. The Blitzkrieg was also a method of waging war which would avoid the misery which war seemed destined to bring to the civilian population. The prolonged war of 1914–1918 had inflicted catastrophic economic burdens on many of

[1] A. J. P. Taylor, *The Origins of the Second World War*, introduction to the second edition.
[2] A. J. Brown, *Applied Economics*, p. 23.
[3] W. K. Hancock and M. M. Gowing, *British War Economy*, pp. 19–20.

the combatants. By basing military strategy on a short war, starting with surprise, and ending with a quick victory, the failures of the First World War would be avoided. At the same time as Germany's better preparedness for war could be made to tell against her opponents, her weaknesses in the event of a long war based on mass-productive resources would not be disclosed. The Blitzkrieg allowed Germany to play the part of a great power, which she no longer was. It was a method of avoiding the total economic commitment of 'total war'. It was the Blitzkrieg in its profoundest sense for which Germany and Hitler were prepared in 1939. For such a policy 'armament in width' rather than 'armament in depth' was necessary.

It may be arguable that by revealing the small degree to which Germany's economy was geared to war in 1939, by illustrating the extent to which a civilian economy operating under peace-time conditions survived in Germany well into the war years, by revealing the muddled inadequacy of much German economic administration during the war, Klein and the Bombing Survey, rather than redressing the historical balance, have weighed it down too heavily on the other side. The tendency of their work has been to suggest that the lack of a war economy in the early years of the war was a serious handicap to Germany. But after all, under Blitzkrieg economics Germany achieved one of the most remarkable periods of conquest in modern history. The Blitzkrieg was responsible for the conquest of Belgium, Holland, Scandinavia, Poland, France, Yugoslavia and a large area of Russia. As long as Germany relied on Blitzkrieg economics she was winning the war. Once engaged in a long-drawn-out war of economic attrition, such as her opponents always wished to engage her in, she was losing.

Nevertheless it is very pertinent to ask: what factors led Hitler to the Blitzkrieg? The origins of Blitzkrieg economics were entangled in the deepest roots of the National Socialist State and the Hitlerian dictatorship. It was, in a very profound way, conformable to the tenets and principles on which the Hitlerian dictatorship was based. It reached down into the grass roots of pre-1939 Germany and drew its strength from there. Firstly, it was conformable to the *ad hoc* administrative methods of National Socialism. Secondly it was conformable to the fissi-

8

parous, centrifugal, tendencies of the National Socialist Party itself, or that wing of it from which sprang most Gauleiters and local officials. Thirdly, it was conformable to the idea of a dictatorship. Fourthly, it was economically an escape from the seeming impasse of 'total warfare', a means of waging war which did not bear too heavily on the civilian and therefore did not perturb a régime none too sure of its own standing. Fifthly, it was economically convenient in that it seemed to preserve the fundamental physical weaknesses of the German economy from exploitation by the enemy. It seemed to offer a way in which Germany, no longer economically a great power, could wage war as though she were such a power. And lastly it was strategically highly convenient. Whatever Hitler's ultimate war aims, Germany's situation in Europe appeared to be such that they could be gratified by a series of short-term sudden wars against powers much weaker economically. In this context it is even possible that Hitler convinced himself that Russia was a weaker power economically than Germany.

It was a regular part of National Socialist administrative practice, when something really important needed to be done, to appoint an *ad hoc* administrative committee to do the job. The way in which the system worked was that the thrusting individual would create around him his own machine and then cast around for some sphere of responsibility which he could take over. His 'own' administrative machine might then be filling very much the same sort of role as the ministries had done in the parliamentary republic. In fact many surviving ministries were left to compete in a similar way with such essentially 'private' organizations as the *Organisation Todt*. The whole career of Fritz Todt is a splendid example of the rise to power of the individual and his particular administrative group. The Four-Year-Plan Organization was just such another private group, controlled by Göring as his personal machine although fulfilling a fairly important function in the administration of the State.

The running of the German war economy therefore was originally left in the hands of a number of competing administrators and administrative organizations. To have reorganized the economy for a full-scale war would have meant abandoning

9

these administrative practices which were not only comfortable ones, but also became, in themselves, a vested interest resisting change. When the Blitzkrieg failed it became necessary to have a Ministry, and Minister, of War Production with overriding powers. And this, when it was forced on Hitler by circumstances, proved very difficult to achieve, because the whole structure of the German administrative body was one of competing individuals and competing machines which by 1942 represented a powerful collection of vested interests each unwilling to relinquish its control of its own small part of the war economy. Such centralization and rationalization was against the whole spirit of National Socialist administration; the Blitzkrieg economy, however, imposed no such need for rationalized efficiency, and could be operated very easily within the scope of National Socialist administrative method.

When, from 1942 onwards, attempts were made to put Germany's war economy on a more rational basis and to increase her output of raw materials some of the most insuperable opposition came from local National Socialist Party organizations. Beneath the veneer of unity imposed by the 'Führer-Principle' the Party was very local in its affiliations. Gauleiters had their own regional machines and in some cases—that of Thuringia is a striking example—they objected strongly to the centralization process carried on by Albert Speer. The Blitzkrieg was very much in the interests of the Gauleiters and regional organizations. They were always the loudest and most influential in their cries if standards of civilian living were threatened by any kind of restrictions on the output of consumer goods. Of course their finger was very much on the pulse of the small Party member who had voted Hitler into power, possibly as a protest against declining standards of living. But, even so, many Gauleiters displayed a tendency towards the practice of regional economics. They would defend the skilled workmen and the plant of works in their areas against the depredations of rationalizers and redistributors who wished to centralize production of important armaments. At the same time many of the more fanatical, more ideological, more 'revolutionary' sections of the Party, from which the Gauleiters often emerged, objected on ideological grounds to the machinery by which centralization was imposed after 1942. The control of Albert Speer from 1942 onwards was exercised indirectly through committees of private business men. Such committees could easily, sometimes justly, be suspected of acting in their own private capitalistic interests rather than in those of the Party. Fundamentally however, there were strong centrifugal forces in the National Socialist Party, which found the whole idea and system of the Blitzkrieg immensely more attractive than a full-scale war economy which would need centralized direction.

Thirdly, the Blitzkrieg suited Hitler's personal position as a dictator. Also, dictatorship could obviate some of the more prominent disadvantages of a Blitzkrieg economy. The idea of the Blitzkrieg was of a series of short wars geared to short but intensive bursts of economic effort. Given a situation in which only a certain unchanging sector of the economy was consecrated to war production purposes it would be necessary to change the composition of the output of this sector according to the war to be fought. The attack on France was preceded by an abnormally heavy production of vehicles and mobile armour, that on Britain by an increased production of naval equipment and aeroplanes. The attack on Russia was preceded by an all-out production effort in the field of general army equipment. None of these increases in output involved an overall increase in the output of that sector of the economy committed to war production. Each increase was achieved by throttling back in other, no longer wanted, branches of armaments production. Consequently, although the size of the sector committed to war production did not change, there were violent switches of priority within that sector. Even before the French campaign was over, production had been diverted away from that campaign towards the next. Before the winter of 1941–2 military production had already been reduced in anticipation of a victory in Russia. It was only possible to achieve such violent shifts of priority by having the responsibility for such decisions clearly defined. This was achieved by the 'Führer-Command'. Any executive order issued by Hitler was promulgated in official form as a Führer-Command, and issued as such to the administrative departments concerned with its execution. All Führer-Commands became, as soon as they were issued, top priority requests. The democratic states found it desperately difficult to solve the whole question of priorities, discovering that a small number of divisions never worked, and that priorities lay within priorities. The ruthless simplicity of the Führer-Command solved these issues, cutting cleanly through the red tape surrounding them. And this was all the more necessary as the economics of the Blitzkrieg was very much an economics of priorities. The lesson learnt in Britain, that government had to be simplified by the creation of a very small war cabinet, did not need to be learnt in Germany.[1]

The files of the office of the Berlin President of Police were well stocked with fearful anticipations of the political unrest that would be caused by the negligible hardships of Germany's capital investment programme. Whether these anticipations were valid, or even plausible, does not matter very much in assessing their influence on Hitler's mind. It was the wish to achieve for as long as possible a war which did not entail restrictions on consumer goods production that caused Hitler to hesitate so long before committing himself to a thorough-going war economy. He was reluctant to admit that, after the failure of the invasion of Russia, 'guns *and* butter' had failed as a policy. At the same time, especially in the earlier years of the war, Hitler exercised much of his power through the medium of Party organizations, who, out of self-interest, opposed any attempt to restrict civilian living standards. The Blitzkrieg succeeded for two years in producing the kind of war which made, for Germany, 1914–18 seem a folly of inefficient statesmen, and also it served to dispel political criticism of the régime.

In a deeper way the Blitzkrieg was well adjusted to the fundamental strengths and weaknesses of Germany's economy. In any long-drawn-out war, especially a war of mass-productive resources, Germany was bound to suffer from her inherent raw material deficiencies. Coal was the only vital raw material essential for war with which Germany was well endowed. The Four-Year-Plan was an attempt to remedy this situation by increasing the production of *ersatz* rubber (*buna*), and of benzine and oils by the hydrogenation and Fischer-Tropsch processes.

[1] See, on these topics, J. Ehrman, *Cabinet Government and War 1890–1940*.

At the same time it had aimed at the increasing utilization of Germany's low-grade iron ores. But Germany was still dependent on 10,000,000 tons of iron ore every year from Sweden. She produced no chrome and no nickel, both essential ingredients of armaments steel; no tungsten, essential for high-speed machine tools. Although molybdenum and manganese were not so vital, serious weaknesses would appear if, as seemed likely, imports were cut off by enemy action. Zinc and lead came into the same category. National reserves of copper and tin, the first extremely important, had been used up in Spring 1939 as foreign credits had been difficult.[1] It was partly on such potential shortages that the United Kingdom Ministry of Economic Warfare tried to concentrate the blockade once war had started. For a short war such problems inherent in the German economy could be overcome by stockpiling, in the long run they might prove serious weaknesses. On the most general level, overall economic strength is roughly the equivalent of war potential, but, in the short run, war potential is much more closely tied to the volume of capital goods produced by the economy. On this short-run calculation Germany was very favourably endowed and this also pointed the basic suitability of Germany's economy to a series of Blitzkrieg campaigns. For a short period Germany could play the role of a great power, a role which, in the long run, was reserved for those powers with greater overall economic strength.

Finally, the Blitzkrieg answered the needs of Germany's diplomatic situation. Ringed by powers which, taken in isolation, were economically less powerful than herself, Germany could ally this idea to Hitler's aggressive diplomacy. Given her long-run weaknesses both economic and political, Germany could not afford to engage in a war against any strong combination of powers. A war on two fronts would mean the death of the Blitzkrieg, and, in the end, that was what killed it. But an economy in which there was always a relatively high level of armaments ready to use, but which, at the same time, appeared to the civilian as a peace-time economy, could provide a useful

[1] FD 1434/46 (No. 168), OKW/WiRüAmt, 'Die Tätigkeit des WiRüAmtes bei der Sicherstellung der Munitionsversorgung der Wehrmacht-Teile von 1938 bis zum Waffenstillstand mit Frankreich', p. 10.

support for a diplomatic policy which needed to be carried out over some length of time and was aimed at isolating Germany's neighbours. In such an economy mobilization was easy and war entailed no great change. In this way the Blitzkrieg was highly successful and only needed to be abandoned when Hitler was faced with a two-front war against powers economically stronger than Germany, and, in the long run, better prepared for war.

Hitler's acceptance of the Blitzkrieg as a method of waging war meant that only a moderate portion of Germany's total resources was committed to rearmament purposes. Therefore preparation for war was a question of mobilization methods rather than of long-term planning. Consequently the development of the German economy from 1933 to 1939 sheds less light than is often supposed on Hitler's more precise intentions. German rearmament proceeded very roughly in step with the economic recovery from late 1933 onwards. The high levels of public expenditure initiated by the von Schleicher and von Papen governments were maintained at an even higher level by the National Socialists. But these expenditure levels were strictly combined with exchange control, import regulation, and wage and price restrictions to check inflation. Central government expenditure, 22·9 per cent of the Gross National Product in 1934, rose only to 24·5 per cent of Gross National Product in 1937.[1] Its record peace-time level occurred in 1938, the year when Hitler could be said for the first time to have really invested heavily in rearmament.

But civilian levels of consumption also improved during the same period of economic recovery. House-building in 1937 was roughly comparable with the 1929 level, although, here too, 1938 shows some change of direction of investment.[2] Even in 1938 production of many consumer durables was above the 1929 level. Klein's classification of German investment for the period 1933–8 puts over half the total investment outside military facilities or the basic industries.[3] The current value of those investments in 1938 was equal to that of 1928. Not only

[1] S. P. Andic and J. Veverka, 'The Growth of Government Expenditure in Germany since the Unification', *Finanzarchiv*, vol. xxiii, 1964. See also, R. Erbe, *Die nationalsozialistische Wirtschaftspolitik 1933–39 im Lichte der modernen Theorie.*

[2] B. H. Klein, *Germany's Economic Preparations for War*, p. 13.

[3] Ibid., pp. 14–15.

was this so, but, in accordance with Blitzkrieg economics, such investment as might be said to be for war purposes was on armaments rather than on basic industry. Expenditure on government buildings and road building was annually higher than that on mining, transportation, and steel making.[1]

But although estimates of the size of the German army at the time of the reoccupation of the Rhineland usually put it well over its actual 500,000, from that time onwards its real size began to approach much more nearly to its imaginary one. The original conscription programme, promulgated in March 1935, was quickly outdistanced by the intensified programme of summer 1936.[2] This conscription programme coincided with the developments foreseen by the Four-Year-Plan of September 1936. Therefore the Four-Year-Plan came to be associated closely with the rearmament programme. The basic investment aims of the Plan were limited to a few specific raw materials, and even in these they were not particularly successful, owing to the confusion of economic and political motives. But the idea of the Blitzkrieg did not require any extensive building-up of the productive capacity of German industry, except in the two very important areas of synthetic fuel-oil production and synthetic rubber production. In those two areas the Four-Year-Plan was vital. Elsewhere what mattered was ready armaments. Hence the rearmament programme of 1936 was more important for the future than the Four-Year-Plan, in spite of the bellicose language in which the latter was proclaimed.

From 1936 onwards German armaments production was probably at a higher rate, and also qualitatively more modern, than that of the other powers, until the later months of 1939 when Britain caught up with German monthly totals in many important fields.[3] German expenditure on defence rose, both as a proportion of Gross National Product, and as a percentage of total expenditure, regularly from 1935 onwards.

Such figures are expressive and, in the absence of accurate statistical information on German armaments output before

[1] Ibid., p. 15.
[2] C. Meinck, *Hitler und die deutsche Aufrüstung, 1933–37*.
[3] This statement does not apply to Russian production, the levels of which remain unknown. All comparative statements of this kind are difficult because of the lack of precise information about the rate of British pre-war output.

1939, they must be made to do more work than, perhaps, they ought. Detailed output figures are available only for aeroplane production. From 1936 to 1939 German aircraft production ran at about 400 a month.[1] Undoubtedly in 1939 this rate increased slightly. But such figures can be misleading, for air power was very important in the idea of a Blitzkrieg and expenditure was possibly concentrated in that direction more than elsewhere.

Government expenditure on defence as % of total expenditure[2] and of G.N.P. 1935–38

Year	% of total expenditure	% of G.N.P.
1933	8·7	3·2
1934	8·8	3·4
1935	15·8	5·5
1936	22·6	7·6
1937	28·2	9·6
1938	42·7	18·1

Given a diplomacy which would make the Blitzkrieg feasible, that is to say one which would avoid too strong a combination of economically powerful nations against the Reich, all Hitler needed to deal with his immediate neighbours was an Air Force of about 2,000 planes and an Army of about 70 divisions. When eventually he went to war against Russia he aimed at an Army of 180 divisions, but this was to be achieved by throttling back production in other armament areas. All these calculations about the possibilities of a Blitzkrieg depended on two things. Firstly the Wehrmacht had to have a ready supply of armaments to give it a short-term superiority over any possible opponent; it had to be ready for war. Secondly, there had to be great flexibility in the system. The Blitzkrieg could be used against any opponent. But each possible opponent would require a different kind of war. And each war would require a different kind of Wehrmacht. Therefore the economics of Blitzkrieg had to be highly flexible. In a situation where only a certain area of the economy was committed to rearmament this was feasible. It

[1] United States Strategic Bombing Survey, *The Effects of Strategic Bombing on the German Economy*, p. 149.
[2] Extracted from S. Andic and J. Veverka, op. cit., table A.21.

is even arguable that basic investment, 'armament in depth', would have inhibited this very economic flexibility on which Hitler's strategy so much depended. The economic machinery had to be such that production could be switched quickly from one sector of the Wehrmacht to another. How was this flexibility achieved?

At the head of this machinery was Hitler himself. He was the supreme authority on all questions of economic policy. In any matter in which he chose to intervene he could formulate or alter decisions on the spot. Therefore the economics of Germany's pre-war and wartime policies must be considered his own personal choice. However, his interventions were inconsistent, erratic, and impulsive. It is thus important to know as exactly as possible what Hitler thought about the general issues of economic strategy. Owing to the destruction of archives this question can only be answered from material dating from after 1942.

The system of work of the Ministry of Armaments from 1942 onwards provided for a regular series of conferences in which Hitler and Speer discussed overall economic issues and also matters of almost insignificant detail affecting armaments construction and policy. Such a mixture was partly inevitable because, although an Armaments Minister, Speer also had a general control over the working of the German economy. But admitting the dichotomy inherent in this situation the 'Führer-Conferences' must be held to reveal many of the weaknesses in Hitler's thinking on economic matters. He could never distinguish between overall decisions which governed future economic policy and short-term decisions of far less ultimate economic significance.

The subjects of discussion at the Führer-Conferences with his Armaments Minister leap in a disconcerting, jumbled, way from the ballistic possibilities of rifles to the quarterly planning of steel production. Hitler displayed great interest in top-level economic decisions which seemed to affect most immediately the Armed Forces, such as the size of the call-up and the relative size of the different services. Below this level there was a large area of important decision in which Hitler merely ratified the plans of Speer and others. This area included such matters as the degree of utilization of raw materials, quarterly allocation of raw materials, stockpiling, the general behaviour of the economy, prices, labour conditions and so on. Rarely in the three years of the conferences did Hitler fix his attention for very long on such things. When he did so he was nearly always ready to bow to expert advice and concede the argument. At a still lower level there was a mass of day-to-day questions, particularly relating to types of armaments, in which Hitler displayed unbounded interest. He had a very good detailed knowledge of armaments and liked to discuss and direct their development and manufacture. On such issues almost the whole of a three-day conference between Hitler and Speer was often spent. In its most specific sense war production received a great deal of attention from the Führer. But on the mechanics of organizing war production, on the level of war economy, Hitler was utterly vague.

It is impossible not to feel that when he was concerned with such issues Hitler lacked an adequate sense of proportion. Before the advent of a full war economy Hitler had had two prosperous years of warfare without any top-level economic planning at all. He knew well enough that, faced with Russia and the U.S.A., this would not do. But his sense of constriction, of irritation at being confined within the framework of a definite economic policy, broke through from time to time. Some of his more foolhardy essays in policy, like his thwarted attempt to increase the allocation of iron to the civilian sector of the economy in Summer 1942, can be seen as a protest against this circumscription.[1]

So long as the German economy operated on Blitzkrieg levels of output no one person or organization was sufficiently strong to seize control of the area of economic decision which Hitler abandoned to others. The machinery of economic policy and of war-production was extremely complicated and all areas of important decision were criss-crossed by administrative borderlines.

On the local level German industry had already been organized in 1933 on a basis of 'groups' and 'chambers', associations of allied businessmen and industrialists. Such organizations

[1] See below, p. 88.

could easily be fitted into the new régime.[1] But above this level responsibility for economic affairs was not clearly determined.

Theoretically the application of economic development in the military sphere came within the scope of the Reichs Defence Council. The Reichs Defence Committee which was more particularly concerned with economic affairs served as a subcommittee of this organization. But the reality of power did not rest with these formal bodies. The Reichs Defence Law of 1935 had established a Plenipotentiary-General for War Economy. This office was at first held by Schacht. However, it was agreed that even in the event of a war the production of all military armaments would remain the responsibility of the Wehrmacht. The factories would be controlled by soldiers, Schacht's powers being more concerned with the general functioning of the economy. In fact when Funk succeeded Schacht in 1938 this office ceased to be of any importance.[2]

There were three possible organizations which might have supplied the direction of a war economy: the Four-Year-Plan Organization, the Ministry of Economics, or the Wehrmacht itself.

The Four-Year-Plan, promulgated on 9 September 1936, had been put under the overall direction of Göring on 18 October. It arose from a secret memorandum by Hitler written some time in August in which he expressed his own views on the economy in opposition to those of his Minister of Economics, Schacht.[3] The memorandum concluded, 'the German economy must be on a war footing in four years'. It was Göring's job to achieve this. But the contrasting intentions of the Four-Year-Plan, and its quite limited objectives, cast doubt on the meaning of Hitler's words. Ultimately the Four-Year-Plan would save foreign exchange by concentrating domestic production on oil, rubber, and low-grade iron ore. And at the same time this would make

[1] K. D. Bracher, W. Sauer and G. Schultz, *Die Nationalsozialistische Machtergreifung*, pp. 627–55.
[2] There was even some dispute as to Funk's actual title, I. T., Nürnberg, *Trial of the Major War Criminals*, xiii, 105. Royal Institute of International Affairs, *Hitler's Europe, 1939–46*, p. 174, n. 3.
[3] W. Treue, ed., 'Hitlers Denkschrift zum Vierjahresplan', in *Vierteljahrshefte für Zeitgeschichte*, 1955.

Germany's strategic position less precarious in the event of a war. But the Plan went no further.

Theoretically the Four-Year-Plan Office was confined in its administrative responsibility to the limited aims of the Plan. But Göring had received certain overriding economic powers in April 1936, which were later taken over by the Four-Year-Plan Office. On top of this his importance as a statesman, and the fact that he was Commander-in-Chief of the Air Force, gave his 'personal' machine greater importance than its official responsibilities for the Four-Year-Plan. Göring rivalled, and then succeeded, Schacht as a potential economic dictator. The two men personally detested each other. When Schacht was interrogated after the war he was asked whether Göring had any knowledge of economics. 'Not the slightest glimmering', he replied.[1] It must be conceded that he was right. A mixture of economic ignorance and increasing distaste for work prevented Göring from seizing the area of power which, in 1936, seemed to be his for the taking.

However, in those areas of the economy covered by the Four-Year-Plan Göring's organization remained powerful. When in 1938, the 1936 planning on oil output was seen to be insufficiently imaginative, the Four-Year-Plan Office introduced the *Karin Hall Plan*. The 1936 Plan had anticipated a 1940 output of 4·3 million tons; the *Karin Hall Plan* aimed at 11 million tons for 1944,[2] although the 1940 target was lower. Capacity for synthetic oil production was increased more than twofold between 1936 and 1939. But the 1939 output was 45 per cent below what had been envisaged. In steel production the Four-Year-Plan Office was no more successful. Germany's 1939 steel output only exceeded that of 1929 because plant in Austria and Czechoslovakia which she had occupied, had given her an extra 3 million tons a year capacity. Only in the field of synthetic rubber production was the story different. Here the building of new plant increased production of synthetic rubber from 22,000 tons in 1939 to 69,000 tons in 1942, which was more than adequate for civilian and military needs.

Planning activity in the Four-Year-Plan Office thus did not

[1] FD 3055/49, 2nd Preliminary Investigation of Dr. H. Schacht, p. 5.
[2] B. H. Klein, *Germany's Economic Preparations for War*, pp. 39 ff.

cease with the expiry of the four-year period but continued in 1940 and 1941. This proved very troublesome to the other economic agencies because the Four-Year-Plan Office had an area of undisputed control, but Göring's overall powers were extremely vague and ill-defined. He could, when he chose to, demand to be consulted on, and to approve, many decisions. And since he did not assert his authority consistently the situation was even more confused.

With Schacht's verdict on Göring as an economist the Reich Ministry of Economics would have heartily concurred. It would also very gladly have been rid of the whole apparatus of the Four-Year-Plan. The Ministry was a survival from the parliamentary state. Its functions had been slowly whittled away since 1933. Schacht held the post of Minister until his supersession by Funk. In theory the Minister was the primary adviser to the government of the Reich on all economic problems, although Hitler does not seem to have taken Funk's advice on anything. He was also responsible for appointing the chairmen of the various 'groups' and 'chambers'. In fact the Ministry of Economics found itself confined to matters of trade and commerce, banking, and foreign exchange. It had also had a nominal control over the Ministry of Agriculture and the Ministry of Labour; although the latter acted in a quite independent way. Only in so far as it was concerned with the importation of essential raw materials did it directly impinge on the direction of the German war economy.

This was even more true after 1938 when Funk was Minister. Schacht's attempts to control overall policy had led to disputes about the financing of rearmament. These disputes had been resolved by Schacht's departure from the government. Thenceforth the Ministry of Economics never extended its empire beyond the limits where it could act without coming into conflict with the Four-Year-Plan.

There remained the Wehrmacht itself. After 1919 the Army had been the first to start any form of economic planning with a view to rearmament.[1] After the seizure of power by the National Socialists it retained control of the 'shadow' armament

---

[1] FD 386/46, Gen. G. Thomas, 'Grundlage für eine Geschichte der deutschen Wehr- und Rüstungswirtschaft 1923–44', Anlage IV, 1.

factories and became responsible for the national network of armaments inspectors, whose task was to strengthen the links between armaments contractors, the Wehrmacht, and other organizations concerned with the economy, in particular to keep an eye on the fulfilment of contracts.[1] The Wehrmacht exercised its control at the top level, after 1935, through the High Command of the Armed Forces (OKW),[2] a specially pliable tool of the Führer and under the control of General Keitel. In 1939 part of the personnel of the old-established Army Armaments Branch[3] was transferred into the Office of the Staff for War Economy[4] under the control of OKW. This Office was renamed on 22 November 1939 'War Economy and Armaments Branch' (WiRüAmt).[5]

Through this change one man retained the primary role in the Army's economic planning, General Georg Thomas.[6] His unpublished work, *Grundlage für eine Geschichte der deutschen Wehr- und Rüstungswirtschaft*, gives perhaps the clearest account of these organizational changes.[7] It turns at times into a rather implausible essay in self-defence, and is a long justification of the work of WiRüAmt. None the less it reveals the degree to which rearmament was tied to general economic policy before 1939 and in the earlier years of the war, and gives a coherent picture of a policy which was in the later years of the war to be covered with opprobrium. WiRüAmt functioned in two quite opposing ways. In one aspect it was the economic general staff of the Army, and in that sense it formulated economic plans to fit whatever strategy was being pursued. In another aspect it was merely the executive agent of the Führer, carrying out his decisions recorded in the form of Führer-Commands. Ultimately its only advocate before the throne was the subservient Keitel. Moreover, WiRüAmt was purely an army organization, and in a situation where the different sections of the Armed Forces bid

---

[1] K. D. Bracher, W. D. Sauer and G. Schultz; op. cit., p. 671.
[2] 'Oberkommando der Wehrmacht.'
[3] 'Heereswaffenamt' (HWA).
[4] 'Amtsgruppe Wehrwirtschaftsstab.'
[5] 'Wehrwirtschafts- und Rüstungsamt', referred to throughout as 'WiRüAmt'.
[6] Under the Army Armaments Branch Thomas had been Head of 'Wehrwirtschafts- und Waffenwesen'.
[7] FD 386/46.

in competition with each other for the ear of the master the Air Force by virtue of the position of its C.-in-C. Göring, had an advantage. WiRüAmt and its predecessors therefore had stressed to Blomberg when he had been War Minister, and later to Keitel, as Chief of OKW, the need for some more comprehensive control over economic policy. This control would, of course, be provided by the Army.

The last of these representations made in peace time was a proposal by WiRüAmt at the beginning of September 1939 for a planning committee to adjudicate between the economic needs, purely of the Wehrmacht, and those more generally concerned with the defence of the Reich.[1] There were too many separate agencies all trying to go ahead together in rearmament. Thomas characterized it in a memorandum at the time:

> At the moment in Germany there rages a war of all against all . . . the result is that it is demanded on all sides that no reserves should be held back but that the total amount of raw materials available should be consumed. . . . So long as Their Lordships, the Commanders-in-Chief, are allowed to do everything as they please without contradiction we shall never arrive at any clear solution.[2]

The Army had two motives for advocating this planning committee. It desired an extension of its own power to conduct a political struggle in the economic field. At the same time it genuinely disagreed with Hitler on the type of rearmament and war to be undertaken. As regards the first motive Blomberg's refusal to put the proposals to the Führer may have been well-considered shrewdness. Hitler proved increasingly unwilling to allow the Army any widespread economic powers. When such powers eventually became essential they were given to civilians and not to generals.

As to the other motive, the Army thought that the Hitlerian concept of war was dangerous to the State, and entailed a fearful risk. In the first place, it was not satisfied with the extent of Germany's immediate superiority over her potential opponents. Her aircraft production in Autumn 1939 was only equal to that of Great Britain, although her Air Force was much larger. The naval construction programme started in 1938 was not due to

---

[1] FD 1434/46 (No. 168), OKW/WiRüAmt, pp. 15–16.
[2] Ibid., pp. 23–40.

finish until 1944.[1] Only 26 submarines were suitable for operation in the Atlantic.[2] On land Germany was strong in terms of mobilized manpower; but in armaments production her rivals were gaining. Britain's tank production was greater on the eve of the war than that of Germany although Germany possessed more tanks. The Blitzkrieg did not seem to the Army very likely to succeed. In the second place they thought that Hitler's overall strategy was wrong and forecast a time when Germany would face a combination of powers who in absolute economic strength were not only far superior to her but who had also geared their economies to war production in a far profounder way than Germany. These powers, in short, would have conceded Germany an immediate short-run superiority in return for their own overwhelming long-run superiority. Linking these two fears together was the idea that if there was to be war it could not be fought with such little effort, particularly the Army's part of it.

But Thomas and the WiRüAmt had no very precise idea of how far a peace-time economy could be changed into a thoroughgoing war economy, of how far 'armament in depth' was possible. Nor were they certain what war was to be fought. Nor were they very knowledgeable on the exact mechanisms by which the German economy could be changed into what they regarded as a correct war-economy. They feared, for instance, that workers already working overtime would not be able to stand the strain of extra shifts.[3] They had none of the precise statistical information so essential for the kind of economic planning which they envisaged. They were dealing with 'the art of the possible', as they always claimed.

An all-out preparation for an imminent war is impossible. The unforeseeable duration of the war, the exorbitant cost of such an armaments effort and the danger of the equipment becoming obsolete or lost are the chief reasons for this.[4]

---

[1] *Führer Naval Conferences*, 'Reflections of the Commander-in-Chief, Navy, on the outbreak of war, 3 September 1939'.

[2] H. Le Masson, 'Les constructions navales allemandes', in *Revue Maritime*, 27 (nouvelle série), July 1948. F. H. Hinsley, *Hitler's Strategy*.

[3] FD 4457/45 HWA, 'Die Rüstungslage Deutschlands wie sie sich augenblicklich und voraussichtlich in den nächsten Jahren im Falle eines Krieges darstellt', p. 4.

[4] Ibid.

Therefore Thomas argued that Hitler would be taking an unjustified risk if he were to plan a war before the German economy was ready. He asserted repeatedly in memoranda and notes that Germany was not arming for the right sort of war, that there must be drastic cuts in the production of consumer goods, an increase in munitions plant, greater numbers of women employed, and an agency for deciding the all-important question of priorities.[1]

On this last point WiRüAmt was wrong. The cumulative effect of all this seemingly cumbrous economic machinery was to produce extreme flexibility. If widespread economic planning had been needed such machinery would have proved unworkable. But outside certain limited objectives Hitler wished to dispense with long-range economic plans. All priorities were, in fact, decided by the simple device of issuing a Führer-Command. On its way down the administrative ladder this was translated into top-priority requirements. Most Führer-Commands were concerned with adjustments in the level of armaments; in a situation where there were so many unexploited reserves in the economy these adjustments could be effected in this highly empirical way. There was hardly any accurate statistical evidence on armaments output because very little was needed. The lack of documentary evidence on economic and military planning before 1942 indicates how little of such planning there was.

Such lack of precise economic evidence could sometimes produce scathing comments from the Führer on the inefficiency of the three branches of the Armed Forces in conducting their own economic affairs. WiRüAmt, and its fellow organizations for the Navy and the Air Force found that their control over civilian industrialists had to be exerted through large staffs. The Berlin office of WiRüAmt, according to Speer, had a staff of 1,000 to 1,200.[2] When the Army in 1914–18 had achieved a degree of control over the economy greater than that it was ever to obtain in the Second World War, the directing body for industry had managed with a much smaller staff than that. One of WiRüAmt's great difficulties was attracting suitable people into the organization. Many of its staff were first and foremost career generals.

[1] FD 1434/46 (No. 168). OKW/WiRüAmt, pp. 11–15.
[2] Speer Report No. 1, p. 1.

Its recruits from industry itself were often second-rate. How little it needed to depend on its long-term planning is revealed by the gross mistakes that were made. Its production-study for a Panzer-army in 1944 foresaw by that year a monthly capacity of 800 to 1,200 tanks and *Sturmgeschütze*.[1] Otto Saur who later became Deputy to the Minister of Armaments and Munitions, calculated that it would have taken the whole machine-tool industry two complete years to produce the necessary tools, provided, in the first place, 100,000 specialists had been recalled from the Army.[2] More celebrated is the WiRüAmt estimate for quarterly copper demand from the Army which appears to have been greater than the total annual world copper output. During the Blitzkrieg such arithmetical errors could willingly be tolerated as the price for political ease. What could not be sacrificed was flexibility.

The essential requirement was occasional decisions from Hitler on the level of production of each armament, and, providing the level of total production of armaments did not vary much, then shifts within this total according to the kind of war to be fought, could be achieved with deadly simplicity. This flexibility had to be allied to accurate, very speedy, and secret mobilization plans. A considerable amount of ingenuity and planning went into the details of military mobilization, and also some rueful thinking about the errors of 1914.[3] In general the tangled machinery and apparent lack of direction of the war economy was the inward reflection of the strategical policies which Hitler pursued; it was only another aspect of the idea of Blitzkrieg.

Compared to her neighbours in September 1939 Germany's strength was very great. Her armaments were ready. The United Kingdom, faced by a double threat from Germany and Japan, had begun to rearm in depth. The basis of German production had recently increased as a result of a long period of territorial expansion; the steel and oil of Austria, the steel and armaments of Czechoslovakia, the coalfield of the Saar, all had been considerable accretions of strength. In 1938 greater Germany produced 22,000,000 tons of steel, one-quarter as much

---

[1] A type of self-propelled assault gun.   [2] FD 3049/49 (Folder No. 1).
[3] See the discussion by E. M. Robertson, *Hitler's Pre-War Policy and Military Plans 1933–39*, pp. 88–90.

again as the United Kingdom and France. Her coal resources in the Saar, Silesia, and the Ruhr, were much greater than those of France and the United Kingdom. Her machine-tool industry was the strongest in Europe. She had, in that field, a considerable export trade, while her imports were exiguous, although her manufacture was partly dependent on imported raw materials. When Göring became Director of the Four-Year-Plan he boasted, 'We are already at war, but there is no shooting'. It was not an idle boast. No nation had ever previously spent so vast a sum in peace time on preparations for war.

These were Germany's short-run advantages. Her disadvantages were almost all long-run. And though there were basic economic inferiorities between Germany and Russia or the United States, Hitler hoped to avoid a situation where he was caught in a war whose ultimate result depended on mass-productive resources.

From Hitler's point of view there was everything to be said for the Blitzkrieg and not much against it. Albert Speer, and other writers since, have argued that one of the principal causes of Germany's failure was the failure to commit herself to a full-scale war economy in the early stages of the war. Beside such an advocate as Speer, General Thomas and General Hanneken, opponents of the Blitzkrieg at the time, seem pedestrian. But in spite of them all Germany obtained astonishing military successes with the Blitzkrieg. Germany overran half of Europe with an economic system which Thomas, quite justifiably, called 'a war of all against all'.[1]

[1] FD 1434/46 (No. 168), OKW/WiRüAmt, p. 15.

CHAPTER II

The Working of the Blitzkrieg

THE Blitzkrieg phase of the German war economy lasted from the outbreak of war in September 1939 to the recapture of Rostov-on-Don by Russian troops in December 1941. During this period the overall production of armaments remained fairly steady, and was certainly running at a lower rate than that of the United Kingdom. At the same time the total output of consumer goods did not fall, and, indeed, in some important industries it actually rose, even allowing for the inflation of these years.

Output of Consumer Goods, 1940 and 1941[1]

Group of industries	Net production value in million marks	
	1940	1941
Glass industry	440	466
Ceramic industry	361	383
Printing industry	917	927
Foodstuffs	3203	3241
Brewing and malting industry	1098	1183
Sugar-producing industry	444	482

This table refers only to goods produced within the area of the greater German Reich and consequently does not indicate the fact that by the end of 1941 goods from contracts placed in the occupied territories were reaching the German market in steadily greater volume. The policy of Blitzkrieg economics appeared in 1941 to have been justified up to the hilt, at least by

[1] Wagenführ, '*Aufstieg und Niedergang der deutschen Rüstung*' (manuscript) (FD 3057/49), p. 13. This is a slightly different manuscript version of the book published by Deutsches Institut für Wirtschaftsforschung, *Die Deutsche Industrie im Kriege 1939–45* (Berlin, 1954). Wagenführ was in charge of the Statistical Office in the Planning Office from 1943 onwards. His manuscript was captured at the end of the war.

outward results. It is, however, in its inward effects upon the economy that it must be examined. How successful was the Blitzkrieg as a method of avoiding the intense economic pressures of modern war?

There can be little doubt that the impact of the war on the German people over these years was very small. The start of the war against Poland, although undertaken in the knowledge that it might provoke a general war, witnessed the silent dropping of any plans or machinery still in existence for creating a more extensive war economy than already existed. Funk's theoretically strong powers as 'Plenipotentiary-General for War Economy' were allowed to lapse.[1] Funk himself explained the situation in a speech at Vienna on 14 October.

> In war, however, most things turn out quite differently from the way they were foreseen; that is especially the case in this war and, for Germany, in a very fortunate way. The plans previously drawn up are therefore to be considerably altered, particularly in this respect, that economic life does not need to be readjusted so fully as the mobilization plans foresaw.[2]

'Business as usual' was the motto, and propaganda was not long in rejoicing that the usual impact of war on a nation's economy had been avoided. Ley, head of the German Labour Front, boasted that the economy was working 'normally'.[3] The assumption that the war would not be a very long one was widespread and industrialists felt optimistic about the post-war market. Even when the war rapidly became more generalized few restrictions which had not been already in existence before the war were imposed on the civilian sector of the economy. In 1942 consumers' expenditures, in terms of 1939 reichsmarks, stood practically equal to 1937 when the civilian population was almost the same size.[4]

The monthly allocation of finished steel in thousand metric tons between the various sectors of the economy indicates the essentially stable balance which was preserved between the civil

[1] Funk later claimed he had always been mere 'Plenipotentiary-General for Economy'. *I.M.T. Nürnberg*, xiii, 105.
[2] *Die Deutsche Industrie im Kriege 1939–45*, p. 22.
[3] Ibid., p. 26.
[4] U.S.S.B.S., *Effects*, p. 23.

sector of production and production for the armaments and war industries.[1]

Monthly allocation of finished steel 1939-40
(in thousand metric tons)

	1939	1940			
	4th qtr	1st qtr	2nd qtr	3rd qtr	4th qtr
Army	306	342	348	305	351
Navy	125	140	122	140	155
Air Force	222	195	160	230	270
Construction	206	247	252	224	241
Exports	173	200	200	258	302
Civil sector	732	780	769	800	908
Totals					
Wehrmacht, etc.	859	924	882	899	1017
Civil Sector	732	780	769	800	908
Absolute total	1764	1904	1851	1957	2227
Civil Sector as a percentage of absolute total	41·5%	41·0%	41·5%	40·9%	40·8%

One of the reasons for this maintenance of the standard of civilian life was clearly the success of the Blitzkrieg itself. Germany was able to draw heavily on occupied territories for supplies of raw materials, manpower, and food. The effects of German occupation on the economies of the occupied countries are still unknown except in the broadest outline, certainly less well known than the political effects of occupation. But it is already clear that there was a complete absence of systematic planning in the German 'New Order'. The systematic plans so often discussed in theory were all fundamentally concerned with preserving the Greater Reich as the heavy-industrial and manufacturing centre of Europe while concentrating the production of consumer goods and foodstuffs in the occupied territories.

This division was even more fundamental in the case of armaments production which throughout the war was overwhelmingly located within the political boundaries of the Reich.

[1] Ibid., extracted from appendix 69, p. 248 (OKW, 'Rohstoff-Bilanzen').

Yet beyond this simple practical distinction between the Reich and the occupied territories there seems to have been little attempt to rule Europe as an integral economic unit, except on paper. For this reason the main value of the occupied territories to Germany was as an area for exploitation, in the least sophisticated sense. The true economic foundation of Germany's victories was her already existing economic base.

Many of the occupied territories had stocks of raw materials which proved useful in sustaining the Blitzkrieg. Some were producers of those raw materials, such as non-ferrous metals, in which Germany was deficient. Molybdenum supplies to Germany came largely from the Knaben mine in Norway. France had great reserves of iron ore, Belgium had stockpiles of non-ferrous metals. Also Germany's victories enabled her to exert great pressure on neutral powers. Supplies of nickel and chrome could be obtained from those Balkan areas which became economic dependencies of Germany. Spain and Portugal supplied wolfram in the same circumstances. Both occupied territories and neutral countries supplied additional strength to the German labour force.

The Blitzkrieg economy was not successful because of the occupation of large areas of territory. There were deeper reasons for its success. It was pre-eminently suited to the structure of the National Socialist State. It was the system of warfare best suited to the character and institutions of Hitler's Germany. For a democratic country such a method of waging war would have presented immense difficulties, for Germany it was politically and economically convenient.

There were no far-reaching changes in the economy, only changes of emphasis from one section of armaments production to another, to suit the needs of each particular campaign. Many economic crises arose; but these must be seen against the background of the great quantity of unexploited reserves in the economy, although in Germany the idea was widespread that these reserves could not be developed. But the presence of such reserves of manpower, floor-space, machines, and raw materials meant that economic factors did not impose limits on military, naval, or air strategy. For instance, the job of WiRüAmt, fundamentally, was to provide the equipment for whatever kind of campaign the Army might be ordered to undertake. No economic planning such as preceded the Anglo-American invasion of France preceded the German invasion of Russia. The criterion was one of military possibility rather than economic possibility. This had its reflection in the fact that what control over armaments production existed outside the armaments industry itself lay largely in the hands of service personnel. When economic factors, later in the war, began seriously to limit strategy, civilians steadily ousted the service personnel from this control. By 1945 the criterion of strategy had become solely one of economic possibility. This process culminated when the Minister for Armaments sent letters to military commanders in the field telling them what they could or could not do.[1] Such control by one ministry was unthinkable and unnecessary in 1940.

Also the system had one very important quality built into it, flexibility. The fact that production priorities could be violently and speedily shifted from one sector of the armaments industry to another obviated the kind of difficulties which proved so troublesome to the United Kingdom in this period. A simple scale of priorities there proved quite insufficient: it was soon discovered that there were priorities within priorities and more priorities within those. Given great unexploited reserves in the economy the system of Führer-Commands proved simple and workable in Germany until Winter 1941–2. There was no questioning the few top-level decisions that had to be made once they had been made. Looked at in the files of bureaucrats the Blitzkrieg economy can be mistaken for a complicated muddle. There is no doubt that all the agencies responsible for war production wasted much time and paper competing with each other. But the flexibility of the machinery to some degree compensated for this and the large safety margin within which the war economy operated permitted quick transfers of men and materials to eliminate any bottlenecks.

It was not until a week after the military mobilization of 25 August 1939 that the 'X-order' for the economy was promulgated. This was in effect the first of the important Führer-

[1] FD 2690/45, Vol. 9c, Speer to Guderian, 15 November 1944.

Commands of the war, that of 3 September 1939.[1] War supplements to certain taxes were introduced and a wage and price freeze came into operation for a short time. There were to be increases in the production of the Ju. 88 bomber and in torpedoes.[2] These were the only comparatively large increases of production necessary to defeat Poland. The battle was over before Allied intervention on anything but the smallest scale was possible. By the end of September the Führer had decided to attack his western enemies.[3]

The campaign was to begin on 12 November, but through a mixture of bad weather and military opposition to a winter campaign the attack was eventually called off until Spring 1940. In fact no significant switch in armaments production was ordered before 12 November. But once the decision to wait until the spring had been taken Hitler began to rearrange armaments production within the framework of the Blitzkrieg. This rearrangement was effected by the Führer-Commands of 29 November 1939 and 6 December 1939.[4]

The background to these Führer-Commands had been complaints from the Army that there was not enough iron and steel to produce the requisite quantity of military armaments and munitions. Thomas complained at a meeting on 21 October about the quota of iron and steel allocated to the Army. As long as each steel consumer got less steel than he asked for but more than he needed then essential consumers like the Army, he declared, would be deprived, and this was the real answer to the difficulties in carrying through the munitions programme. Hitler suspected that the real answer was more competent administration on the part of WiRüAmt. The Führer-Command of 29 November prescribed exactly the production figures for different calibres of munitions and armaments. The calculations had perforce to be based on First World War figures. Top priority in production for the attack on the West was to be army munitions; accordingly some of the productive capacity directly

[1] FD 1434/46 (No. 168), WiRüAmt, 'Die Tätigkeit des WiRüAmtes bei der Sicherstellung der Munitions-Versorgung der Wehrmachtteile von 1938 bis zum Waffenstillstand mit Frankreich'.

[2] FD 1434/46 No. 169, WiRüAmt, 'Anlagen zur Munitionsversorgung'.

[3] See the discussion of this in A. Bullock, *Hitler, a Study in Tyranny*, p. 512.

[4] FD 1434/46 No. 169, WiRüAmt, Anlage 16. FD 1434/46 No. 168, pp. 28 ff.

controlled by the Navy would have to be surrendered to the Army. This involved particularly the release of plant for producing the heaviest munition upwards from 24 cm, as well as the smaller 21 cm mortar munition. In order to cut off English imports mine-production would be greatly stepped-up. To achieve this the Air Force and the Navy were to produce a combined plan utilizing their own share of the productive resources. Production of explosives was to be increased from the December output of 18,000 tons to 47,000 tons per month, and of powder from 7,000 tons to 20,000 tons. It was these last calls which proved the only unrealizable ones and eventually on 12 December they had to be modified by the *Orangeplan*. The *Orangeplan* was drawn up on the basis of the Führer-Command of 6 December. A monthly output of 55,050 tons of explosive was then settled for, but this was to be reached by monthly increments ending by the beginning of 1942. Powder requirements were reduced to 18,970 tons per month.[1]

On the same day, 29 November, General Thomas was given the task of convincing the *Reichsgruppe Industrie* of the need for such increases.[2] His speech here and his later speeches reveal that he was still as ardent an advocate of 'armament in depth' as he had ever been. After describing with fairness Hitler's strategy, and pointing out that Britain was arming for a long-term war and should therefore be crushed before her economy was ready for such a war, he expressed his opinion that Germany's production was still too low. Apart from this what had emerged so far in Germany, in spite of all that propaganda might say to the contrary, was 'no war economy, but a transitional economy'.[3] The attitude of both people and party to the war had so far been quite wrong.

We do not need to look far for the reasons why that has happened, they are primarily of a political nature, and were based principally on the false hope of the German people that the war would be over by Christmas. . . . The bans on production were not published, the majority of the factories persisted in their peace-time production, raw materials were still utilised in production which was unimportant for

---

[1] FD 1434/46 (No. 168), p. 30.
[2] FD 5454d./45, speech of General Thomas, 29 November 1939.
[3] Ibid., p. 2.

the war, each factory manager sought to retain his reserve of skilled workmen, all in the hope of a quick peace.[1]

This attitude, Thomas urged, must be changed. The latitude allowed to factory managers should be severely restricted and the idea should be abandoned that it was possible to 'defeat England with radio-sets, vacuum-cleaners and cooking-stoves'.[2]

I say to-day quite openly what I have urged for several years; our war-economic organisation with its multiplicity of bodies interfering daily in the war economy, was, even in peace-time, an abortion, for war it is impossible.[3]

Hitler's views on this matter of policy were just as firm. Thomas had suggested stockpiling a certain quantity of steel and non-ferrous metals for the first quarter of 1940.[4] Two days after his speech Keitel replied to this suggestion saying that all-out mine warfare gave Hitler every hope of a decisive success in the shortest possible time against Britain. Therefore it was the Führer's intention that everything possible should be done to build up still further immediate supplies for the Armed Forces even at the cost of the future.[5]

WiRüAmt remained unshaken in its conviction that the intended scale of war production was impossible to achieve, without certain important reforms. One possibility would be to abandon the customary single-shift working in factories and introduce not merely a second-shift but night work as well. Another possibility would be to employ more women in munitions production. The 30,000 women who disappeared from the labour market between October and December 1939 could have resolved the unskilled labour shortage.[6] Worse problems than this arose with the shortages of skilled labour, most of them due to lack of labour mobility. *Waffenamt*, the armaments executive of WiRüAmt believed that the chemical industry was not producing at a sufficient rate to keep the munitions industry busy,[7] but Keitel refused even to mention to Hitler the question of awarding a special priority to the production of military ammunition.[8]

---

[1] Ibid., p. 3.   [2] Ibid., p. 5.   [3] Ibid., p. 5.
[4] FD 4809/45, File 2, Beauftragter für den Vierjahresplan, p. 273.   [5] Ibid., p. 7.
[6] FD 5446/45, WiRüAmt, Thomas to Syrup, 22 February 1940.
[7] FD 1434/46 No. 168, p. 37.   [8] Ibid., pp. 40–41.

Hitler in fact was supremely confident that the targets he had set could be reached. His only doubt appears to have been whether they ought not to be slightly increased to provide a greater margin of safety. It may have been the decision to invade Norway and Denmark before attacking France that finally persuaded Hitler to ask for further slight increases in the production of all kinds of munitions. Final military and naval plans for the invasion of Scandinavia were concluded in the two long conferences between Hitler and the Commanders-in-Chief on 1 and 2 April.[1] The Führer-Command for increases in munitions output over the months between April and October was issued on 3 April.[2] In spite of the gloomy prognostications of WiRüAmt no difficulties occurred that lasted long enough to impede seriously the flow of vital armaments. Some of the earlier problems had been caused by the very severe winter of 1939–40 which had caused delays in the transfer of raw materials, large quantities of which were customarily moved by canal. The coming of spring released raw materials which had been delayed and allowed production to go ahead more rapidly.

By the last week in April the Norwegian campaign was as good as won. The long-postponed attack on France could now be launched. For such an attack an increase in the size of the Army was necessary. The Führer-Command of 22 April ordered the Army to be increased to its greatest size yet. It required a base of 120 divisions, plus 20 motorized divisions, 15 'occupation divisions', and 6 mountain divisions.[3] This increased number of men required further expansion in the output of general army equipment. The invasion took place on 10 May. Its critics both military and economic were confounded by the speed of its success. On 5 June after the British and French northern army groups had been pushed into the sea at Dunkirk the German armies swung southwards across the Somme and advanced on Paris.

The second stage of the invasion of France was regarded by the Führer merely as a mopping-up operation. On 7 June a new

---

[1] W. Hubatsch, *Die deutsche Besetzung von Dänemark und Norwegen 1940*, p. 54.

[2] FD 1434/46 No. 168, pp. 43–45. The revised production schedules for the Air Force were issued on 6 April 1940.

[3] FD 5447/45, Führerbefehl, 22 April 1940.

Führer-Command ordered war production to proceed on the assumption that in the near future France would be completely beaten.[1] Therefore for the moment the Army's task in the war was completed. Men and materials would be withdrawn from army production and transferred to other sectors. Nine days later Pétain came to power in France expressly for the purpose of concluding an armistice.

Hitler was now face to face with the strategic problems involved in pursuing a war against Britain. The extreme flexibility of the Blitzkrieg economy was excellently shown in the way in which preparations were first made for a war against the United Kingdom and then abandoned in favour of an eastern land war. The directive for the invasion of Britain was issued on 16 July 1940. The decision had been taken some time earlier, and the week before the issue of the directive was occupied with conferences on the naval and military problems involved. General Jodl's 'First thoughts on a landing in England' were submitted on 12 July.[2] The next day Hitler discussed final plans with Generals Brauchitsch and Halder at the Berghof, agreed with them, and ordered the preparations to begin immediately. On the same day, 13 July, German war production was diverted into its new channels.[3]

The needs of a campaign against Britain were very much naval and aerial and to keep within the framework of the Blitzkrieg it was essential that increases in such fields should be achieved by sacrificing a certain amount of army production capacity. Therefore army production was to proceed on the assumption that the Army would once again revert to its previous full-time strength of 120 divisions. The men freed would be used in a variety of ways. Older men would simply be released; some younger ones would be transferred to the Air Force; skilled and semi-skilled workmen would return into industrial production on 'ticket-of-leave'. Whether for an invasion of Britain or of Russia a greater number of divisions would need to be motorized. But this redistribution of strength within Germany's armed forces was to take place strictly on the existing

[1] FD 5447/45 WiRüAmt, Führerbefehl 7 June 1940.
[2] R. Wheatley, *Operation Sea-Lion*, pp. 33–36.
[3] FD 5447/45 WiRüAmt, Führerbefehl 13 July 1940.

raw material base, and increases in the output of tanks and troop-carriers would be gained by cutting back on munitions production.[1] Production priorities were also placed on the output of the Ju. 88 bomber, of mines, and of torpedoes.

In practice the monthly increases in aircraft production looked a formidable task.

July 1940. Required increases in certain types of aircraft[2]

Type	Output June 1940	Monthly output demanded
Ju. 88	235	345
Ju. 87	55	60
Me. 109	180	300
Me. 110	117	175
Ju. 58	35	40
DFS. 230	20	160

It was estimated that an extra 110,000 men would be required in the aircraft production industry alone.[3] Increases in naval construction would require a further 50,000 men. The increased output of heavy armour needed 380,000 men more. For all other purposes WiRüAmt added 100,000 to the list and arrived at the grand total of 640,000 more men needed in war production. The total labour force that could be switched from its current employment in the production of munitions, combined with those workmen released from the Army, amounted to 210,000. Again the task was forecast to be impossible. In fact WiRüAmt's estimates of the labour requirements of the new programme were an outrageous exaggeration and they were left to get on with the job.

The result was striking. The speed with which the Blitzkrieg economy could be adjusted to a quite different campaign was never better illustrated than in this instance. Detailed instructions for the switch-over were sent out by WiRüAmt on the day after the Führer-Command.[4] Five days later the decisions on which

[1] FD 5447/45, WiRüAmt, 'An alle Wirtschaftsorganisationen', 14 July 1940.
[2] FD 5447/45, WiRüAmt, 'Umsteuerung der Rüstung', 9 July 1940.
[3] FD 5447/45, WiRüAmt, 10 August 1940.
[4] FD 5447/45, WiRüAmt, 13 July 1940. FD 5447/45, WiRüAmt, 'Richtlinien für die Umsteuerung der Rüstung', 14 July 1940.

the transfer of firms from the control of the Army to that of the Navy depended had been taken.[1] The circulars which were sent out to the factory managers were prefaced with a succinct account of the principles of Blitzkrieg economics emphasizing the importance in war of paying close attention to those fundamental social and political factors which governed the economy.[2]

The Führer-Command of 13 July was concerned primarily, but not solely, with orientating the German war economy towards a war with Britain. Some of the dispositions made reflected the Führer's growing unease about Russian activities on the eastern front. The increased proportion of motorized divisions would be equally necessary in the case of a war with Russia since the land front in such a war would be so long. Initially Hitler seems to have considered a war with Russia in the Autumn irrespective of the state of the war in the West. But his opinions on the western war veered with the different estimates of the success of the air attacks on Britain. Final economic commitment to a war against Russia could only be undertaken at the expense of the arrangements now under way for the invasion across the Channel.

The well-known excerpt from General Halder's diary for 31 July indicates that by that date Hitler had firmly rejected the idea of an autumn and winter campaign in Russia, and had decided that May 1941 was a wiser date if there was to be an invasion. To leave a projected invasion till then would give time for the great increases in the size of the Army. It would also leave more time before the winter for the success of the Blitzkrieg tactics to be employed. For whatever Halder's diary proves about the firmness of Hitler's decision to launch a war on Russia, the decisions announced at the military conference on 31 July indicate very clearly the *kind* of campaign envisaged.

The quicker we smash Russia the better. Operation only makes sense if we smash the state heavily in one blow. Winning a certain amount of territory only does not suffice. A standstill during the

[1] FD 5447/45 WiRüAmt, Minutes of meeting of WiRüAmt, 19 July 1940.
[2] FD 5447/45 WiRüAmt, 19 July 1940. Typically enough the Four-Year-Plan sent round circulars at the same time saying the same thing, FD 5447/45, Beauftragter für den Vierjahresplan, 13–18 July 1940.

winter hazardous. Therefore better to wait, but decision definite to dispose of Russia. Necessary also because of situation in the Baltic. No use for a second Great Power in the Baltic: May '41. Five months' time for carrying out. Preferable still in this year. Can't be done, however, if it is to be carried out as a single operation.[1]

It was such a Blitzkrieg that Hitler had mentioned to Brauchitsch on 21 July.[2] And the point was again clearly made in the directive for 'Operation Barbarossa', as the invasion was called.

The German Armed Forces must be prepared to crush Soviet Russia in a quick campaign even before the end of the war against England.[3]

Ribbentrop, the Foreign Minister, considered eight weeks sufficient time.[4] Former critics of the Blitzkrieg strategy were made less rather than more voluble by the boldness of these plans. It seemed that to engage in a long war of attrition with a power whose economic strength was as great as that of the USSR was to court disaster. If there was to be a war the Blitzkrieg offered the only hope of success. Only in aircraft had Germany's losses so far been great. Her army was battle-hardened. The Russian Army was thought to be numerically no stronger than in 1914 and inferior in quality since the great purges.

Nevertheless an overland invasion on such a scale would still mean changing the order of priorities given to war production by the Führer-Command of 13 July which had placed priorities on aeroplanes, mines and torpedoes. Economic preparations for the war against Russia were therefore intimately bound up with the state of Hitler's war against Britain. In mid-August Hitler finally decided that 'Operation Sea-Lion', the name given to the cross-Channel invasion, could not take the form of a large amphibious landing operation on a broad front. The landing would have to be smaller than at first thought, and could only take place if massive air attacks had first had their effect.[5] On 15 September the most massive of the bomber raids on London was repulsed with heavy losses. On 17 September the invasion

---

[1] *Documents on German Foreign Policy 1918–45*, Series D, x, 373.

[2] I am indebted to Mr. E. Robertson, and to Mr. B. Melland of the Cabinet Office, for permission to read some unpublished work of Mr. Robertson's on German planning for the invasion of Russia.

[3] A. Bullock, op. cit., p. 625.

[4] *Ciano's Diplomatic Diaries, 1939–43*, p. 559.   [5] R. Wheatley, op. cit.

was postponed indefinitely; it clearly could not be reconsidered until Spring 1941. On 28 September a new Führer-Command ordered economic preparations to begin for a Blitzkrieg on Russia.[1]

By May 1941 the Army would have a size of 180 divisions. Munitions production would therefore have to be restored to the levels of June 1940 with some further increases. Tank production, armoured car production, and all forms of artillery for motorized divisions would be stepped up. The transfer back to war production for a land war was bound to be difficult because the Navy and the Air Force would still be involved on the western front, but the solution found was to concentrate production very heavily on certain aspects of naval and air production and transfer resources from the less immediately relevant aspects of these sectors of production. There were to be reductions in the output of bombs and landing craft. Fighter production could not be allowed to drop, and anti-aircraft guns had to be produced in greater quantities. U-boat production was to be given high priority over the construction of all other ships and the Navy was instructed to prepare its capital ships for battle.

Once again the most immediate problem was that of labour. The only real solution was a great increase in the number of foreign workers to be brought into Germany, and this was ordered. At the same time the men who had been released from the Army in the summer on ticket-of-leave had to be recalled.[2] There then began an inquiry into those men who had been graded 'indispensable' (UK)[3] and consequently were exempt from conscription. If they could be replaced by semi-skilled men, or older men, then they were to be called into the Wehrmacht. In any case the UK grade was to be confined to armaments factories engaged in essential production.[4]

Wagenführ argues that very little development of the war economy took place before the invasion of Russia.[5] He cites in evidence the drop in production of most forms of equipment after the start of the invasion. These figures are indisputable and

---

[1] FD 5436c/45 WiRüAmt, Führerbefehl 28 September 1940.
[2] Ibid.   [3] *Unabkömmlich.*
[4] Ibid., p. 3.
[5] *Die Deutsche Industrie im Kriege*, p. 32.

in the light of the war as a whole his argument is surely correct. But it must be remembered that the main effort took place before the invasion, in the winter and spring of 1940–1. The Army was intended to be in Moscow for Christmas 1941.

Except in the production of aircraft nearly all the necessary target figures had been reached before the invasion of Russia. But the difficulties under which the Blitzkrieg economy was functioning are reflected in the failure of aircraft production to maintain its monthly output during the autumn of 1940. Once resources in September 1940 had been diverted to U-boat and tank production a sharp fall is apparent in the numbers of air-craft produced.[1]

Aircraft production, Autumn 1940

Type	Sept.	Oct.	Nov.	Dec.
Ju. 88 (fighter)	232	189	146	146
Ju. 88 (reconnaissance)	83	61	46	32
He. 111	90	98	41	69
He. 126	35	23	12	7
Bf. 110	112	100	73	43
Ju. 87	57	62	57	31
Bf. 109	195	144	60	115
Ju. 52	47	41	37	30

Not only do these figures show a total decline but they are also a long way below the target figures demanded. The executive orders drawn up on the basis of the Führer-Command of 13 July had stipulated a target for Ju. 88 of 345 per month and of Ju. 87 of 60 per month. The Führer-Command of 28 September had not modified this.

But the picture in the aircraft production industry was gloomier than elsewhere, and the experience of war pressures was forcing administrators to find quicker solutions to their problems. In June 1941 an attempt was made to concentrate armaments production into a smaller number of factories, primarily by bringing the production of components under the

---

[1] Quartermaster-General, 6. Abt. 28 June 1945. These are figures of aircraft 'accepted'. Because of delivery delays they do not tally with the exact monthly production figures. But the figures for aircraft production proper are very frag-mentary.

same roof as the production of the finished armaments.[1] This proved a total failure; nine months later there were still 174 separate important armaments production managements.

On the eve of the invasion of Russia the decision was taken to reduce the level of armaments production.[2] Within the context of the Blitzkrieg this was an entirely rational decision. It was also a way of trying to solve the difficulties of the aircraft industry. All the resources set free were to be transferred to production for the Air Force. Aircraft production was now given top priority, followed by tanks and U-boats. These changes were effected by the Führer-Command of 20 June 1941. But this Command had only a short life before becoming embedded in the more important Führer-Command of 14 July, which restated production priorities. Aircraft production was still top-priority, but it was now followed by increases in raw material production, particularly mineral oil. The U-boat programme, all that remained of the Navy programme of 28 September 1940, was unchanged. But anti-aircraft gun production, under the joint control of Army and Air Force, was placed equal in priority with tank production. Even so, by May 1942 there were to be 36 divisions supplied with the Panther tank.[3]

Quite large increases in aircraft production were in fact obtained, although the underlying strain of an insufficient basis of productive capacity is perhaps revealed by a tendency to a falling away in November and December 1941.

Aircraft production, 1941[4]

Type	May	June	July	Aug.	Sept.	Oct.	Nov.	Dec.
Ju. 88 (fighter)	160	135	186	253	253	206	168	176
Ju. 88 (rec.)	8	53	69	83	52	45	41	49
He. 111	60	73	111	90	100	100	100	100
Do. 217	13	16	37	33	35	35	16	22
Ju. 87	22	54	37	26	10	25	38	49

The output of certain types which were now less essential fell more severely. That is true of the Bf. 109 where the output fell

[1] FD 1434/46 (No. 170) WiRüAmt, 'Umstellung der Rüstung', March 1942, p. 11.
[2] Ibid., p. 2.   [3] FD 5452/45 WiRüAmt, Führerbefehl 14 July 1941.
[4] Gen. Qu. 6. Abt. op. cit.

from 391 in May to 192 in December, and of the Bf. 110 where the comparable figures were 93 and 1.[1]

The unforeseen economic factor in the invasion of Russia was the heavy losses of equipment on such a long front. These losses combined with a fall in army armaments production below the limit permitted by the Führer-Command of 14 July. One of the purposes of that decree had been to secure a stricter definition of production priorities, which WiRüAmt considered had been rather confused by the decree of 20 June on aircraft production.[2] When the decree of 14 July had been first promulgated WiRüAmt had been of the opinion that changes in priority of such an order were only possible if all the 'mobilizable strength in the Greater German area is mobilized as quickly and as fully as possible'.[3] At any rate the implementation of the programme proved immensely difficult. The minutes of a meeting on 16 August between General Keitel and the heads of the different Wehrmacht armament branches are very revealing.[4] Keitel defined the principles of the Blitzkrieg as being, in the first place not to increase armaments production capacity, in the second place not to utilize any greater supply of raw materials than previously, and in the third place not to increase the labour strength of the armaments industry. The experience in Russia, maintained Keitel, indicated that there was a great deal of surplus infantry equipment. Although all administrative branches concerned with armaments production expressed themselves unanimously against such a policy, a final embargo was placed on the building of any further floor-space for armaments manufacture. Russia's most vital producing area, the Führer believed, would soon be in German hands.[5] The Blitzkrieg must be made to work.

On 11 September a fresh Führer-Command redefined the necessity of keeping strictly to the top priorities of the armament programme.[6] It also reflected a certain uneasy feeling that munitions production was falling too quickly, and attempted to

---

[1] Ibid.   [2] FD 1434/46 No. 170 loc. cit. p. 2.

[3] FD 5452/45, WiRüAmt, 'Richtlinien des Führers vom 14.7.41 für die künftige Kriegführung u.s.w.', 19 July 1941.

[4] FD 5450/45, WiRüAmt, 'Niederschrift über die Rüstungs-Besprechung Chef OKW u.s.w.', 11 September 1941.

[5] Ibid.   [6] FD 1434/46 No. 170, loc. cit., p. 27.

remedy this by creating arbitration procedures for disputes concerning spheres of authority. The value of light infantry munitions produced in April 1941 was 12·9 million reichsmarks; in December it was 6·3 million.[1] The value of artillery ammunition produced in February 1941 was 69·1 million reichsmarks; in December it was 15·7 million. These figures are not far different from those for weapons production over the same period.

German armament production before and during the
Russian campaign[2]

Weapons group	Month in which 1941 maximum reached	Decline from maximum by December
Light infantry arms	April	− 38%
Heavy infantry arms	August	− 49%
Army artillery	April	− 67%
A/C armament	August	− 36%
Tank guns	December	− 0%
Flak	November	− 17%
Weapons total	July	− 29%

Had the U.S.S.R. collapsed, as Hitler had hoped, before the end of 1941, the Blitzkrieg would have justified itself. But when, on 26 November 1941, the Russian armies began the counter-attack that led to the recapture of Rostov-on-Don the Blitzkrieg was doomed. It was some time before this was recognized in Berlin. The Blitzkrieg had been highly successful and there was great reluctance to abandon it. The story of the autumn of 1941 is primarily the story of the attempt to drive the existing German war economy to its last gasp before reluctantly taking the decision to abandon those principles on which the National Socialist economy was based and to commit Germany to a full war economy.

During the Russian campaign it was becoming evident that the resources which Germany had committed to the war in the East were barely sufficient. Her economic base was not adequate to force the defeat of Russia in five months. It is therefore worth considering at what points the Blitzkrieg economy was most highly strained.

[1] *Die Deutsche Industrie im Kriege*, op. cit., p. 33.　　[2] Ibid., p. 32.

One of the most noticeable features of 1939–41 was Germany's constant labour problems. Single-shift working was the almost universal practice in Germany, therefore machines and tools were very often under-utilized. If single-shift working was to be maintained more skilled and semi-skilled men were needed for the Blitzkrieg to function smoothly. If double or triple-shift working were to be introduced to step up output and utilize the machines, a still greater number of skilled men, or a programme of labour dilution, could not be avoided. Double or triple-shift working would have been against the whole spirit of the Blitzkrieg, machines were therefore left under-employed. The shortages of skilled men were often local, but direction of labour was also against the whole spirit of the Blitzkrieg economy. The local shortages of unskilled labour which occurred from time to time could have been avoided by employing more women. But the Party was the victim of its own subservience to, and propaganda for, the idea that the place of the woman was in the home. Hitler held quite decided views that the employment of women would not only make industrial relations more difficult, especially in the special problems it would bring before supervisors, but would also be biologically harmful to the race.[1] In February 1942 Speer calculated that at least 80,000 women had left industry proper since July 1939.[2] This in fact was an overestimate; the number of women employed in all industry did not vary by more than 300,000 throughout the war; between Summer 1939 and Spring 1942 it decreased by about 40,000.

The most dramatic drop in the total labour force revealed by these figures is that caused by the initial sudden withdrawal of labour by the armed forces at the beginning of the war. Here the impact of war was felt with great keenness, even by the civilian sector of the economy. In the first two and a half years of war the armed forces drafted more than seven and a half million men from the available labour force.[3] During this period Germany absorbed 3,800,000 workers from foreign territories. It seems likely that of all categories of the labour force that of

[1] FD 1434/46 No. 167, WiRüAmt, Speer to all Gauleiters, 18 February 1942. This is also a frequent theme of Hitler's conversations. *Hitler's Secret Conversations, 1941–44.*
[2] Ibid., p. 2.   [3] Ibid., p. 31.

'handwork' suffered the most severe depredations.[1] Distribution services lost 1,400,000 workers in this two and a half year period. Pre-war administrative services were probably overswollen and did not lose too much from this letting. When seen as an exercise in the redistribution of manpower the Blitzkrieg appears as a considerable economic effort. A large number of difficult administrative problems were solved in this sphere long before 1942. Yet it was in this sector that the Blitzkrieg economy showed the most strain.

Germans in industrial labour force 1939/44[2]

(in thousands)

	Total Force	No. of Women
31 July 1939	10,405	2,620
31 May 1940	9,415	2,565
30 November 1940	9,401	2,615
31 May 1941	9,057	2,613
30 November 1941	8,861	2,626
31 May 1942	8,378	2,580
30 November 1942	8,011	2,493
31 March 1943	7,893	2,576
31 July 1943	8,099	2,808
30 November 1943	7,948	2,787
31 January 1944	7,782	2,781
31 March 1944	7,720	2,745
31 May 1944	7,715	2,737
31 July 1944	7,515	2,678

The Ministry of Economic Warfare in the United Kingdom had surmised that the weakness of Germany's economy was really her excessive dependence on supplies of raw materials from overseas.[3] The Ministry's hopes of exploiting this weakness faded fast as Germany conquered new material bases and captured enemy stockpiles. Also, of course, Germany's constant success put her in a much stronger bargaining position in relation to neutrals such as Sweden or Turkey.[4] One of the

[1] Ibid., p. 204. *Handwerk*, or domestic crafts and industry, such as the putting-out of tailoring and umbrellas, had always occupied a larger proportion of the German labour force than the British.

[2] U.S.S.B.S., *Effects*, op. cit., p. 209.

[3] W. N. Medlicott, *The Economic Blockade*, p. 32.

[4] Ibid., ii, p. 53.

motives for the Norwegian campaign had been to secure the supply of the annual 10 million tons of iron ore from Sweden. Many of Germany's more chronic raw material shortages were overcome by experiment and substitution, but a great deal more of this kind of technological triumph was achieved after 1942 than before. And there can be little doubt that the Allied policy of blockade was fully justified. In fact the Blitzkrieg drove stocks of vital raw materials down to dangerously low levels. This kind of wholesale utilization of stockpiles is one of the strongest testimonies to Hitler's confidence in the Blitzkrieg. It was to create many serious problems after the Blitzkrieg had been abandoned.

Non-ferrous and ferro-alloy metal supplies and consumption[1]
(in thousands of metric tons metal content)

Metal	1939	1940	1941
Copper			
annual addition to stock	312·0	318·0	329·0
consumption	324·0	292·0	372·0
Tungsten			
annual addition to stock	2·7	0·9	1·0
consumption	4·2	3·7	3·4
Lead			
annual addition to stock	216·0	248·0	224·0
consumption	248·4	224·0	277·0
Nickel			
annual addition to stock	8·5	13·7	8·8
consumption	10·1	11·6	9·2
Molybdenum			
annual addition to stock	1·4	0·3	0·5
consumption	3·4	2·2	1·8
Chrome			
annual addition to stock	58·1	13·8	11·2
consumption	48·1	35·3	43·3

Discussion of Germany's raw material base leads naturally to the last and probably the most dramatic reason for the failure of the Blitzkrieg economy. Germany's economy from 1939 to 1942 became steadily less national and more European. But she never in these years evolved any effective system of amalgamating

[1] U.S.S.B.S., *Effects*, op. cit., p. 264.

these various national economies into one German economy. The 'New Order' was an extension of the Blitzkrieg economy to the occupied territories.[1] It was the economics of 'smash and grab' performed less efficiently on a much larger scale. The occupied territories were regarded merely as areas to be plundered in the simplest way. Germany might well have imposed on the civilian population of these areas economic burdens of the kind which were not imposed on the German people themselves: but although the occupations were harsh they were not systematic. This was certainly one of Germany's great failures.

The competing economic administrative machinery of Germany, the absence of top-level planning, the administrative insistence that a war economy was merely an economy to produce a certain fixed quantity of armaments, the whole apparatus of the Blitzkrieg machinery was transferred to the occupied territories.[2] There were the same kind of disputes as in Germany about who controlled what in the economy. And so the German disputes of 1939 were scrawled gradually across the face of Europe. One striking illustration will suffice.

The hard winter of 1939–40 brought difficulties with the transport of Roumanian oil up the Danube to Germany. These difficulties were exacerbated by activities of the British Ministry of Economic Warfare.[3] Readjustment of the Russo-German partition-line in Poland, on 28 September 1939, had entailed German withdrawal from the Borislav-Drohobycz oil region, thus aggravating German dependence on Roumanian supply. The monthly figure for German oil imports from Roumania had been fixed on 20 December 1939 at 130,000 tons.[4] On 11 February 1940 Roumania had despatched only 100,000 tons of

[1] There was much discussion, at the time, of the 'New Order' as a system of European economic organization, both by National Socialist propaganda and by foreign economists taking their information from that source. See, for instance, P. Einzig, *Hitler's New Order in Europe*, and other books by the same author; O. Nathan, *The Nazi Economic System*; and C. W. Guillebaud, 'Hitler's New Economic Order for Europe', in *The Economic Journal*, l, 1940. In the light of post-war evidence a lot of this discussion is very inaccurate and misinformed.

[2] A. Dallin, *German Rule in Russia, 1941–45, passim*. Easily the best study of German rule in an occupied territory.

[3] W. N. Medlicott, op. cit., p. 254.

[4] FD 4809/45, WiRüAmt, 'Mineralöle und die Versorgungslage im Kriege', 31 August 1941, p. 72.

crude oil to Germany, whereas Britain had received 255,000 tons.[1] Britain, Holland, and the United States controlled about 52 per cent of the capital in the Roumanian oil industry[2] and although in the long run German pressure was bound to force the Roumanian oil traffic up to the required figure, anti-German pressure could, for the moment, place Germany in difficulties. Later the situation was again made difficult by occasional Allied sabotage and the great fire at the Standard Refinery on 15 July.[3]

A meeting of the chiefs of the different Wehrmacht economic divisions was held to discuss the situation on 27 March 1940, under the auspices and chairmanship of Göring in his capacity as Commissioner for the Four-Year-Plan.[4] Whereas the nominal imports from Roumania should have been 130,000 tons per month, 30,000 tons of this was allocated to the Protectorate of Bohemia and Moravia, and 5,000 tons to the Danube fleet itself. Consequently even if the Roumanians delivered the full quota only 95,000 tons was available for distribution in Germany. Actual deliveries for the first quarter of 1940 amounted, after the deductions, to only 50,000 tons.[5] From Russia there came 80,000 tons. Thomas's calculations about the economy's need for fuel oil indicated that supply was falling short by 50,000 to 60,000 tons monthly.[6]

Here was a neat problem to be solved. Under the 'New Order' some readjustment of the supply to the occupied territories might have been expected, better still a speeding-up of development and investment in the Austrian oilfield. But there was no authority except Hitler higher than the committee which met on 27 March to decide on this issue. Consequently all the Wehrmacht economic representatives present realized that one of them, or all of them, would have to surrender some of their allocation of crude oil. Therefore they all hastily demonstrated that by now their allocations had reached an irreducible minimum. The Reichs Economics Ministry turned the attack on the Navy by pointing out that they had much greater reserves of furnace

---

[1] Ibid., p. 74.   [2] W. N. Medlicott, op. cit., i, p. 250.
[3] FD 4809/45, op. cit., p. 77.
[4] FD 4809/45, Beauftragter für den Vierjahresplan, 'Sitzung betr. Mineralölversorgung unter Vorsitz des Herrn Generalfeldmarschall', 27 March 1940.
[5] Ibid., p. 2.   [6] Ibid., p. 4.

oil than seemed warrantable.[1] There now began a long struggle to force the Navy to part with some of its reserves.

The complexity of having so many administrative branches involved in the dispute enabled the Navy to evade the issue temporarily. They were further helped by the reopening of the Danube in the spring and the increase in the flow of oil which resulted. But the Ministry of Economics continued to press for some surrender of naval stocks of furnace oil. On 12 July 1940 the Navy seized and appropriated to its own use 10,000 tons of diesel fuel in Holland during the occupation.[2] This oil had been destined for a holding company whose task was to transfer foreign oil stocks to Germany.[3] On 16 July the holding company protested about the Navy action.[4] On 17 July the Reichs Economics Ministry supported the protest and suggested that the amount seized in Holland should be compensated for when the amount of oil to be allocated to the civilian economy and the Navy was fixed. Also it was suggested that the compensation should be obtained from the 13,000 tons of diesel fuel to be imported in August from Sweden mainly for naval use.[5] On 13 August the Navy persuaded the High Command of the Armed Forces not to agree to that solution.[6] The Navy's reserves of oil were unresistant to low temperatures and would not be much use for agricultural purposes. But the holding company was now demanding to know precisely from which of its stores the Navy would release the compensatory 10,000 tons of oil. They pressed WiRüAmt to act on their behalf since it had a greater degree of control over the economy than any other organization. This led Thomas to suggest a compromise whereby the Navy should surrender certain quantities of ingredients of furnace oil out of their allocation. 5,000 tons of pit-coal-tar furnace oil would be surrendered to the Pölitz works and 11,400 tons of lignite-tar furnace oil to the Leuna synthetic oil plant.[7] This compromise was rejected as useless by the Navy on the

[1] Ibid., p. 2.
[2] FD 4199/45, OKM to WiRüAmt, telegram, 12 July 1940.
[3] Zentralbüro für Mineralöl G.m.b.H.
[4] FD 4199/45, Zentralbüro für Mineralöl to OKW, 16 July 1940.
[5] FD 4199/45, Reichswirtschaftsministerium to OKW, 17 July 1940.
[6] FD 4199/45, OKM to OKW, 13 August 1940.
[7] FD 4199/45, Thomas to OKM, 31 December 1940.

grounds that the system of blending then in operation would make the total loss of furnace oil much greater.[1]

The dispute had now raised the issue of who controlled the German war economy both within and outside the German frontiers. Admiral Raeder wrote personally to Thomas on 15 January 1941 to say that he would not give up any oil from naval stocks without a signed order from the Führer.[2]

I would like to repeat emphatically that I am fundamentally unable to agree to a surrender of oil from navy stocks or a decrease in agreed supplies of oil, except on the basis of an order personally sent to me by the Führer.

Lest the letter should not sufficiently convey its point Raeder had added 'personally' in his own hand afterwards.

Raeder, however, was by this time fighting a losing battle. The day before he wrote, the High Command of the Armed Forces, in fact Keitel himself, had decided to end the impasse by diverting on his own initiative 37,000 tons of furnace oil, much of which had been allocated to the Navy, straight to the Pölitz works.[3] In return the Navy would be offered 90,000 tons of Esthonian shale-oil which could be worked up into a much smaller quantity of diesel fuel. It had taken in all nine months to reach this solution at a time when oil was a highly valued commodity. In a continuous series of such disputes Germany squandered away the advantages of the territories she had occupied. Failure to exploit these territories systematically drove her into the administratively simpler habit of merely living off the country. Consequently the German occupations came to resemble gigantic looting operations. There was little that was new and less that was orderly in the 'New Order'.

This incident also focuses attention on the weaknesses of German internal economic administration and the Blitzkrieg economics which it served. The practically unregulated competition between bureaucrats and the three separate armament agencies of the Wehrmacht was bound to be disastrous should any development into a fuller war economy prove necessary. Only in decisions on armaments priorities was there any top-

---

[1] FD 4199/45, Raeder to Thomas, 15 January 1941.
[2] Ibid.   [3] FD 4199/45, Keitel to Raeder, 14 January 1941.

level planning. As long as the level of armament was not too high, and the system like that which prevailed before 1939, the machinery worked. Private manufacturers negotiated directly with the three armament agencies of the Armed Forces and Hitler decided from time to time what level of armament these agencies were entitled to demand. WiRüAmt tried to exercise some control over navy and air force production but each service was concerned with its own factories. Guns are not made without steel, and no one had any overall control over steel production. Steel, and most raw materials were allocated on the basis of quarterly requests by all having a claim. Those responsible for each sector of production demanded more steel than they could use. They then got less than they had asked for, and often more than they needed. Some more rational method of allocation would have to be introduced if the Blitzkrieg had to be abandoned. This system had creaked from the start of the war once it was a question of raw materials in shorter supply than steel, oil for instance.

A war geared to sudden spurts of economic effort will be a war fought in strategic bursts. This was how Hitler had conducted his foreign policy from 1936 to Autumn 1941. Each military campaign was planned by the Führer as a concentrated drive to one goal. Production had to be allied to that drive at the cost of sacrifice in other spheres of armament production. This could work when Germany fought on one front only. Russia's ability to survive the 'five-months war' committed Hitler to a struggle on two fronts. One front was primarily military, the other was largely naval and aerial. Thus the Blitzkrieg became impossible.

CHAPTER III

Fritz Todt

WHEN Albert Speer, German Minister of Armaments and
Munitions, surrendered to the Allied armies in 1945 he
proved the most valuable of all their prisoners. He
brought with him a bulging briefcase of documents from his
Ministry.[1] He was only too willing to discuss his role in the war
with Allied interrogators. He had been Minister of Armaments
and Munitions for just over three years. In these years he had
been responsible for what was later termed the 'armaments
miracle', the almost constant increases in production from early
1942 to late 1944 which had so taken by surprise Germany's
opponents. In these years he had changed from being Hitler's
personal friend to being the most powerful and successful member of the government, and then into being a bitter and determined opponent of the National Socialist régime. He had an
amazing story to tell. To whom should he tell it?

Speer was transferred to the reception centre for important
prisoners, 'Dustbin'. Once there a spate of people and agencies
were eager to interview this important and talkative member of
the vanquished government.[2] For political reasons it proved
impossible to allow only those people who could do so with
profit to interrogate the prisoner. The committee in charge of
permissions to interrogate was inundated with requests; and
was often forced to grant permission according to the importance of the petitioner. Nevertheless, the reports of these interrogations have proved one of the best sources for the history
of Hitler's régime.[3] The reports were at first issued in chrono-

[1] C. Wilmot, *The Struggle for Europe*, p. 820.
[2] I am indebted for an interesting account of these events, and for certain information relative to Speer and to the system of interrogation, to Mr. (formerly
Major) E. Williams, of the Credit Assurance Company, London.
[3] They were used to great effect by H. R. Trevor-Roper, *The Last Days of Hitler*.

54

logical order and merely numbered in sequence from the first exploratory interviews to the much more detailed questionnaires which came later. After a while attempts were made to impose some order on the process. But many subjects were omitted and many repeated several times.

The upshot was that Speer soon discovered he had some control over this situation. He was infallibly polite to, and cooperative with, all comers. But he chose his answers, in particular the level of his replies, to suit his interrogators. On vital subjects he is responsible for much of our knowledge. Where it has proved possible to check documentary evidence it has almost invariably justified not merely his statements of fact but his opinions as well. However, in the extraordinary situation in which he found himself he would hardly have been human had he not given from time to time a misleading slant to his story. And it was perfectly possible to do this without distorting fact, all it needed was a few omissions.

It must be admitted that there are not many to whom history is as indebted as Speer, especially for the preservation of documents. Yet in two particular ways he gave a false impression. Firstly he indicated that his original appointment as Minister of Armaments and Munitions had been one of those wayward impulses to which Hitler was prone; that he himself had neither angled for the job, nor even expected it; that, in fact, a more unlikely man to receive such an appointment in the spring of 1942 could scarcely be imagined. This was not entirely true. Speer's appointment, although unexpected, was not astonishing. He had been working in the recently created Reichs Ministry for Armaments and Munitions as chief constructional engineer and architect, and he was also the 'official' architect to the Third Reich.

Speer's own version of events was as follows. After his appointment, he perceived that the only hope for German success was to go over to a full war economy. For this, absolute powers were necessary for some ministry to control the economy. Consequently he converted the small and not particularly significant Ministry of Armaments and Munitions into the controlling force behind the German war economy. Therefore the dividing point between Germany's Blitzkrieg economy and Germany's full war economy was really the moment of Albert Speer's appointment as Minister of Armaments and Munitions. In fact, Speer's powers were still fairly limited until 1943, therefore he sometimes gave the impression that Hitler was not converted to the new policy until after the defeat at Stalingrad. The armaments increases of 1942 could be attributed to Speer's personal abandonment of the Blitzkrieg in those spheres of production for which he had responsibility.

This may be the source of some confusion of thought on German war strategy. There is some indication of such confusion in the United States Strategic Bombing Survey.[1] Klein places the abandonment of the Blitzkrieg quite firmly after the defeat at Stalingrad.[2] It was, he claims, Germany's Pearl Harbor. Nothing could be more misleading. The Blitzkrieg was abandoned as soon as the first serious setbacks in Russia occurred. From the winter of 1941–2 Germany was arming for a long war and abandoning the economic policies she had previously pursued.

Those authors who have set the end of the Blitzkrieg in early 1942 have tended to link it entirely with the appointment of Speer. Wagenführ divides his book into a pre-Speer era and a post-Speer era. Again this is misleading because it places Hitler's change of heart on war strategy as late as February 1942, whereas in fact it had come earlier and in a more gradual way.

This would have been seen by a study of the work of Speer's predecessor as Minister of Armaments and Munitions, Fritz Todt. Pretty well all that can be discovered about Todt from the Bombing Survey is that he died in an air crash on 8 February 1942. The importance of his death, it appears, was that Speer followed him in office, and everyone was now able to get on with the job properly. Klein takes exactly the same view, which he borrows directly from Speer,[3] who maintained to his interrogators that Todt was not interested in expanding his Ministry at all.[4]

---

[1] U.S.S.B.S., *Effects*, op. cit., p. 18.   [2] B. H. Klein, op. cit., p. 202.

[3] 'Todt was more interested in his construction work than in becoming involved in disputes with General Thomas, the army procurement agencies, or Hitler and Göring. According to Speer, then one of his assistants, Todt spent only one or two days a week in Berlin'; B. H. Klein, op. cit., p. 152.

[4] Speer Report No. 1.

In fact the first architect of Germany's change to a war economy was Fritz Todt. He was a very able and efficient minister, responsible for the preparatory work on, and in some cases the initiation of, many of the reforms of the German economic administration which have been attributed to Speer. He was destined to be the powerful figure who would exercise some measure of overall control over the war economy when he met his untimely death in an air-crash. It was his death which robbed him of much of the credit which he deserves for his work.

Todt was born in Baden, at Pforzheim, in 1891. His early life does not distinguish him in any way from the typical convert to National Socialism.[1] He served in the First World War and returned to work for a firm of constructional engineers in Munich. By 1922 he had adopted a complete loyalty to the Party which was to remain unshaken for the rest of his life. He worked within the Party on a scheme for ending unemployment by the construction of fast motor roads. These were to become the *Autobahnen* of the 1930s, and Todt was put in charge of their construction. In this job he made a reputation for technical efficiency and disregard of red tape. He was a skilful administrator who always insisted on giving the expert a free hand and had no use for bureaucratic punctilio. He was to prove exactly what Hitler was looking for later on. In May 1938 he was put in charge of the western fortifications. In December he became 'Plenipotentiary-General for the Control of Building'.[2] By this time the *Organisation Todt* had been established out of the building workers on the West Wall. At the time this was not much more than a title, but with the outbreak of the war, the OT developed into a large para-military formation.[3] Todt was building up his own private empire in the recognized National Socialist way.[4] In February 1940 he received a special commission as a trouble-shooter from Hitler, to enforce economy in

[1] E. Schönleben, *Fritz Todt*, pp. 28 ff.
[2] 'Generalbevollmächtigter für die Regelung der Bauwirtschaft.' FD 3049/49 (Folder No. 1), 'Ministerium Todt'.
[3] W. Kumpf, *Die Organisation Todt im Kriege*.
[4] Speer accused Todt of filling his organization with men from Sager and Wörner, a firm of engineers in Munich, FD 3250/45, Speer Report No. 20, Supplement 3.

the use of metals, especially copper, by the armaments industry.[1]

Copper requirements in early 1940 could not be met from the almost exhausted stocks. The problem had come to the surface when the Army had tried to induce the Air Force to reduce its copper demands. Göring maintained that Air Force consumption was lower than the figure given by the Ministry of Economics. Todt was appointed to resolve the dispute and at the same time speed up technical innovations which would reduce the consumption of copper. This he succeeded in doing by implementing the already developed process of substituting iron driving-bands for copper ones in munitions. His appointment had been within the Four-Year-Plan as 'inspector-general for special tasks of the Four-Year-Plan'.[2] In such a position, Göring was his chief. But part of his responsibility was to stop the Air Force encroaching on Army production plant, and it was in this respect that he came to earn the hostility of Göring.[3] This same hostility was later transferred to Speer.[4] Thanks to his success Todt became on 17 March 1940 the first Reichs Minister for Armaments and Munitions.[5]

The powers of this Ministry were very limited and its tasks very specific. But Todt's appointment meant a faltering step towards a greater degree of collective responsibility in the field of munitions production. More important, it meant that a new organization, and an efficient one, was reinforcing the pressure for administrative reform already being exerted by WiRüAmt. By his very position, which depended on increasing Army production, Todt was bound to attempt some rationalization in economic matters. Walter Rohland[6] said of him,

I believed I had found in Dr. Todt, in contrast to my previous experience, a man of such character as to admit healthier criticism, both of measures taken by him and of politics, and who would him-

---

[1] FD 3049/49 (Folder no. 1), 'Ministerium Todt'. FD 3298/45, Dr. W. Bosch, 'Organisation and Function of the Reichs Ministry for Armaments and War Production'.
[2] 'Generalinspekteur für Sonderaufgaben des Vierjahresplanes.' FD 5454a/45.
[3] FD 3298/45, W. Bosch, 'Organisation and Function etc.'
[4] Speer Report No. 1.
[5] FD 5445/45, 17 March 1940, 'Erlass des Führers und Reichskanzlers über die Bestellung eines Reichsministers für Bewaffnung und Munition'.
[6] Chairman of the main committee for iron production.

self possess the courage to pass on these criticisms and his own to the highest authority without any consideration for his own person.[1]

His relations with WiRüAmt and with OKW were uneasy; the Army regarded him as a civilian interloper who was taking power from them. On 24 January 1941 Todt attempted a New Year settlement with Keitel.[2] Quite correctly he identified the major cause of friction as competition for the prestige of having the first word with the Führer and, consequently, of eliciting favourable decisions from him. They therefore arrived at an agreement whereby they would notify each other previously of all important matters which they were taking to Hitler for decision.

One of Todt's difficulties with the Army was his desire to 'debureaucratizc' production. He wished to hand over even more completely the technical control of, and responsibility for, production and design to the factory managements themselves, thereby emancipating them from the loose control of the Wehrmacht. To quote Rohland's opinion again:

> He very soon recognised these weaknesses and attempted to build up the armaments industry on the basis of his own experiences during the construction of the West Wall—by mobilising the many experts that were available in the whole of industry.[3]

The particular method which Todt adopted was that of controlling the armaments industry by a series of committees. This system of tiers of committees, the most distinctive feature of the German war economy, is invariably attributed to Speer as one of his most important reforms.[4] In fact it originated in the summer of 1940 in the munitions industry and was the work of Todt. Saur describes the setting-up of this first committee and its purpose.

> In the course of the first weeks of the Ministry a Special Committee for Munitions was set up under Director-General Kessler in contradistinction to the previous procedure of finally channelling armament tasks through military branches . . .

[1] Speer Report No. 66.
[2] FD 1434/46 No. 167, Todt to Keitel, 24 January 1941.
[3] Speer Report No. 66.
[4] U.S.S.B.S., *Effects*, p. 7, 'Speer set about replacing the existing machinery of control with a new organization'. B. H. Klein, op. cit., pp. 220–5.

The job of the Committees was to ally the strongest parts of the industry to these production aims and, particularly, to supervise technical questions of production in the fields concerned.[1]

It is important to examine the committee system and see how it functioned, for it was around this early experiment in the munitions industry that Germany's war production was ultimately to be so successfully planned. The abandonment of the Blitzkrieg was to be not only the abandonment of a whole strategy in the field, but of a whole method of fighting the war. Without completely new machinery there could have been no change to a full war economy. Therefore the first symptoms of the abandonment of Blitzkrieg economics are administrative ones. It is to the machinery of administration that we must now turn. In this context Todt's early experiments in the munitions industry set up a prototype of the machinery which was to be universally copied in the winter of 1941–2.

The munitions industry was to be controlled by a main committee (*Hauptausschuss*) and a series of special committees (*Sonderausschüsse*). The main committee would control all factories making munitions. Its powers of control were very extensive.[2] It could force the different firms to pool their knowledge of production techniques, and also of means of rationalizing production. The committee was to carry out a census of the productive capacity of all the plant under its control and then regulate all plans for the purchase of new machinery. Machinery and labour could be transferred from one plant to another in order to enable certain factories to reach their targets. The manufacture of certain types of munitions and components was centralized on those factories which could produce them most efficiently. The responsibility of the main committee ended with the completion of production. Transport and acceptance were the responsibility of the relevant Wehrmacht Ordnance Department.

The special committees functioned as sub-committees of the main committee. Each individual type of munition was assigned to a special committee. The chairmen of these com-

---

[1] FD 3049/49, (Folder no. 1), 'Ministerium Todt'.
[2] FD 3298/45, W. Bosch, 'The Organisation of German Industry for War Production'.

mittees were usually chosen from the ranks of factory managers, often from that factory which had evolved the most efficient method of manufacture, although this was not always the case. Dietrich Stahl, manager of the most efficient tracer munition factory, became chairman of the special committee for tracer munition.[1] The special committees were not in any way under the authority of the purchasing departments of the Services; all chairmen were appointed by the Minister of Armaments and Munitions and received their directives straight from him.

The way in which the system was supposed to work was this. Demands for munitions had first to be sanctioned by the Führer. They then were laid before the main committee for munitions. Later on, as the power of the Ministry of Armaments and Munitions increased it became an essential intermediary, but in 1940 and 1941 demands were laid by the Wehrmacht directly in front of the main committee. The main committee, which, of course, contained Wehrmacht representatives, would decide how best the demand could be executed. It would then split the order up among the factories under its control, according to their various production capacities, and notify the ordering agency of the ratio in which the order had been placed among different enterprises. The Wehrmacht agency would then write out individual orders for these firms so that after the orders had been delivered, the individual firms could receive payment direct from the ordering agency. Raw material allocation for fulfilling orders was always strictly supervised by the main committee, so was the achievement of delivery dates. The main committee had very wide powers over the firms in the industry with regard to those problems.

This system of industrial control left complete freedom within the factory to the industrialists themselves. For this reason it was ultimately given the title 'Self-Administration and Responsibility of German Industry'.[2] But it had within it the germ of a strong indirect control by a civil ministry of armaments production. In fact the system was to turn into a more elaborate

[1] Speer Report No. 32, p. 2.
[2] 'Organisation für die Selbstverantwortung und die Verantwortlichkeit der deutschen Industrie.'

structure. The elaborations, however, were always on the basic theme of Todt's munitions committees of 1940.

By the Summer of 1940 Todt was already planning to extend his committee system to tank production. A main committee for tank production was finally established in September 1940.[1] The initial comparison of production methods which the committee carried out revealed some startling information. Consumption of raw materials, utilization of machines, and time taken for the completion of orders, even demand for power, could vary between plant and plant by as much as 300 per cent.[2] There were also striking differences in the quality of the finished product.

These reforms of Todt's were not, of course, concerned with putting the war economy on a broader footing. His object was to ease the flow of production and at the same time to cheapen its cost. Nor were these reforms immediately successful in every case. The gap separating many of the central departments responsible for economic administration from industry itself proved difficult to leap. Todt appointed special commissioners to achieve the necessary liaisons. On the whole this was successful but occasionally the new men busied themselves unnecessarily, as far as the committees were concerned, in the actual drawing-up of the programmes.[3] Their position was very similar to that of the *Wirtschaftsführer* who had been appointed by Thomas to bridge the gap between WiRüAmt and industry, and whose main function was now to attend the annual beer-parties in Berlin.

During the autumn of 1941 Hitler became convinced that the Blitzkrieg, which seemed to be running into difficulties, could be preserved if the rationalization of production methods was thoroughly undertaken. He saw the real obstacle to rationalization of production in the vested interests of the less efficient industrialists, and that a system of 'self-government for industry', such as Todt had begun to apply to production, could be applied equally well to development.[4] Certainly the system by which the military, naval and air force requirements for generally used articles had to be met to individual specifications

---

[1] Speer Report No. 66.　　[2] Ibid.　　[3] Ibid.
[4] FD 3049/49 (Folder no. 1), 'Ministerium Todt'.

was wasteful of time and productive capacity. Therefore a system of development committees was set up in the tank industry, the munitions industry, and in weapon production. It was a replica of the production committee system, concerned solely with development and not with the technique of production at all. Wehrmacht requirements were to be first sifted by the development committees, which would achieve as much standardization as possible. At the same time they would try to simplify design as much as possible. Calculations indicated that if 100 per cent of effort was needed to meet a specification 100 per cent, only 30 per cent of effort was needed to meet the same specification 90 per cent.[1] Representatives of the Wehrmacht, scientists, economists, specialists in administration, and manufacturers were to pool their knowledge on the development committees to achieve the kind of result envisaged by these calculations. In this way the three separate Wehrmacht armaments agencies, for instance, would be forced into some sort of co-operation. No longer would each service develop its own heavy gun requirements, each demanding its own particular type of heavy shell. The weapons committee, under Dr. Müller, does not seem to have made the impact of the tank development committee under the wayward and advanced Professor Porsche.[2] In fact Porsche's committee's success seems to have assured the initial success of the whole system. Its later success was not so striking, in fact some of the later development committees appear to have done nothing at all

There can be no doubt that the machinery of 'Self-Administration and Responsibility of German Industry', which Speer claimed as his own, and to which his success has been attributed by later writers, was not his idea but Todt's. Todt's reforms of the administration had shown the way, even during the Blitzkrieg, to a better system, should the German economy have to be changed to a policy of full-scale war production.

Such a change-over could come only on the Führer's decision. To write an accurate history of the autumn of 1941 and the winter of 1941–2, so vital a period for Germany's war economy, we should need an insight into Hitler's mind which is

[1] Speer Report No. 27.
[2] FD 3049/49 (Folder no. 1), 'Ministerium Todt'.

only rarely vouchsafed to us. Consequently the timing of many decisions in this period is difficult to fix exactly. Hitherto Hitler had resisted all military pressure for a policy of total war. He may have feared the effect on the popularity of his rule of savage restrictions on the output of consumer goods. The Four-Year-Plan Organization always included in its summaries of the economic situation opinions that it was necessary to move slowly and cautiously. These opinions were based on evidence in reports from the President of Police in Berlin.[1] The Goebbels concept of 'total war', even though largely verbal, was often under criticism from the Gauleiters; sometimes they objected to the committees' transferring machinery between plants in different *Gaue*. All opponents of the Blitzkrieg had been silenced by events, which seemed to prove that Hitler had evolved the correct strategy. It is conceivable that the Blitzkrieg would have been successful again had the Central Army not been halted before Moscow in order to strengthen the attack in south-east Russia. Hitler does not seem to have been convinced of the need to abandon it until December 1941.

As the German advance squelched to a halt on Russian mud, and as for the first time serious losses of equipment, losses which were exceeding production, made themselves felt, the advocates of 'armament in depth' were heard with louder voices. The story of these weeks is one of determined efforts to drive the existing war economy to its last effort, followed by the sudden revolution which placed the whole economy on a different basis. The most important figure in this revolution was not General Thomas, as might have been expected, but Fritz Todt.

The main target for criticism in the Blitzkrieg economy was the 'system' of control of levels of production, which was supposed to be achieved by varying the allocation of raw materials to different sectors of the economy. This was certainly so inefficient as not properly to constitute either 'allocation' or 'control'. It was simply a scramble by vested interests for what was available. As the situation became tighter a meeting was held in the Ministry of Economics in November 1941 to try to start a new system of quarterly allocation of metallic raw materials.

[1] FD 3438/45. Generalbevollmächtigter für den Vierjahresplan, reports from the Berlin Chief of Police.

The majority of those present argued that the economy was working at its limit and that any attempt to increase production could only be achieved by cutting down elsewhere.[1] A vocal minority felt that the limit was a purely artificial one. All, however, agreed that it was necessary either to have a greater stock of raw materials, or to have a more authoritative way of allocating them. WiRüAmt were convinced, as they had always been, that a full war economy was the only way out of the difficulty. The idea of a direct approach to the Führer to report the feeling of dissatisfaction at the meeting was shelved, mainly on the advice of General Fromm, who perceived that 'in the end it must come to swearing by Adolf Hitler'.[2]

On 3 December 1941 the first of a series of Führer-Commands on rationalization was promulgated.[3] The decree warned that the coming military and economic situation demanded a greater degree of rationalization of production and restriction of consumer goods. The decree listed three methods by which this rationalization could be achieved. Firstly modern methods of mass production were to be introduced on a greater scale than before, together with simpler designs for equipment. Secondly production was to be concentrated in the plants with the best and most economical working methods.[4] This was the basis of Porsche's early work on the tank development committee. Thirdly there would have to be a limited programme of construction of additional floorspace to replace the losses of general military equipment in Russia. The principles on which standard equipment for all three services was to be produced were specified. This Command was to be implemented by the Minister of Armaments and Munitions and the Head of OKW. The outcome, of course, was the confirmation and extension of the development commissions.

This Führer-Command did not imply conversion to a full war economy. Hitler was trying to find his solution in a more rational Blitzkrieg economy. Not until the end of December and

[1] FD 3049/49 (Folder no. 4) 'Gewaltaktionen—Kartei des Technischen Amtes', I.2.
[2] Ibid., I.3.
[3] FD 1434/46 No. 170, WiRüAmt, 'Umstellung der Rüstung', p. 15. FD 3049/49 (Folder no. 4) op. cit., I.3.
[4] FD 1434/46 No. 170, op. cit., pp. 15–17.

the beginning of January did German armies suffer their first major defeats. These defeats, combined with the American entry into the war, changed Hitler's mind.

Todt took the Führer-Command of 3 December as constituting implicit approval of his methods. By 22 December development and production committees for general army equipment had been established.[1] At the same time there was established a new headquarters for the Ministry of Armaments and Munitions, where the officials of the Ministry and the committee chairmen could meet regularly; a sign that the method of control by committee had become a system rather than an expedient. This was eventually to become the central headquarters of Germany's war economy, from which a systematic control could be exercised over the execution of Führer-Commands.

In the last resort Todt, almost as much as WiRüAmt, depended on Keitel. His ministry was an Army ministry; many of the agencies with whom he negotiated were under Keitel's control. In December 1941 he was far from exercising the supreme direction even of production for the German Army. But he had the advantage over WiRüAmt of not having been discredited by events. Nor did he come under Hitler's strong suspicion of everything military. He was an ardent National Socialist. Personally he stood on much firmer ground in his relations with the Führer than did General Thomas. At some date between 3 December 1941 and 10 January 1942 Hitler decided that the current degree of war effort was inadequate, and that the Blitzkrieg was to be abandoned. During the same period he decided that the administrative machinery of the Blitzkrieg must be scrapped, and that, in its place, the civilian Ministry of Armaments and Munitions, under Todt, must be given wider powers.

The Führer had a low opinion of American society's power to hold together,[2] and his response to the American entry into the war was a demand on 13 December for an increased call-up and a greater production of Army equipment.[3] A further 508,000

---

[1] FD 3049/49 (Folder no. 1) op. cit., p. 8. FD 3049/49 (Folder no. 4) op. cit., I.3.
[2] *Hitler's Secret Conversations*, p. 196 and passim.
[3] FD 1434/46 No. 170, WiRüAmt, op. cit., pp. 32 ff.

men were to be conscripted, 300,000 of them into the Army. WiRüAmt, who had made up their minds in November that this would be impossible in present circumstances were now forced to come into open opposition again. On 23 December they presented an analysis of the situation in a memorandum to the Führer.[1] The analysis pointed out that a draft of this size would mean more skilled men being called into the Wehrmacht and a consequent intensification of the labour shortage. No matter how many Russian prisoners were set to work in Germany they could not compensate for the loss of the skilled labour. The planned targets for output of aeroplanes and munitions could not be obtained. The new target for U-boat construction would only be achieved at the cost of all other naval construction.

From these statements it follows that small-scale measures are no longer sufficient to meet the needs of the present situation. New incisive directions are therefore necessary to define clearly the armaments tasks for the year 1942.[2]

The memorandum ended with an appeal to Hitler to sanction the prosecution of the war on a full-scale basis.

This unwelcome Christmas present for the Führer was followed by a similar memorandum submitted on 3 January 1942,[3] which drew attention to the decline in munitions output in Autumn 1941, and contrasted this with the great increase both in consumption and losses of munitions in the field. It was impossible, WiRüAmt concluded, to continue to increase the size of the Armed Forces without at the same time securing the output of raw materials on which such increases depended. Therefore those parts of the economy running at their peace-time level must be severely checked.

By 10 January Hitler seems to have been convinced. The Führer-Command 'Armament 1942'[4] of that day marked the vital break with the economics of Blitzkrieg.[5] Great increases were ordered in mobilized troops and their equipment, in heavy anti-tank guns and in munitions of nearly every calibre. Whilst the needs of the western coastal defences of France and Norway

---

[1] Ibid., p. 34.   [2] Ibid., p. 34.   [3] Ibid., p. 36.   [4] *Rüstung 1942.*
[5] Ibid., p. 4. FD 3049/49 (Folder no. 1), op. cit.

must continue to be met they must share top-priority with U-boat production to meet the demands of the new phase which was beginning in the battle of the Atlantic. Increases in the output of aircraft and of flak were demanded. The output of light alloys, of mineral oil, and of *ersatz* rubber was to be stepped-up. The necessary machines and machine-tools would be made available to meet the needs of this programme.

'Armament 1942' implied an abandonment of the Blitzkrieg as far as an alternative to it could be achieved. The big question now was, how was this to be done. The days from 10 January to 21 January 1942 were filled with meetings and conferences to which the background was the Russian advance on Kerch. WiRüAmt was determined at the least to retain, if possible actually to increase, the Army's control over the economy. On 15 January General Hanneken issued a circular to all branches of WiRüAmt which declared that the Blitzkrieg was over and done with. A long war would ensue. 'As for the economy, it is a matter of prime importance that it should definitely be reconstructed on the basis of a long war.'[1]

The Führer had given permission to proceed with the armament programme which WiRüAmt had always advocated. But the soldiers were to have less, not more, control. Todt's advice to the Führer over this period had been much the same as that of the Army. The long conferences of January were concerned just as much with the question of who would control the German economy as with the question of what sort of an economy it would be.

The most important of these conferences was that of armament inspectors in Berlin on 20–21 January.[2] This represented a last bid for economic power by WiRüAmt. The armament inspectors were to produce recommendations on the way in which the German economy could be converted to a full war economy and on how WiRüAmt could maintain its control. Thomas made a long speech in which he hailed the coming of the genuine war economy which he had so long advocated. He could not help referring back to his speech before *Reichsgruppe Industrie* on 29 December 1939, in which he had advocated so many of the measures now accepted everywhere. 'Within the

[1] Ibid., p. 42.   [2] Ibid., p. 43.

next two months we must finally complete the closure of those industries which are unimportant for war, and must redistribute their strength.'[1]

The minutes of this conference show how far-reaching the changes which Thomas had discussed the day before at the Berghof with Hitler, were likely to be. But the initiative had slipped from WiRüAmt.

One of the measures decided on by Hitler was the introduction and establishment of a 'fixed price' for war contracts.[2] WiRüAmt had long advocated this reform,[3] but by December Todt had tentatively introduced it in some spheres.[4] The system known as 'L.S.O.' had survived the first years of war.[5] Its guiding principle had been that when the contract was completed the total expenditure was paid back by the contracting agency plus a profit of between three and six per cent, which was reckoned on the size of the contractor's expenditure. Obviously no armaments manufacturer operating under such a system would be keen to reduce his expenditure; the more he allowed the contract to cost, the greater his profit. For this costly system Todt substituted a system of price fixing, under which the contractor had the option of three price categories. Should he choose the lowest, he would not have to pay taxes; if he chose the second he would be taxed; the third category, the equivalent of the second category plus approved costs, could only be selected if enough evidence could be provided of great transport or geographical difficulties, or of heavy encumbrances with mortgages or loans. The Four-Year-Plan office opposed the introduction of this system as bitterly[6] as the 'fixed price' was opposed in the United States. Nevertheless, it was already being operated extensively in December 1941 and cannot be attributed to Speer as it universally has been. Its extension to cover

[1] FD 5444/45, p. 7, 'Vortrag des Herrn Amtschefs des WiRüAmtes im OKW, Gen. Thomas, gelegentlich der Besprechung der Rüstungs-Inspekteure und Rüstungskommandeure am 21.1.1942 in Berlin, über die militärische und wirtschaftliche Lage und die sich hieraus ergebenden neuen Forderungen bezüglich der Rüstung.'

[2] Ibid.   [3] FD 1434/46 No. 170, op. cit., p. 52.

[4] Speer Report No. 90, pp. 3–4.

[5] 'Leitsätze für die Selbstkostenabrechnung bei öffentlichen Aufträgen' (Guiding Principles for Settling Prime Costs in Public Contracts).

[6] Speer Report No. 90, p. 4.

every form of war production was one of the measures which Todt laid before Hitler in February 1942. Saur claimed that Todt attempted to introduce the 'fixed price' into munitions contracts as soon as he took office but that nothing could be done until Göring signed the executive order in October 1941. But for this there is no corroborative evidence.

Although committee control over production and the 'fixed price' system were vital to the introduction of a full war economy, they did not represent the full extent of Todt's plans. He wanted a strong centralized control which could give the necessary impulse to the new autonomous régime in German war industry.[1] Efficiency demanded that production must be confined to fewer and larger factories; armaments and their components could not afford to travel hither and thither about the countryside whilst still awaiting completion. This problem was especially knotty with regard to components. Most components were produced in small factories scattered over the Reich which practically defied regular control of production by the committees. It was centralization in his own hands which Todt was after and which Speer ultimately achieved.

Todt had his recommendations before the Führer at the end of January.[2] All the evidence indicates that many of the powers which Speer claimed to have won from the Führer in the first few days of his appointment as Minister were in fact granted to him by virtue of his being Todt's successor; many of them had already been granted to Todt, others were about to be granted. The great increases in munitions production which started with Speer's assumption of office were due to the period of reform which had gone before. The overall increase in armaments production of 55 per cent between February and July 1942 was the result of the administrative reforms introduced by Todt. It began too early to be the work of Speer.[3] Walther Rohland told his interrogators,

> Dr. Todt had already recognised the necessity for centralising all branches of industry directly or indirectly necessary for war produc-

---

[1] FD 3049/49 (Folder no. 1), op. cit.   [2] FD 3049/49 (Folder no. 4), op. cit., I.3.
[3] The U.S.S.B.S. was of the opinion that the increase 'must have been largely the result of earlier plans or simply of the changed attitude towards the war'. *Effects of Strategic Bombing on the German War Economy*, p. 7.

tion and had paved the way for this by discussion with Hitler. The actual decisions for the creation of a sort of War Ministry under the leadership of Dr. Todt were taken shortly before his death.[1]

On 6 February 1942 Todt was chairman of a meeting of all the chairmen of committees at the new central headquarters.[2] It was the first time such a meeting of all those in charge of war production had been held at a central ministry. The meeting discussed the changes in administration which had taken place and how they might be furthered. Saur records that as a result of this meeting preparations and detailed work, some of which had stretched over years found recognition at last, and how the 'long-superannuated bureaucratic' military administration suffered a visible collapse in prestige.[3] It had suffered such a collapse indeed. Speer on taking office was able to alter the whole structure of the economic general staff of the Army. To soften protests against the changes by Party officials and to indicate the greater powers which the Ministry of Armaments and Munitions now possessed Todt decided to issue monthly bulletins to all the Gauleiters.[4] These bulletins would explain and justify the severe restrictions placed on civilian production. In fact it fell to Speer to issue the first of these which had been put together by Todt.

By February 1942 Todt had achieved a considerable degree of centralization. The economic machinery of the Blitzkrieg was being rapidly dismantled. Germany was arming for a long and painful war and adapting her administration to the new situation. The first great period of expansion of German war production had just begun. Great changes were under way and Todt was the man of the moment in the Party hierarchy. The outward and visible sign of his new status was the meeting of 6 February.[5] The moralist might well brood on Todt's career; two days later he was killed in an air crash on the Eastern front.

[1] Speer Report No. 66, p. 5.
[2] F.D. 3049/49 (Folder no. 4), op. cit., I.3.   [3] Ibid.
[4] FD 1434/46 No. 167, Speer, 'An alle Gauleiter', 18 February 1942.
[5] FD 3049/49 (Folder no. 4).

CHAPTER IV

Albert Speer

Todt's death slowed down the reconstruction of German economic administration. But thanks to the extraordinary qualities of his successor its effect was only short-lived. All attempts to use the dramatic death of the Minister to weaken the new position of the Ministry of Armaments and Munitions failed before the strong personality and skilful political manoeuvring of the new Minister. In his first few months of office Speer extended the powers of the Ministry even further and introduced for the first time an efficient central control of the economy. It was these changes in the institutional framework of the German war economy which made possible the brilliant successes of German war production between Spring 1942 and Summer 1944 and so confounded Germany's opponents.

This was the high summer of German economic achievement. An index of overall armaments production based on January–February 1942 averages equal to 100 gives figures of 153 for July 1942, 229 for July 1943, and 322 for July 1944.[1] How was this achieved? There are three principal reasons. The first is the obvious one that there was a great deal of slack to be taken up in the economy and any action to do so would initially give dramatic results. Todt's initial dose of rationalization was responsible for a 55 per cent increase in the index between February and July. Secondly the extraordinary ability of the Minister of Armaments himself played a great part. Thirdly, and most importantly, must be ranked the completion of the movement towards central control of the economy begun by Todt. The power and speed of the executive from 1942 to 1945 could not be in stronger contrast to its weakness and dispersion before

[1] Appendix 1.

1942. Speer created a simply-operated machine for controlling Germany's war production by indirect but enormously effective pressures. This machine dragged Germany at top speed from being a nation economically in a state of peace into being a nation able to survive for over three years against a combination of all the powers economically stronger than herself. The way in which this machine was created and the way in which it operated are therefore of primary importance.

The dominant figure was Albert Speer. An architect by profession, he had been early a member of Hitler's circle of fireside acquaintances at the Berghof. He had been at first subordinate to Troost as Hitler's personal architect and after Troost's death had become responsible for the construction of the Reichs Chancellery. Speer was socially captured by Hitler; after all at twenty-nine, in a minor professional role, he had been suddenly introduced into the world of power. He was also personally captured; he found Hitler fascinating and dynamic. Eventually he became one of Hitler's firm 'artistic' friends.

Hitler did not like to get his friends mixed up with the members of his government and Speer provides the one outstanding example of Hitler's breach of this principle. He was a 'surprise' choice of Minister of Armaments, but he gave his interrogators an exaggerated picture of the situation which overstates the impulsiveness of Hitler's decision and Speer's own political innocence before 1942.

The day when Dr. Todt was killed I happened to be at Headquarters. Hitler got the news at about 9 a.m.; at 11 he summoned me and disclosed to me that I was to be Todt's successor. My protests had no effect. They were altogether well founded, since I knew nothing about either constructional engineering or armaments. He assured me that 'I would manage' and that he had confidence in me. I was a typical outsider; in this case with the soldiers as well as with the Party and industry.[1]

The statement is certainly very misleading.[2] Speer was not a brilliant amateur who achieved success where stupid or hidebound professionals had failed. He had already been responsible

[1] Speer Report No. 19, p. 3.
[2] See, for instance, Speer Report No. 5, p. 7. H. R. Trevor-Roper, op. cit., pp. 82–83.

for the doubling of floorspace available for aircraft production.[1] It was important for Hitler to have a man who knew the way the system had worked under Todt, who was loyal, and, most importantly, was, like Todt, not identified with any of the vested interests whose competition with each other had up to now been such a feature of the German war economy. Hitler needed an outsider for the job. And Speer was a fairly experienced, loyal, and very able outsider. But it would be inhumane to hold such misrepresentations against a man fighting for his life. It was surely the acute pressure of circumstances at 'Dustbin' in 1945 which made Speer put about the idea that he was not politically committed before 1942.

At any rate the outcome says a great deal for Hitler's choice of men. He could not have picked a better for the job than Speer; he proved himself to be far more outstanding as an administrator than as an architect. Part of Speer's skill was political; he was able to outmanoeuvre politicians of much longer standing than himself. But he had also the capacity to survey from outside the struggle for power in which he was himself engaged and comment on the various motives of those taking part. His speculations on the nature of National Socialism are of great interest to the historian although some of the evidence which he has provided is intended for self-justification. If he was vain he had something to be vain about. By any standards he was a very able, intelligent, and brave man. He calculatedly risked his life in 1945 by telling Hitler to his face that the war was lost and submitting a memorandum in the same vein after being given time to reconsider his words.

Like many men not themselves fanatics he was not averse to having powerful and ruthless men around him who could carry out the tasks which he felt himself not suited for. Men like Saur, Sauckel, and Milch all collaborated easily with him. But there is evidence that his personal judgement of people was not too sure. Geist, whose ignorance shocked his interrogators,[2] was described by Speer as 'a very good expert'.[3] The invariable comment on all possible rivals is 'ambitious'.[4] Even so he accu-

---

[1] Speer Report No. 5.   [2] Speer Report No. 53.   [3] Speer Report No. 13, p. 3.
[4] Ibid. (Saur is described as 'too ambitious and not a realist but good in secondary or tertiary positions'.)

mulated round himself, in what came to be called the 'Speer Ministry', a band of able men who all agreed with him fundamentally on the way the German war economy should be run.

The timing of events for the two months after Todt's death is vital for the history of the German war economy; but some events still remain obscure. Many influential figures still felt that Hitler's decision for 'armament in depth' was unnecessary. They felt that Germany's hope lay in a gathering of her strength and another mighty blow at Russia which would either overthrow the Soviet government or place the bulk of its agricultural and manufacturing capacity in German hands. That the important decision of January 1942 was not rescinded was due to Speer's clarity of thought and ability to argue with Hitler on his own terms.

Speer's own account of events was this. After Todt's death he was summoned to Hitler's presence.[1] There, the Führer told him he had been chosen to succeed Todt in all Todt's jobs. Speer felt reluctant, on the grounds of his own inexperience, and because of his reluctance to be drawn into enmity with Göring.

He overcame his reluctance on being given a clear assurance by Hitler that he would be supported in whatever measures he might feel obliged to undertake. How long a delay elapsed between the offer of the Ministry and its acceptance Speer does not say. 'A few days later',[2] that is to say after he had become Minister of Armaments and Munitions, he was invited to attend a meeting of the economic branches of the three wings of the Wehrmacht. The meeting was called by Funk and Milch, the Director of the Air Force Economic Branch, to discuss means of co-ordinating war production. Speer apparently felt nervous, or, as he puts it, 'not at home in his new surroundings'.[3] Therefore he asked Hitler if he might be excused from attending the meeting. Hitler insisted that Speer should attend and gave him a guarantee that, should decisions taken at the meeting mean any curtailment in the powers of the Minister of Armaments, a second meeting would be held, with Hitler in the chair, which would rescind all such decisions. As it turned out no such decisions were taken at the first meeting, although Funk pushed for

[1] Speer Report No. 1.   [2] Ibid.   [3] Ibid.

Milch to be appointed as co-ordinator in chief for the war economy. If the Wehrmacht wished to regain control of war production they could not have done better than put forward Milch who was in the much-favoured Air Force and also a very able man. But according to Speer he was placed in no danger from this rival candidate because Göring was invincibly opposed to any individual, even an Air Force general, having such powers within the state.

Nevertheless, a second meeting was held with Hitler in the chair. At this meeting it was decided that Speer should have the decisive role in war production, and to overcome the difficulties with Göring's empire a special post of Commissioner-General for Armaments Tasks in the Four-Year-Plan Office was created for Speer. Apparently the head of the Four-Year-Plan Office was not present at the meeting to oppose Speer's appointment—according to Speer, because of 'an oversight'![1] When Göring heard of the appointment he threatened to disband the Four-Year-Plan Office altogether.

The dates of these events are imprecise. Independent witnesses and corroboration are patchy. Saur declares that Speer was installed as Todt's successor on the day of Todt's death, and that, on 13 February, Hitler, in a personal interview, promised Speer extraordinary powers over armament agencies.[2] The decree formally appointing Speer as Minister was signed on 18 February. Saur says that Speer received his post in the Four-Year-Plan Office at almost the same time as he was created Minister. Speaking at a meeting in April Speer said this decree had not been signed by Göring, thus making it valid, until 1 March.[3] Thus it may have been that three weeks elapsed before Speer was sure that with Hitler's help he had overcome opposition to his appointment.

There is no proof of Speer acting as Minister until 18 February, the day when his appointment was formally decreed by Hitler. On that day he issued his first official bulletin[4] which had in fact been written by Todt. The following day Speer makes his first authentic personal appearance, discussing questions of

[1] Ibid.   [2] FD 3049/49 (Folder no. 4).
[3] FD 1434/46 No. 167, Speer, 'Rede Gauwirtschaftsberater', 17 April 1942, p. 5.
[4] FD 1434/46 No. 167, Speer, 'An alle Gauleiter', 18 February 1942.

policy with the Führer.[1] These Führer-Conferences, of which this is the first, form an almost continuous historical record until the end of the war. Speer or, later, Speer's deputy, Otto Saur, would discuss questions of policy, some of them very minor, with Hitler and record Hitler's decisions as the minutes of the meeting. As Hitler had an extensive knowledge of the details of armaments, and also a very good memory, a great deal of technical detail of no great significance was recorded in this series. But decisions on strategy and on the general economic level were also recorded, in a somewhat inconsequential way.

At this first meeting on 19 February 1942 Speer's plans for the increase of German war production were endorsed entirely by Hitler. The Führer declared that he attached

the greatest importance to peace-time planning and developments in all firms being stopped immediately. Contemplates heavy penalties and emphasizes that there will be time enough for this after the War, and also that industrialists must not make any sort of attempt, in the organization of their factories, to take account of peace-time purposes at this stage.[2]

To further these ends Speer had already obtained sanctions for a large-scale extension of production committees.[3] It was now decided that the heads of all committees could only be appointed by Speer and, curiously enough, that if they were over fifty-five years of age, they were to have a deputy not older than forty.[4]

If 'armament in depth' was now to be the policy there were radical adjustments to be made to the economy. It was essential to create more floor-space for production and consequently it was essential to have more labour available. This meant modifying the call-up. After some discussion of this question[5] a Führer-Command was issued after the conference, containing important restrictions on the call-up. A number of industries were classified as vital to the war economy. The list included the production of certain scarce raw materials such as oil and non-ferrous metals, the building of railway wagons, the manufacture of powder and explosives, the chemical industry, the power

[1] FD 3353/45 vol. 1, 19 February 1942, 'Besprechungspunkte über Reise zum Führerhauptquartier'.
[2] Ibid., p. 6.   [3] Ibid., p. 3.   [4] Ibid., p. 14.   [5] Ibid., pp. 6–7.

industry, and the particular branches of the construction industry on which these depended. For these industries the old UK grading would be abolished and a new grade 'key-worker' imposed.[1] The Ministry of Armaments was to be allowed to classify certain workers as 'key-workers', which would give them complete exemption from conscription.[2] Below this grading would be the grade of 'highly-skilled worker'[3] carrying a smaller range of exemption. WiRüAmt calculated that from January to March 1942, 244,000 men had been called up from these specified industries.[4] In addition to these restrictions on conscription, Hitler agreed to a more equitable distribution of the labour-force between the three armed services. This meant preventing air force production from getting an excessive share due to Göring's influence.[5]

There were, however, certain great weaknesses in Speer's position. In the first place Todt had left a residual problem of some importance. What was to be done with the superseded WiRüAmt? So long as it was in existence its co-operation with the Ministry of Armaments was likely to be uneasy. In any case almost all its main functions had passed to Todt. Secondly it was the functions of WiRüAmt only that the Ministry had acquired. Naval and air force production was still quite outside Speer's control. Thirdly the vital issue of who was to control the distribution of the German labour force had not been tackled. And, fourthly, Speer had to ensure that he had the decisive control at all times of the long-term rearmament now being undertaken. Such control could only be obtained on a level higher than that of the administration of war production. It had to be some form of indirect control over the whole economy operated by Speer himself. The working out of these problems was to occupy another three months.

The WiRüAmt could have been left as a sort of superfluous and harmless appendix in the bureaucracy. This kind of solution was quite common in National Socialist Germany. But Speer did not work that way. Although General Thomas was in

[1] Schlüsselkraft.
[2] FD 1434/46 No. 170, WiRüAmt, 'Umstellung der Rüstung', p. 61.
[3] Fachkraft.
[4] Ibid., pp. 62–63.
[5] FD3353/45 vol. 1, op. cit.

sympathy with Speer's aims he considered him an interloper in military affairs. On 2 March Thomas sounded Speer about his intentions.[1] Speer told him that his conversations over the last three weeks with the Führer and Göring had been for the purpose of creating a greater centralization and unification of the whole economy. The basic rule now was that armaments production was to be the single most important aim of the economy. The whole of the economy must be orientated towards producing increasing quantities of armaments and munitions; the Four-Year-Plan Office had ceased to be 'a deciding body'; its powers had been taken over completely by 'a more statistical and bureaucratic branch'.[2] Speer was to be given still more new and overriding powers by Hitler. Göring had been furious and had wished to resign all his economic responsibilities. A new planning committee would be formed which would be a small body of men gathered around the Reichsmarschall to direct central planning policy. Thomas would certainly be a member; so would the more important secretaries of state. Speer hoped to work very closely with WiRüAmt as he had the greatest faith in it. Thomas assured him of his co-operation; but recorded afterwards in a note of the conversation that Speer had made it very clear that soldiers could no longer be trusted with the direction of the war economy.[3]

Thomas saw that the biggest problem of abandoning in midwar a programme of 'armament in width' for one of 'armament in depth' was that of labour supply. A week after Thomas's meeting with Speer WiRüAmt argued the situation out in a memorandum to Speer.[4] They disagreed, understandably enough, with Speer's policy of reducing the intake into the Wehrmacht, although they agreed that the death or glory tactics on the Russian front were a waste of men. The problem was to adjust the available labour supply within industry. Also they disagreed with the Ministry of Armaments' policy of trying to bring all branches of the armaments industry into large, rationally-operated factories. Not only, they claimed, was it

[1] FD 5454a/45, WiRüAmt, 'Aktennotiz über Besprechung mit Minister Speer 2.3.42', p. 8.
[2] Ibid., p. 9.
[3] Ibid., p. 10.
[4] FD 1434/46 No. 170, WiRüAmt, 'Umstellung der Rüstung', p. 54.

easier to maintain the small and scattered plant when labour was in short supply, but with grim foresight they forecast that a scattered armaments industry would prove better able to protect itself from air attack. In this forecast they were to be proved quite correct by events. Finally WiRüAmt were of the opinion that foreign labour was being thoroughly badly used. Policy in this respect was generally to confine captured territories to the production of consumer goods for Germany and bring skilled workmen into the Reich for use in the armaments industries. In most captured territories consumer goods factories were already working half-time, owing to inability to obtain raw material. This under-employment could be eliminated if fuel and raw materials were transported for industrial production to places with good lines of communication with the Reich. At the moment transport was being devoted to carrying people into Germany to work in German factories where they deliberately worked badly and consumed foodstuffs which had to be transported to them. Furthermore the recruitment of labour was becoming increasingly difficult, and the more difficult it became the less popular were the military governments. Undoubtedly WiRüAmt were swayed in their opinions on this matter by the fact that concentration of war production outside the factories of the Reich would have meant a reversion to a greater degree of control by the soldiers themselves.

The system of *ad hoc* modifications to the call-up could only provide a temporary answer to a problem which was to become more and more difficult with the intensification of Germany's war effort. Nominally, labour supply was directed by State-Secretary Syrup of the Reichs Labour Ministry. Control, however, was virtually in the hands of Ministerial-Director Mansfeld who, at the same time, held the office of Commissioner for Labour Supply in the Four-Year-Plan Organization. Mansfeld was unable to mobilize labour systematically for employment in the armaments industry, since the Gauleiters, by using all their political power, were able actively and successfully to oppose the movement of labour out of their own *Gaue*. Labour mobilization could not be achieved by the Labour Ministry alone; it had become more than an economic problem, it was a problem of political power.

The solution which Speer favoured was that a Plenipotentiary-General should be appointed to enable the Regional Labour Offices to stand up to the pressures of the various Gauleiters.[1] For this post Speer nominated Hanke, Gauleiter of Lower Silesia, a former friend of Goebbels who had broken with him after a quarrel. Ley, head of the Labour Front, was very much interested in extending his own empire by securing this job.[2] According to Speer Hitler was at first ready to agree to Hanke's appointment but later changed his mind and decided to appoint Fritz Sauckel as a compromise between the two parties.[3] This decision was announced to Speer at a Führer-Conference.

The Führer again informed of Dr. Ley's wish to direct manpower, at the same time pointing out that it would be bad administration if the same organisation which represents the worker's interests also represents that of the opposing interests of the State. This would be as if Reichsleiter Bormann simultaneously held Dr. Lammer's post. The Führer fully agreed and decided that Gauleiter Sauckel is to be GBA.[4]

What lay behind this recorded decision was that Hitler had decided that Hanke was too junior, and that Sauckel, a former Gauleiter of Thuringia, would be more capable of exerting authority. Apart from this he had given evidence of considerable economic ability as director of the Gustloff Werke. Bormann, thinking the most important thing was to prevent Ley getting more power, threw his influence against him. Sauckel, who had no machine behind him, was no real danger to Bormann. And in addition Bormann and Sauckel had worked together in Thuringia in the early days of the movement.

Sauckel's appointment as Plenipotentiary-General for Labour gave him a quite independent position. He was anything but a tool of Speer. The consequence was that for the rest of the war, one sector of the economy existed over which Speer had only a

[1] Speer Report No. 19, Part 1, p. 19.
[2] Ley had also tried to get for himself some of Todt's powers when Todt was killed. See *The Goebbels Diaries*, 'Ley, of course, is very sad that the campaign for increasing production was wrested from him by Speer. But there is nothing to be done about it', p. 62.
[3] Speer Report No. 19, p. 19.
[4] Generalbevollmächtigter der Arbeit, FD 3353/45 vol. 4, pp. 4–5. Führerkonferenz, 19 March 1942.

slight control. As he put it later, 'This would have rounded off my otherwise successful endeavours to centralize the control of all factors of production.'[1] The situation was made worse for Speer as a result of Göring's protests. Göring's objections were to Sauckel's operating outside the Four-Year-Plan. Therefore the new post of 'Commissioner-General for Labour in the Four-Year-Plan' had to be created for him. Hitler, not Göring, signed this decree and Sauckel used this fact later to claim special powers. It is possible that with a large measure of goodwill on both sides the separation of labour control from the Speer Ministry would not have proved a handicap. But this goodwill was never achieved. For a lot of the time Sauckel went his own sweet way.

The other weaknesses of the position of the Speer Ministry in the economy were overcome more to Speer's liking. In early 1942 Speer was not strong enough to wrest immediate control over naval and air-force production. But if he could extend the system of control by committee into these areas of production the Speer Ministry would establish itself as the sole intermediary between the High Command and industry as a whole. A Führer-Command of 21 March announced the introduction of the committee system on a much wider basis.[2] It is clear from the Ministry circular of 25 March that Speer regarded this as a revolutionary break with the traditional methods of management in German industry and the economic policies of the National Socialist Party. Apart from its ultimate advantages it straight away ensured that co-operation between managements would inevitably be more frequent.

On 20 March Speer had obtained Hitler's consent to the formation of a main committee for shipbuilding.[3] Speer had already secured the Navy's agreement to a main committee for U-boats. Raeder had personally requested that Speer should name the chairman of this committee, and faced with this Hitler was obliged to accept Speer's nominee.[4] It was also agreed that, in spite of opposition by Göring, anti-aircraft guns

[1] Speer Report No. 19, p. 19.
[2] FD 1434/46 No. 170. 'Umstellung der Rüstung', Verordnung zum Schutz der Rüstungswirtschaft.
[3] FD 3353/45 vols. 4/5. Führerkonferenz 21/22 March 1942.
[4] Ibid., vol. 4, pp. 5–6.

and bombs should also come within the purview of the committee system.[1]

Munitions production was now to be calculated on a long-term basis. Basic production plans were to be drawn-up to replace the old fluctuating and spasmodic demands.[2] For this long-term planning Speer would be entirely responsible, acting through the 'Organization for the Self-Administration and Responsibility of Industry'. The Führer 'likewise confirmed that any changes in the requisitions which reach us from the General Staff or other centres are not binding on us, and I am authorized to refuse such requisitions'.[3] Thus the extension of the production and development committees into naval and air-force armaments gave Speer the reality of control over these areas of production if he did not have control in name.

The most important of Speer's immediate objectives still remained; the creation of a branch through which his own power would be exercised not only in the sphere of armaments production but in that of the general direction of the economy. He had spoken to Thomas of 'a small body of men gathered around the Reichsmarschall to direct central planning policy'.[4] During the Blitzkrieg military strategy had always dictated economic planning although at times they had been confused with each other. The new committee, Speer told Thomas, would plan for the economy as the General Staff planned military operations.

On 4 April the Führer agreed to the formation of a planning board to be called Central Planning.[5] Speer's 'small body of men' had become a committee of three, over which Speer would have almost complete control, shared only with Milch and Körner, an official from the Four-Year-Plan Organization. Its job was to control allocation of raw materials to each sector of the economy. It would meet at frequent intervals and claimants would have no appeal beyond Speer. The procurement and allocation of raw materials was one of the few functions not concerned solely with foreign exchange and finance remaining to the

---

[1] Ibid., vol. 4, p. 9.
[2] Ibid., vol. 5, pp. 1–2.
[3] Ibid., vol. 5, p. 1.
[4] FD 5454a/45, WiRüAmt, op. cit.
[5] FD 3353/45, vol. 6, p. 16. Führerkonferenz 4 April 1942.

Reichs Economic Ministry. Having lost these functions it was to sink into even less importance. The Ministry maintained an extensive purchasing organization in neutral countries but its machinery for internal allocation varied from rudimentary to non-existent. Central Planning, on the other hand, would be able to control the autonomous industrial groups and all other sectors of the economy by controlling exactly their supplies of raw materials, at the same time eliminating all wasteful competition for existing supplies.

At the same time, I pointed out that allocation of raw materials would be undertaken by this Central Planning Board, since the Minister of Economics is too much concerned with his own interests and less with those of war economics while now, through the increase in the production of ammunition and arms, a considerable redistribution in favour of the armaments industry must be undertaken. The Führer is of the same opinion.[1]

When the Führer raised the question of iron quotas on the same day it was agreed that in future these would be fixed by Central Planning.[2] The decree finally ratifying Central Planning was signed by Hitler on 15 April.[3]

Funk who became a member of Central Planning in November 1943, later left an interesting description of the proceedings:

> They were always opened by a speech from chairman Speer, who invariably asserted that armaments production must go up, up, up. Then, if, for example, the principal subject for discussion was the allocation of iron, Speer would read a statement allocating so much to this and so much to that of the principal claimant agencies. Even before the reading had been completed, the audience would begin to grow restless, and after the chairman concluded, the air was filled by the strident demands of the various representatives who claimed that their sector could not function without larger supplies. At this stage, ... the proceedings were reminiscent of the end of the first act of the *Meistersinger*, when the various contestants sing against one another in vigorous competition. There would be readjustments, claimants A, B and C would get a bit more, and then it would be discovered that claimant X, in the process of redistribution, had been left with nothing. Whereupon all the other claimants would grant to X

---

[1] Ibid., p. 16. [2] Ibid., p. 23.
[3] FD 3353/45 vol. 7. Führerkonferenz 14/15 April 1942.

one per cent of their allocation, everybody would have a schnapps, and the meeting would adjourn.[1]

The minutes of Central Planning have survived.[2] Sadly they reflect nothing of the apparent hilarity of these proceedings. Perhaps Funk was trying too hard for his captors. Funk, it can be seen from the minutes, attended only twice, and neither of the meetings he attended fits his description. But his description conveys the essential point. Central Planning was a committee in which Speer could announce his decisions to applicants for favours.

On 17 April, two days after the formal creation of Central Planning, Speer addressed a meeting of 'economic counsellors' from the *Gaue*.[3] He declared that until the autumn of 1941 the direction of the war economy had been based on the idea of a series of short wars, a concept now abandoned.[4] Because of this change of strategy he had introduced administrative reforms, of which the most important was that central direction of the economy was now in the hands of himself, Milch, and Körner. He explained that he intended to start an all-out drive to introduce a fully-worked second shift into all factories concerned with war production. This speech marks the stage where Speer could review a large body of actual administrative achievement. One of his immediate problems remained.

In the first week of May 1942 WiRüAmt was transferred from the High Command of the Armed Forces (OKW) to the Speer Ministry.[5] WiRüAmt had lost its battle in January; by February it was seeking a compromise with the powerful new Minister. By May Speer was number three in the hierarchy.[6] The whole organization was left intact, even the armaments inspectors became a part of the Speer Ministry. Officially Thomas had only changed masters, but the scope and power of his authority had been already grievously curtailed. Speer's judgement on Thomas is revealing about both men.

He was [said Speer], an able and intelligent man, without special qualifications for his position and too fond of abstract and compre-

---

[1] FD 3062/49, 'Interrogation of Dr. W. Funk'.
[2] FD 3048/49 (Folder nos. 10/48) iii, p. 795/vii, p. 3531.
[3] FD 1434/46 No. 167, op. cit.   [4] Ibid.
[5] Speer Report No. 83.   [6] Speer Report No. 1.

hensive planning. He relied too much on the figures submitted to him without testing their validity, and as they were often prepared by non-experts, Thomas's planning was often based on unrealistic assumptions. Thus his departments persistently over-rated the raw materials requirements of armaments production, and Thomas did not believe in the possibility of expanding substantially and simultaneously armaments production for all three Wehrmacht services.[1]

Thomas's view of his own activities was, not unnaturally, different. On 6 July he attended a meeting of the Four-Year-Plan Organization with the Reichsmarschall to discuss the production of scarce metals. Göring loudly proclaimed that copper production was far too low, largely because of the lack of effort of the workers and managers. He threatened to court-martial all those responsible for the running of the Goldberg mine. Thomas entered a marginal note to his memorandum of the conference.

By this file note I wish to place on record that, even prior to the war, and continually during the war, WiRüAmt demanded that indirect war requirements, especially basic industries, should be more strongly built up. . . . Time and again, iron, raw materials and manpower were invested in direct armaments and production, whereas the requirements of the raw materials industry were given a lower priority.[2]

Speer had one advantage which Thomas never had, power. Thomas's struggle with a clumsy bureaucracy made him seem an ineffective man. Speer's relations with Hitler enabled him to chop into tiny pieces the red tape which had throttled Thomas. But Speer also had a more realistic attitude to the situation than Thomas. When the renewal of German victories in Russia made Hitler wonder whether the abandonment of the Blitzkrieg had not been rash, Speer was able momentarily to swim with the tide. Thomas's persistent failure to agree with Hitler was one of the reasons for his loss of power; the other, perhaps, was that he was a soldier.

May 1942 is the month when the German economic machine was finally ready for the war of attrition. The machinery of economic administration had been completely reformed. The days of the Blitzkrieg had vanished. On the lower levels of war

[1] Speer Report No. 1, p. 3.
[2] FD 4809/45 File 3, WiRüAmt, Aktennotiz, 6 July 1942.

production the committees supervised closely all production and development at every stage. On the higher levels the volume of economic activity in each sector was dictated by the strict quarterly allocation of raw materials supplies by a three-man committee. The old independence of the Navy and the Air Force had been severely restricted. The Economics Ministry, the Organization for the Four-Year-Plan, and WiRüAmt, had become minor intermediary organizations closely controlled by the Ministry of Armaments and Munitions in their few functions of real importance. A new and more powerful body had been set up to solve the labour problem. High policy decisions were taken at meetings held at frequent intervals between Hitler and the Minister for Armaments and Munitions.

Between May 1942 and the end of the war the powers of the Speer Ministry were to increase still more. But the machinery through which it exercised its powers did not greatly alter. It worked well, of that there can be no doubt. But in practice it had certain drawbacks which can be conveniently examined here. The machinery for taking top-level decisions was impulsive and erratic because Hitler's interventions in this field were so spasmodic. The operations of Central Planning did not entirely eliminate wasteful procedures because in some sectors its control, however sensitive, was remote. The system of committees did not work equally well in every industrial sector. And the independent operations of Sauckel in the labour market meant that there were frequent policy conflicts on labour questions.

Hitler proved a difficult man for Speer to live with. Eventually he withdrew his favour and in 1944 Speer found his high position in the hierarchy had vanished. This was not the main problem. Basically the difficulty was that Hitler did not like being pinned down on issues of principle. He grew restive about long-term planning. He liked to improvise and change his mind on matters of armament production. But this possibility was now closed to Germany. Once the machinery of a full war-economy had been set in motion there was no going back. Nevertheless in Summer 1942, with German armies rolling once more on Moscow, Hitler looked back with nostalgia at the Blitzkrieg. This was responsible for a certain falling away of effort in armaments production. The rate of growth slowed down after June although the total level of output was now much higher than it had been in the previous summer.

Even in May Hitler had ruled on the issue of iron stocks that 'The stocks [of iron] in hand would not decide the war, but every available weapon would have a considerable part therein.'[1] On 28 June Hitler called upon Speer to resume consumer goods production at the previous levels.[2] Speer disagreed strongly. He tried to convince Hitler that the days of 'guns *and* butter' had gone for ever. But Hitler could not be diverted by this argument. Finally Speer clinched the issue by stressing the labour shortage. It was then decided that consumer goods production would be increased 'after a few months, and, then, with the foreign labour which Sauckel would provide'.[3] Even then the change-over would only be made within the limits imposed by the transport shortage and the coal shortage. In 'a few months' the Führer was thinking in quite different terms.

Paradoxically, the changed situation on the Russian front was a help to Speer in some ways. On 25 July Hitler agreed to drop the plans for calling-up 100,000 armament workers a month, not because armaments production might be endangered, but because the favourable turn of events in the South Russian campaign made an increase in military strength no longer essential.[4] Three days before this decision the German armies took Sevastopol, two days later they recaptured Rostov-on-Don. On 16 August the Russians evacuated the Maikop oilfields after systematically damaging them. Not until an entire German army was encircled at Stalingrad at the end of November did Hitler abandon his spasmodic attempts to return to the Blitzkrieg. It was during this period of conflicting views that Speer first began to lose Hitler's favour. And these conflicts were reflected in a slackening of the rate of growth of armaments production. Of course Hitler was living in a world of strategic illusion in Summer 1942, but his directives on the economy, although modified by the Speer Ministry,[5] were none the less

[1] FD 3353/45, vol. 10, p. 2. Führerkonferenz 6/7 May 1942.
[2] FD 3353/45, vol. 18, p. 3. Führerkonferenz 28/29 June 1942.
[3] Ibid., p. 4.
[4] FD 3353/45, vol. 20, p. 18. Führerkonferenz 23/24/25 July 1942.
[5] Speer Report No. 28.

real in their effect. Stalingrad was ultimately to convince every-one that the Blitzkrieg was over. The strategic turning-point of the war had come before the psychological turning-point.

Below this top level of decision involving Hitler and Speer operated Central Planning. It was not a committee in the proper sense, but a triumvirate in which only two men were important, Speer and General Milch who had previously been responsible for Air Force production. The principal tasks were the quarterly allocations of coal, iron and steel to the econ-omy. This was done through the Planning Branch[1] which analysed the proposals put before Central Planning. The Plan-ning Branch took no decisions. The initial question of priorities would be decided by Hitler or Speer; the Planning Branch would then work out what any shift of priorities would mean in practice. It operated through five sub-divisional branches, one of which, the statistical branch, provided overall statistics which had previously been ignored or unobtainable. In November 1943 when further functions were transferred to the Speer Ministry from the Ministry of Economics Funk was given a seat on Central Planning. The appointment was merely a sop for loss of face, which Funk clearly recognized.[2] He did not embarrass his fellow-members by attending too frequently. Possibly his non-attendance was an accident since he believed in 1945 that the meetings were held 'every few months'[3] when they were actually held every fortnight. Certainly he was not encouraged to attend; the agenda was only sent to him the day before the meeting. The only real discussion at the meetings was between Speer and the claimants, sometimes as many as forty who would attend to press their requirements.

Milch had an important role which throws into sharp focus one of the failures of the new administrative system. The design and production of aeroplanes was outside the control of the Speer Ministry. As this became a costlier and more important feature of the German war economy so it became more and more essential for Speer and Milch to agree in Central Plan-ning. But even though they did this pretty well their joint con-trol over the aircraft industry was too remote. By cutting down on raw material allocations they tended, not to eliminate waste

[1] Planungsamt.   [2] FD 3062/49 op. cit.   [3] Ibid., p. 2.

and inefficiency, but to retain the same waste and inefficiency with a smaller final output. And this became a matter of more and more serious proportions for Germany as the war progressed. Naval armaments were controlled by production committees but the Air Force would never agree to committees having the same powers in aeroplane manufacture because that would have meant cutting down on its precise specifications for each type of plane.

There was good ground for criticism of the committee system. Most criticism related back to the tasks for which the committees had initially been conceived. Todt had introduced them originally as a trouble-shooting mechanism into industries where irrational methods and inefficiency were plain to see. They did not prove so adaptable to other industries, and although the system was clearly justified by results on a general level, there were drawbacks.

The obvious danger was that the chairmen of committees would be selected from amongst the directors of the largest and most powerful firms in the industry, instead of from the most efficient. The position of chairman of a main committee was vital since he played the key role in negotiations with the Armed Forces procurement branches. Consequently the chairman of a main committee, particularly if he was a powerful man in his own right, had a certain measure of independence from the Speer Ministry. The National Socialist Party itself had certain vague powers over the appointment of committee chairmen. The normal procedure was for whichever department of the Speer Ministry was most knowledgeable on the subject to submit a list of names to Speer.[1] The Chief of the Party Chancellery could reserve for himself the right to veto any name, should he believe the man politically unreliable. In fact many chairmen appear not to have been even Party members and many others only lukewarm adherents.

The pressure of the Party proved easier to avoid than the pressure of the more important industrialists. The chairman of the main committee for weapons, Dr. Tix, had been managing director of Hanomag, Hanover.[2] Hanomag was a subsidiary of

---

[1] FD 3298/45, 'The Organisation of German Industry etc.'
[2] Speer Report No. 13, p. 4.

Vereinigte Stahlwerke. Frydag, who towards the end of the war became chairman of the main committee for aircraft production, was the managing director of Messerschmitt A.G.[1] Küppenbender, managing director of Zeiss A.G., became chairman of the main committee for general equipment.[2] Mauterer, chairman of the main committee for steel structural work, was managing director of another subsidiary of Vereinigte Stahlwerke.[3] The chairman of the executive board of Vereinigte Stahlwerke, Rohland, was chairman of the main committee for steel and rolling-mills,[4] and the managing director of another of its subsidiaries, Deutsche Eisenwerke A.G., was chairman of the main committee for all other aspects of iron processing.[5] They received no financial advantage, for the appointments were all honorary, but their firms must very frequently have gained.

The way in which, in any particular industry, the committees functioned depended largely on the structure of that industry; in some the forming of the committees made little impact. The United States Strategic Bombing Survey undertook an investigation of the way in which this process was carried out in the machine-tool industry.[6] The Machine Tool Manufacturers' Association (VDW), was founded in 1892 and was the first proper trade association in the industry. When the scheme of compulsory 'groupings' was introduced in 1934 VDW became a 'group' (*Fachgruppe Werkzeuge*) in its entirety, under Wirtschaftsgruppe Maschinen. The head of the former 'Association of Machine Manufacturers', the VDMA, a branch of VDW, had become the director of Wirtschaftsgruppe Maschinen. To add to his list of titles he had been able to collect another when the Four-Year-Plan came into operation. The Four-Year-Plan Organization decided that it was necessary to have someone with overriding powers in the machine-tool industry, and solved this problem by making the same man, Lange, Plenipotentiary for Machine Production. When Speer introduced the committee system into the machine-tool

[1] FD 3298/45, 'The Organisation of German Industry etc.', p. 2.
[2] Ibid.   [3] Speer Report No. 13, p. 4.
[4] Ibid.   [5] Ibid.
[6] FD 3876/45, U.S.S.B.S. Interrogation Report on the German Machine Tool Industry.

industry Lange became chairman of the main committee for machine tools. Thus the control already exercised by the employers' association was perpetuated and strengthened.

As a result of this arrangement the group of leading manufacturers represented in Wirtschaftsgruppe Maschinen were able, while disguised as the main committee for machine tools, effectively to resist the demands of the Planning Branch for the reduction of the volume of labour employed on unessential work, for the reduction of unessential machines, for the reduction and standardization of types, and for the integration of the machine-tool industry into the overall planning of the war economy. Pressure could be put on them by negative means, by issuing only special permits, which could easily be recalled, for certain special types of tool, or by withdrawing their supply of raw materials. Later in the war the policy was adopted of forcing large firms to expend 15 per cent of their output on repairs and small firms to work entirely on repairs. But even this proved an unsuccessful way of forcing the larger firms to concentrate solely on war production. As late as August 1944 Saur was threatening to withdraw their labour supplies.

Consequently control of the machine-tool industry resolved itself into a system of continually threatening the large manufacturers, not unlike the system prevailing in many large British industries in the First World War. The fact that in this instance the Speer Ministry spent nearly all its time threatening inhibited all questions of overall planning. This was more harmful within the peculiar conditions prevailing in the German war economy than might otherwise have been the case. One aspect of the change from Blitzkrieg to full-scale war was a change from small-scale production to mass production to keep up with the immense mass-productive resources of the United States' economy. This was resisted by the machine-tool industry in the form of a go-slow in the change from general purpose machine tools to single purpose tools. This did not mean that there were not enough tools at any particular stage of the war, since the policy of 'dispersal' to avoid the worst consequences of air attack often entailed a partial return to small-scale production. Nor can failure to produce enough tools be held responsible for lack of shift working. In April 1942 90 per cent of the German military armament industry was working only one shift.[1] But it seems certain that twenty-four hour working was never so essential in Germany as it was in Britain, since the supply of machine-tools was so much greater. Before the war the German machine-tool industry had been a considerable exporter. In any case there were great advantages in not introducing twenty-four hour working in engineering. Machine-tools need to be replaced proportionately sooner if used without a break and on three-shift working maintenance becomes a problem of manpower also. The real failure of the committee system in the machine-tool industry lay deeper than this. It lay in the lack of variety of tools produced and in the resistance to the development and production of new machines, a dangerous situation in a war of ever more rapidly changing armaments. This failure had a more acute effect towards the end of the war.

No doubt an examination of the precise way in which the committee system worked in other industries would sometimes reveal similar problems. There were undoubtedly too many committees. The temptation to continue forming agencies which so often had an immense initial impact was too great to resist. Some had very little work of importance to do. Sometimes the functions of two committees would overlap, to the confusion of all who had to deal with them. There was too much unnecessary segregation of individual items.[2] Yet the system worked well on the whole, and its limitations were perhaps the curious limitations of political power, whether real or imaginary, in the National Socialist State, which had made the Blitzkrieg initially such a convenient method of waging war.

Whereas the efficiency of the production committees has in some cases been overstated, there seem to have been examples in the development committees of its having been non-existent. Each main committee for production was supposed to have a corresponding development committee where manufacturers, service personnel, efficiency experts, and economists would decide which new types of product would be produced. In its original purpose the idea was excellent because it prevented the Wehrmacht from specifying a great number of different types of guns or motor vehicles. Theoretically guns of the same calibre

[1] Speer Report No. 90.   [2] Speer Report No. 32, p. 5.

and with interchangeable components could now be produced for all three services. Speer had unfortunately very little interest in scientific development; perhaps he had enough problems of production to solve. The result was that the leadership of technical development tended to devolve on Geist, who was responsible for the co-ordination of the work of the development committees. Geist, who was, in any case, a fairly junior member of the Speer Ministry, proved to be not entirely adequate for his job.[1]

But circumstances were heavily against Geist from the start. The domination of production committees by large firms in some industries spread over into the development committees. There were even instances of the same man being chairman of the main production committee and chairman of the main development committee. Again, some of the chairmen of the development committees were weak personalities and allowed too much latitude to the Wehrmacht officials. The military regarded the development committees as inexperienced intruders, and claimed that it was actually the Army Armament Branch which had to advise and assist the Speer Ministry, rather than the other way round.[2] The general military opinion was that the Speer Ministry was too large and unwieldy a machine.[3] Even Geist admitted that the Army Armament Branch (HWA) sometimes approached firms directly with specifications for new types, by-passing the development committees entirely.[4] The opinion of Major-General Henrici was that

> The development committees were varied—some did good work. HWA did not short-circuit development committees by dealing direct with firms—it was normal procedure for HWA to deal with firms both keeping development committees in mind. If the development committee was weak, then HWA called the tune.[5]

If, on the contrary, the chairman of the development committee was a strong personality and a powerful industrialist he would seek his own private interest in letting the soldiers have their own way. Large manufacturers, like Krupp, saw greater

---

[1] Speer Report No. 53.　　　　　　　　[2] Speer Report No. 83.
[3] Ibid. General Henrici said it was 'too big and cumbersome', General Rossmann said it was 'too large and cumbersome'.
[4] Speer Report No. 53.　　　　　　　　[5] Speer Report No. 83.

future profit if they persisted in continually developing new items for production since this was one of their big advantages over their smaller rivals.[1] In 1942 such firms as Krupp were less easily compelled into mass-production of one article than were the smaller and medium-sized firms. Consequently greater profit had to be incorporated in contracts for mass-produced articles in order to induce large firms away from the constant development of complicated types. This alliance between the Wehrmacht and the larger industrialists on the development committees acted to the exclusion of the other vital group—the scientists. The principles on which the committees were formed tended to place too much emphasis on the mere mechanism of production. The German war economy suffered throughout from a lack of skilled scientific direction and fundamental scientific research. Even on the most efficient development committee the scientists were in a small minority. The number of tests considered sufficient for thorough examination of a piece of equipment varied according to which section of opinion held the upper hand at the time. Consequently there was no proper ruling on the point where development finished and production began. Often it was cheaper for firms to let the military carry out their own tests.

The differing dictates of overall strategy never had much effect on the allocation of facilities for fundamental research. Therefore weapons designed to meet a given situation tended only to come into production when that situation had fundamentally changed. In the last resort the failure of German development policy did not lie in the selfish personal policies of generals and large firms. Differences of opinion on which lines of development to follow were bound in any case to exist in wartime. Some control which can operate as a check on such differences of opinion and ultimately as an arbitrator is essential. In Germany this could only be supplied by neutral expert scientific opinion, or by Hitler. Since the system ruled out the first it had to be the second. But Hitler thought in terms of improvement only on certain occasions and along certain lines. As far as totally new forms of armaments were concerned he would become obsessed with the idea of single weapons like V1 and V2

[1] Speer Report No. 45, p. 12.

as panaceas for the whole situation. He envisaged V2 for some time as an unanswerable weapon which might end the war, and he was wrong. There was no one else who could competently and effectively decide which lines of development should be followed and which ignored.

Quite outside the control of the Speer Ministry was one aspect of the German war economy that was unsolved for the whole five and a half years of the war, the problem of labour supply and utilization. Not only was it unsolved but it became ever more vicious as the war proceeded because in terms of sheer manpower Germany was overwhelmingly inferior to her opponents.

At first Sauckel's vigorous activity after his appointment as Plenipotentiary stirred the whole machinery of labour control to new life and provided the armaments industry with a sufficient flow of labour temporarily to cover its needs. For the first six months Speer and Sauckel worked together fairly successfully. But Sauckel was not prepared to submit to the authority of the Minister. Sauckel took his side of the disputes straight to Bormann who carried them to Hitler, whence they returned as decisions which Speer had to accept. Speer never gave up trying to get labour under the control of Central Planning. From time to time Sauckel would accept Central Planning's 'recommendation', but often he would distribute labour to the armaments industry in whatever proportions he himself decided. The labour was allocated to regions and was there split up among factories by the Reichs Labour Offices. Speer wanted this regional distribution done by some regional armaments agency.[1] Sauckel, for his part, objected to committees transferring labour within the same industry from one region to another as though the consent of the Reichs Labour Offices was merely formal. He tried to make this consent more than nominal, thereby slowing down the process. In fact he tried to get his Labour Offices to inspect factories to make sure that their claims for labour were genuine. The argument that factories were making excessive claims for labour appealed strongly to Hitler. So to forestall the appointment of an inspectorate controlled by Sauckel, Speer created the post of a 'labour utilization' engineer in each factory.[2]

[1] Speer Report No. 19, Part 1, p. 19.   [2] Speer Report No. 29, p. 4.

Generally speaking his job was to check on employment levels, and in large factories where there was already a labour manager he would be given this new position as well.

On the question of labour in occupied territories Speer and Sauckel differed greatly. In the industrial areas of France and Belgium Speer believed it was more efficient to keep the workers employed in their own factories unless they were needed for specialized work in Germany in which case a temporary transfer should operate.[1] Sauckel's policy was to bring trainloads of workmen, including skilled artisans, to Germany. The workers' trains were made up to meet a demand from a particular district and the workmen were not divided according to skills.[2] Consequently many skilled artisans were used in general labouring for long periods. The main committees had a representative on the Armaments Branch[3] of Sauckel's organization who collated their labour demands and transferred them to Sauckel, who organized the trains. Speer believed that these methods of forced conscription abroad merely handicapped industrial production in those territories and stimulated direct and violent opposition there. This was quite true. But in spite of these convictions he continued energetically to demand labour from Sauckel.

The estimates of the number of foreign workers brought into Germany by this method vary immensely. Sauckel's figures were, of course, higher than Speer's.[4] This, in turn, led to another dispute. Speer claimed that Sauckel's figures, on which Hitler based some decisions, were twice as large as they ought to have been, since a man working for several firms in one year, as happened in many trades, particularly in dock labour, was always recorded in each job as a new recruit from abroad. Another explanation for Sauckel's figures may be that train-loads were always recorded as complete, no matter how many escaped, or died, on the way. Speer's methods of checking these figures, by means of the Labour Utilization Branches,[5] the customs posts, or on a regional level, were certainly every bit as unreliable as the figures they were checking.

[1] Speer Report No. 19, Part 1, p. 7.
[2] Speer Report No. 29, p. 8.   [3] Rüstungsamt.
[4] Ibid., p. 2.   [5] Amtsgruppe Arbeitseinsatz.

As relations between Sauckel and Speer deteriorated, Sauckel became an outspoken opponent of the whole system of industrial self-government by which the Ministry of Armaments controlled the economy. He took the 'party line' of the genuinely revolutionary wing of the National Socialists. He complained that there was too much free enterprise in the State to be tolerated in wartime and that Party officials should exercise some supervision over industrialists.[1] Speer, he claimed, was deliberately exaggerating armaments increases to stop the Party from punishing recalcitrant industrialists. Bormann backed this opinion entirely.

It is all too easy to paint the issues between Sauckel and Speer as simple blacks and whites, and to assume that Sauckel was a violent ambitious thug trying to wreck Speer's plans. In fact Speer was in a rather fortunate moral position; he did not have to exercise direct responsibility for acquiring foreign labour. Sauckel was behind many efforts to improve the treatment of workers in Germany. This was especially true of the Russians, worst treated of all. Sauckel stopped the system by which almost the whole of their wage was taxed away; as well as this he ended many arbitrary restrictions on their movement. If his methods of acquiring labour were violent, so was the pressure on him. His difference with Speer was a profound one of political opinion. Many *Gaue* had formed combines of factories within the *Gau* boundaries, enterprises which had frequently been 'aryanized'. One of the largest of these combines, the Gustloff-Stiftung in Thuringia, had been managed by Sauckel.[2] This was a reflection of the vague ideology of 'Gau-socialism' which was common on the revolutionary wing of the Party, the wing from which Gauleiters were often drawn. To Sauckel Speer's policy towards the larger industrialists seemed like a betrayal of everything the Party had fought for and still stood for.

Once these structural faults in the administration of the German war economy have been stated, it is not too hard to find excuses for them. Such things are always present in war because the severe pressure brings questions of principle to the forefront. All Speer's work was done under the violent impact of war's immediacy. He had to attempt a fundamental long-term con-

[1] Speer Report No. 19, Part 1, p. 21.   [2] Ibid., p. 24.

98

version of the German economy and, at the same time, to supply a constant day-to-day demand for fresh armaments and more ammunition. Expediency had often to be resorted to when better solutions were impossible because time was short. Beyond this reason, the faults of the system which he created existed within the State itself. All his work was done under conditions in which any change in economic policy immediately became part of a complex battle for political power. In such a situation that Speer should ever have achieved as much as he did is amazing.

CHAPTER V

Qualitative Superiority

BY July 1942 the general index of finished armaments production was 55 per cent above the February level. July marked the end of this first great increase. In October production once more started to rise steeply and by May 1943 had gone up by another 50 per cent. It remained at about the same level until December and then from December 1943 to July 1944 there was a third period of increase, this time of 45 per cent. Production of weapons, ammunition, and aircraft increased over threefold in two and a half years. The production of tanks in the same period increased almost sixfold.

These three periods of increase tally fairly exactly with the three periods of increase in hand armaments. Here the index figures from January 1942 to July 1944 climb from 100 to 384.[1] Not all increases had the same pattern. Tank production rose extremely steeply between March and May 1943 and reached its peak as late as December 1944. The January 1942 index figure is 100; the December 1944 figure is 598.

For the whole of this time Germany was opposed by countries potentially much stronger. No one in responsibility in Germany believed that Germany's production could be raised to the level of her opponents. Germany was not, although committing herself to a long war, hoping to out-produce her enemies. Given the level of German armaments Hitler doubted after Stalingrad whether Germany could win the war in the East by yet another all-out attack,[2] although his opinions appear to have varied from time to time on this issue. But ultimate victory in the war as a whole was assumed to be quite possible, both by Hitler and within the Speer Ministry.

[1] Appendix I.
[2] *Hitlers Lagebesprechungen, 1942–45*, p. 122.

Hitler felt that in the conditions imposed by a long war German society was likely to stand up to the strain much better than Russian or American society. But his strategic calculations were not based on these readily-identifiable prejudices. They were based on the concept of 'qualitative superiority'. Hitler assumed that it was possible for German technology to keep one step ahead of the enemy all the time in armaments. Germany must concede an overall quantitative superiority in armaments production to the enemy; but she could still win a war of mass-production by harnessing her technology and science to the task of keeping a qualitative superiority in many individual armaments.[1] The early part of the war in the East had revealed that Russian heavy tanks were better than German. Nor had the German 5 cm Pak gun been effective against the armour-plating of the Russian T-34 tank. The speed with which Germany had reversed this situation demonstrates that Hitler's theories about qualitative superiority were not without foundation. By Spring 1942 the 7·5 cm Pak gun, which proved highly effective, was in course of production. The Tiger tank was being developed at the same time, thanks to Hitler who had demanded such a heavy tank against the wishes of many of the Army leaders who had thought such vehicles impracticable.

Most German munition was of a better quality than that of the Allies. The inferior quality of Allied munitions and of other armaments was sometimes the result of the simplifications and standardizations inherent in linear-flow production methods which had been carried much further in the United States and in Britain. The German war economy from early 1942 to Summer 1944 operated on the principle that it was possible to draw a line between a useful modification to the end product and a non-useful one, that it was possible to standardize production methods yet avoid a severe drop in the quality of the armaments produced. It was certainly true that before 1942 German armaments had undergone more frequent modification than those of their opponents and that some of these modifications could have been omitted without undue sacrifice of quality. To this extent at least German production policy after 1942 was based on a valid historical experience.

[1] See Speer Report No. 6 for Speer's opinions.

However, granted the acceptance of the principle of qualitative superiority there were several difficulties in putting such a principle into operation. The first was the huge quantitative difference in armaments output between Germany and her opponents which weighed heavily on the minds of all concerned with the German armaments industry. The ultimate quantitative superiority in the field of munitions alone was perhaps 9 : 2 in favour of the Allies.[1] After the first German failure in Russia and the entry of the United States into the war a Führer-Command was put out forbidding any official discussion of Germany's long-term prospects of keeping up with the Allies' production. No information on Allied war production could be circulated to government branches, even those with a pressing official interest.[2]

Secondly there was the difficulty of maintaining technical superiority over an enemy who was able to copy any armament captured in battle. A Führer-Command of 3 January 1943 declared that qualitative superiority could, and therefore should, only be ensured for very limited periods, and never longer than one year.[3] Germany's temporary superiority in heavy tanks gained by the Tiger would soon cease, and it had already become necessary to get the heavier Tiger and the Mäuschen into production. There was no point in introducing any development of a weapon which represented a very great advance since the enemy, by copying, would be able to pass over the intermediate stages of development. Assuming that German armaments were superior, research should be based on the concept of keeping just one step in front of the enemy. The application of this principle touched the German war economy in one of its most delicate spots, the development committees.

Another difficulty was that the concept of qualitative superiority would have been useless if confined solely to development and production. It extended into the use of the armaments produced, a matter in which the Speer Ministry had only an advisory role. The concept had equal importance in the strategic

[1] A. J. Brown, op. cit., calculates the superiority in munitions of the U.S.A. and Britain at a ratio of 5 : 2.
[2] Speer Report No. 6.
[3] FD 3353/45, vol. 29, Führerkonferenz 3/5 January 1943.

and economic fields; indeed one of its greatest weaknesses was that it needed a close agreement between the High Command and the Ministry of Munitions.

For instance, one of the ways in which qualitative superiority would be most likely to tell was in air warfare. It might have been possible for Germany to develop defensive aircraft superior to those of the Allies and thus lessen the threat from aerial bombardment. But this would only prove possible should Germany concentrate her comparatively limited resources solely on the problem of fighter production. Important men in the Air Force, Milch and General Galland, supported this. But Hitler and the Air Staff insisted for a long time on a policy of retaliation, at least against Britain. To Speer this was absurd. It cost roughly nine times as much to produce a bomber as a fighter.[1] Consequently, if every fighter lost shot down one bomber, the Allies' losses in terms of armaments, men, and morale, would be far more severe than those of Germany.

Galland's tactical idea was to keep 'assault groups' of fighters in reserve in bases in central Germany and throw them at the mass-bomber formations when the fighter escorts were no longer able to follow.[2] This sort of tactic was essential if qualitative superiority was to mean anything. In July 1944, according to Galland, he and Speer made a joint approach to Hitler to prevent the Führer sending any more fighters to France. Speer was told to confine his activities to war industry and Galland to executing orders.[3]

Speer had no control over strategy, and without regard to strategy economic policies exist in a vacuum. The use of fighters in the way suggested by Galland may have been economically desirable, even economically essential, but the problem was much more than how best to utilize German aluminium production. It was not such logical principles, but the pressure of events, that drove the Air Force General Staff to concentrate almost exclusively on the production of defensive aircraft. In September 1940 Germany had 1,162 fighters and 1,871 bombers. In September 1944 German strength in Western Europe

---

[1] Speer Report No. 6, p. 3.
[2] A. Galland, *Die Ersten und die Letzten,* trans. *The First and the Last* (1955), pp. 350–1.　　　　　　　　　　　　　　　[3] Ibid., p. 353.

was 2,473 fighters and 209 bombers.[1] Germany was forced to abandon altogether the production of a new heavy bomber. It was only the pressure of events that drove the Air Force General Staff into opting for qualitative superiority.

The way weapons were used was equally important for ground forces. The principle on which arms were distributed to ground forces was that 90 per cent of new armaments went to newly-formed and inexperienced divisions, only 10 per cent was used for re-equipping units already in the line. Newly-formed divisions naturally lost great quantities of equipment in their first experience of battle. The whole mechanism of distributing arms to the front was faulty. During a visit to Kesselring's Army Group in Italy, Speer found that it was 1,500 machine-guns below strength when monthly production was running at 30,000. The qualitative superiority of Germany in tanks on the Eastern front was often nullified by the fact that tanks would be captured by the advancing Russian armies because of missing engine parts. Not until it was too late could the High Command be persuaded to devote transport space to tank-motors rather than to tanks; ten tank-motors could be conveyed in the space needed by one tank. All such considerations touched qualitative superiority closely. In such a policy deployment of arms was as important as their development and production.

Heavy losses of equipment tended to nullify the superior quality of German arms. German armaments production in 1944 was equivalent to the complete equipment of 250 infantry divisions and 40 tank divisions[2] while Germany only had the equivalent of 150 full divisions of 12,000 men each in the field. In spite of this there was a steady decline in the weapons strength of these divisions; losses must have played their part in this decline.

The shortage of certain raw materials also made qualitative superiority harder to achieve. Effective substitution often compensated for shortages of metals. Acute shortages of fuel-oil could sometimes be overcome by more efficient use of fuel-

---

[1] Lord Tedder, *Air Power in War*, writes 'I believe this unbalance of the Luftwaffe to have been . . . one of the main causes . . . of Germany losing the war. It was, I believe, a symptom of deep-seated misconceptions.' But it is difficult to see what other policy could have been followed.

[2] Speer Report No. 6.

consuming armaments. But these solutions were not always possible. In 1944 supplies of tungsten carbide tips for high-speed machine tools could only be maintained at the necessary level by cutting back the production of carbide-core anti-tank ammunition. Production of carbide-core anti-tank ammunition of 5 cm calibre was allowed to continue, as experience had shown that such 5 cm shells could just, if only just, pierce the armour of the heavy Russian tanks. With the exception of one other calibre the production of all carbide-core calibres was stopped and all stocks were recalled to provide several tons of tungsten for machine-tool tips. Generally speaking, the policy of keeping one qualitative step in front of the enemy placed a heavy strain on the machine-tool industry, each change-over requiring a large new capital investment.[1]

Faced with so many problems in maintaining a superior level of quality, and saddled with an inadequate machinery for the development of such weapons and their improvement Germany was driven into producing not superior armaments but completely novel ones. The secret weapons were Germany's last answer to the mass-productive resources of the U.S.S.R. and the U.S.A.

Admittedly the idea for the weapon which came to be known as V2 had been conceived by von Braun as early as 1934. But in its original version he had regarded it as having a peaceful purpose, possibly the speeding-up of long-distance postal services. Development of the V2 had been a small army project, but in 1942 it became a priority project. The site at Peenemünde was always controlled by the Army, and was outside the committee system. The V1 was an Air-Force development initiated in 1942 out of rivalry with the Army.[2] The V1, which had Göring and other influential people against it, was mainly a propaganda weapon. Economically it was justifiable. It was made of steel, not aluminium, and therefore did not compete with aeroplane production. The V2, however, was a much superior weapon. Yet within the context of the German economy its production interfered with the production of weapons of a more orthodox type. It needed twenty times the production cost of the V1 to

[1] Speer Report No. 50, Part IV, p. 6.
[2] Speer Report No. 2, p. 6.

carry a warhead of about the same size. In mass-production each of these rockets cost 250,000 reichsmarks.[1] For this money and effort at least six high-performance fighters could have been turned out. The complex electrical equipment of V2 retarded the production of vital electrical equipment for U-boats, and the development of a more efficient radar system. Plant capacity for oxygen supply for the V2 proved a major difficulty and was one of the main reasons for the failure to reach production figures of 900 missiles a month. The maximum number ever produced in a single month was 700. Furthermore the V2 also required very high-quality sheet metal, a commodity already in great demand. The development and production of entirely new weapons proved to be incompatible with the policy of keeping one step ahead with existing ones.

Eventually, in Autumn 1944, before the Ardennes offensive, the concept of qualitative superiority was abandoned, in favour of an all-out utilization of every available resource to stave off disaster. This last phase marks the period when the war was tacitly admitted by most planners to be lost. It also marks the time when planning had ceased to have any real meaning since all Germany's decisions were virtually being made for her by her enemies. Until that final stage Germany's hopes of winning the war were placed on the assumption that in qualitative terms her war economy could out-perform the combined economies of her opponents.

Yet, even in 1944 when German armaments production was so high, the economy could not be called a full war economy. The list of consumer goods still produced in 1943 would have made interesting reading for the United Kingdom war cabinet in that year. The production of certain consumer goods actually increased between 1943 and 1944. On 6 October 1943 Speer told the Gauleiters in a speech at Posen:

For example, we still produce in a year 120,000 typewriters, 13,000 duplicating machines, 50,000 address machines, 30,000 calculating machines and accounting machines, 200,000 wireless receivers, 150,000 electrical bedwarmers, 3,600 electrical refrigerators, 300,000 electricity meters.[2]

[1] Ibid., p. 5.
[2] FD 3353/45 vol. 81, 'Rede Reichsministers Speer', 6 October 1943, p. 11.

Using to its full advantage one of his subsidiary offices, that of Inspector-General for Water and Power, Speer had insisted on a policy of dispensing with gas, electricity, and water meters, and of forcing the suppliers to negotiate general agreements with the consumers.

As so often the most glaring examples of wasteful production were in the Armed Forces themselves. The Wehrmacht supply agents were unlikely ever to be reproached for having too great numbers of any article of equipment, and their demands for large supplies of general equipment provided a constant stimulus to firms inessential in a war economy. Watch production, for instance, could be maintained nearly at the peace-time level because of the extraordinary demand for officers' watches.

At present there are still being made for the Wehrmacht 512,000 pairs of riding boots a year, 312,000 pairs of officers' boots a year, 360,000 service bags for women signal assistants, 364,000 spur straps, 250,000 rucksacks . . . I really don't know what they use them for. The Wehrmacht needs 440 millions of the total yearly new production of bottles of 730 millions. The Wehrmacht needs 620,000 of the new production of closets which reaches a figure of one million yearly. Out of the production of stamping surfaces for ink-pads the Wehrmacht needs 6,200,000. The scissors production is reserved entirely for the Wehrmacht, they receive 4,400,000 a year.[1]

Even in 1943 Germany was still producing 12,000 tons of wallpaper, to say nothing of 4,800 tons of hair tonic. The Navy had just had a demand for 50,000 officers' daggers rejected.

Shoe production[2]

(in million pairs)

	1942 quarterly av.	1943 quarterly av.	1944 1st quarter	1944 4th quarter	1945 1st quarter
Footwear for working and vocational purposes	3·0	3·5	4·2	3·2	2·2
Leather street footwear	10·0	10·4	10·0	4·3	3·6
Light street footwear	6·0	9·3	11·2	8·1	3·6
Slippers, gym shoes, etc.	7·5	7·0	5·3	3·7	2·1

[1] Ibid., p. 13.
[2] FD 3353/45, vol. 106, 'Lederproduktion', p. 2 (compiled for Speer's annual report).

Speer's Posen speech threatened drastic reductions of consumer goods production. The level certainly fell as a result of his actions. But on the whole the process was rather uneven and even where there were drops in the figures productive resources were often wasted on manufacturing a variety of patterns.

The final drop in footwear production received extra impetus from the severe decreases in raw material supplies. The production of pottery and glass, which suffered less from a curtailment of raw material supplies did not decline so severely.

Ceramics output[1]

(in tons)

	1942	1943	1944
Household pottery	210,000	184,000	178,000
Sanitary pottery	45,000	40,000	30,000
Plates	130,000	90,000	50,000
Tiled stoves and stove tiles	95,000	95,000	95,000

Glassware production[2]

	1942	1943	1944
Bottles for drinks (million pieces)	600	560	490
Preserving jars (million pieces)	160	150	135
Packing glass (in 100,000 tons)	100	100	100

The Speer Ministry's greatest achievement in the reduction of consumer goods production lay in the textile industry. Here both Wehrmacht and civilian production was drastically cut. In some regions all textile production was closed down and the floor space converted to other purposes.[3]

Such figures as these show clearly enough that consumer goods production was restricted from 1942 onwards. However, the overall impression is that Germany's war economy was not as 'total' as might have been expected. In spite of this Germany's economic machine showed a capacity to solve problems far more difficult

[1] Ibid., 'Keramik', photostat page no. 3222.
[2] Ibid., page no. 3223.
[3] See Table, p. 109.

Textile factory output[1]

Class of products	1943 Wehrmacht	Civilian[2]	1944 Wehrmacht	Civilian[2]
	(in million metres)			
Cotton weaving mill output	337	339	185	235
Wool weaving mill output	65	52	44	41
Woven linen and heavy materials (*Schwerweberei*)	82	30	45	34
Silk and velvet woven products	59	61	45	41
Clothing	(in thousand pieces)			
Men's wear	10,791		1,933	
Women's wear	19,033		8,253	
Working clothes (both sexes)	22,567		22,494	
Underwear	14,106		7,410	
Babies' underwear	4,100		5,007	

than those which had initially impeded rearmament. Each successive production increase brought new problems which were enormously intensified by Allied bombing. Although between the different kinds of problem faced it is a little misleading to draw any lines of demarcation, since each problem was intimately concerned with others, for the sake of convenience they can be divided into problems inherent in the German economy and becoming apparent because of the tremendous production increases, and problems due to external interference in that economy by the Allies. This second group of problems can be postponed for separate consideration. The problems inherent in the German economy included those factors, other than enemy action, which slowed down the rise of output and, indeed, over certain periods, as from July 1942 to October 1942, and from May 1943 to December 1943 caused the overall monthly average of armaments production to remain at about the same level. Even these factors are difficult to isolate. Doubtless given more iron and more labour an even greater production of cases, shells, and fuses for ammunition would have been obtained. But this, in itself, would have been useless without a considerable expansion of the chemical industry. And this in turn needed a considerable increase in constructional labour.

[1] Ibid., p. 3224. [2] Including workmen's clothes.

At the end of 1941 a shortage of copper was the deciding limitation in U-boat production. Later there was so much copper surplus that quantities were set free to be used in infantry munitions. In January 1943 there was an acute shortage of skilled labour, in the autumn lack of raw materials was the main problem.[1] Of course, the ultimate limit to war production was a physical one, the amount of labour available. But Germany was very far from reaching this ultimate physical limit.

The three most persistent bottlenecks in armaments production were: firstly, the insufficient production of high-grade steels; secondly, the difficulty of procuring supplies of components; and thirdly, the shortage of skilled labour.[2]

Overall steel production in Germany was high but war production is much more closely tied to the output of certain specialized kinds of steel. There was an insufficient output of high-grade steels and an insufficient output of both high-grade and low-grade steel plate. The shortage of high-grade steel was complex in its incidence. In particularly short supply were forged pieces and drawn tubes. These shortages did not become apparent until February 1942; and the problem persisted because the solutions never quite kept pace with the increased demand. Ultimately this represented a failure to invest sufficiently in the steel industry between the wars. Investment at that time had been diverted into the exploitation of low-grade ores on an uneconomic basis because of political pressures. The urgency of the demand for finished armaments beginning in 1942 prevented any long-term investment in capital industries of this type; the need for such investment was not realized until it was too late.

The problem of the supply of armaments components was that they were manufactured by a great number of small-scale producers scattered through the countryside. Often they were made in workshops employing no more than thirty men. In such circumstances mass-production was almost unthinkable. 'The components[3] industry' [said Speer] 'forms *the* bottleneck for us. . . . If we cannot increase the industry to the necessary

---

[1] FD 3049/49 (File no. 1). Interrogation of Saur, 9 August 1945, p. 10.
[2] Speer Report No. 55, Part II, p. 8.
[3] 'Zulieferungen.'

large scale, then all our efforts will be absolutely useless.'[1]

A great deal of improvement was brought about by standardizing component parts as far as possible. But such a policy had inherent limitations; any sudden change in the armaments programme might often result in fairly large stocks of useless components.[2] Nor could such a solution ease the transport problems connected with the structure of the armaments industry.

The third serious bottleneck, and the one which was not so clearly attributable to pre-war developments, was the availability of skilled labour. As early as 1937 armaments factories in central Germany had had difficulties in attracting skilled labour.[3] Conscription caused this problem to redouble in intensity, and increases in armaments output after 1941 augmented its seriousness. Apprentices were likely to be called-up as soon as their training was over and thereby the readiest stream of skilled labour was dammed at source. In 1943 and 1944 emergency drafts called up into the Armed Forces skilled artisans who until that date had been deferred. There were acute shortages of gauge-makers, tool-makers, locksmiths, fitters, and welders.[4] Even more acute was the shortage of skilled supervisors and foremen, a factor which impeded the development of shift-working.

The Labour Offices started a series of training schemes as a way of overcoming the difficulty, but the schemes were mainly devoted to getting people up to semi-skilled level.[5] In co-operation with the Labour Front firms themselves started technical-training crash programmes. But that the problem never became insuperable was due to the work of the production committees who were quick to transfer labour from one factory to another as soon as a contract was completed.

The imports of foreign labour were largely wasted since no attempt was made to diversify this labour force according to different skills, except that the strongest and healthiest were sent down the mines.[6] Once a man had been misdirected in this way it was very difficult to get him away from his original employer who did not want to lose his labour. The larger firms

[1] FD 3353/45 vol. 81, op. cit., p. 5. [2] Speer Report No. 50, Part III, p. 8.
[3] Speer Report No. 39, Part 1, p. 3. [4] Speer Report No. 50, Part II, p. 7.
[5] Ibid., p. 6. [6] Speer Report No. 39, Part 1, p. 3.

were forced to attract highly-skilled engineers from abroad by approaching them directly[1]—a method which could apply only to very small numbers of specialized recruits.

The priority systems for exemptions from call-up, which had been overhauled in February 1942 when the old UK grade had been further differentiated, had ceased to have much meaning by 1943, although the oldest method, that of allowing men out of the Wehrmacht on ticket-of-leave still existed and was used in certain special cases. From 1942 all labour requirements for the armaments industry, so long as they were considered urgent, had been submitted to the Labour Offices with a 'red label' which had given them top priority on Sauckel's instructions.[2] In the course of 1944 Sauckel and Speer worked out a compromise whereby 'red labels' were issued only for a part of the requirements, about 50,000 to 80,000 a month.

All such measures, apart from being ameliorations rather than solutions, ran up against the steady deterioration of the labour force as a whole. Although Germany always had only a low mobilization of women those who were employed proved less valuable workers than the men they replaced. This also applied to the old people who were employed. Several methods of improving the performance of a deteriorating labour force were tried.

The most obvious of these was the introduction of piece-work. But this was too severely handicapped by the shortage of skilled artisans. There was too little skilled labour to determine the rates of pay justly.[3] Should the basis be too low and bear no relation to the true working capacity of the worker, he would do no more than necessary to fill his quota, as there was a fixed ceiling for piecework. There would in such a situation be no possibility of reward for higher efficiency. Towards the end of the war great increases in fighter output were achieved partly through efficiency bonuses. Workers compelled to work a twelve-hour day were supplied with good food, liquor, and tobacco, and the opportunity to buy additional consumer goods.

It was not merely the domestic labour force which deteriorated in quality as the war progressed but the foreign labour too.

[1] Ibid., p. 4. [2] Speer Report No. 50, Part 1, p. 16.
[3] Speer Report No. 45, p. 13.

There is little doubt that the vast quantities of foreign labour fed the needs of German industry merely in terms of bodies, and that was not enough. A great many of them were used inefficiently in SS schemes outside the control of the Speer Ministry, and a great many were used in agriculture. Furthermore Sauckel's methods of procuring labour were self-defeating and resulted in a steady decrease of foreign labour just when the need was greatest. 2,100,000 foreign workers were brought to Germany in 1942–3; between May 1943 and May 1944 the net inflow was only 900,000.[1] This deterioration in supply coincided with heavy losses of men in the Wehrmacht.

Strength and losses of the Armed Forces 1939–44[2]
(in thousands)

Date	Strength	Losses	Total mobilized
1939, 31 May	1,366	—	1,366
1940, 31 May	5,600	85	5,685
1941, 31 May	7,200	185	7,385
1942, 31 May	8,635	800	9,435
1943, 31 May	9,555	1,680	11,235
1944, 31 May	9,100	3,285	12,385
1944, 30 Sept.	9,125	3,875	13,000

Foreign workers (civilians and prisoners of war)[3]
(in thousands)

Date	Total	Foreign civilians[4]	Prisoners of war
1939, 31 May	300	300	—
1940, 31 May	1,150	800	350
1941, 31 May	3,020	1,750	1,270
1942, 31 May	4,120	2,640	1,470
1943, 31 May	6,260	4,640	1,620
1944, 31 May	7,130	5,300	1,830

On 20 November 1944 Speer urged a fundamental redistribution of German manpower in order to stave off the point of decision between concentration on production or on soldiers, and so to continue 'armament in depth'. According to his statistics the allocation of manpower in the economy at that time was:[5]

[1] U.S.S.B.S., *Effects*, op. cit., p. 33.   [2] Ibid.   [3] Ibid., p. 34.   [4] Including all Jews.
[5] FD 2690/45 vol. 5, Speer to Hitler, 20 July 1944, pp. 2–3.

Army production	1,940,000
Air-Force production	2,330,000
Navy production	530,000
Shipbuilding	250,000
Mining industries	970,000
Iron industries	470,000
Trade, banks, insurance, catering, etc.	3,180,000
Domestic work	1,450,000

These figures left about three million people engaged in civil and military administration. If the figures of manpower utilization within the Wehrmacht were broken down a similar maldistribution was apparent. Out of 10,500,000 men called up to the Army or Waffen SS only 210 combat divisions, about 2,500,000 men in all, were maintained. In fact, according to Speer, a manpower crisis could be avoided only if the whole structure of the German Armed Forces were re-aligned.

I am attempting now to carry out a survey of the machinery which Ludendorff as Quartermaster-General during the First World War had at his disposal for the Army and the Air Force, and would like then to compare that machinery with that which is necessary today for the same number of soldiers.

That which formerly was done by one Colonel Bauer, is today done by innumerable generals strewn over all branches of the Armed Forces.[1]

Speer's plan was to draft into the front line all conceivable reserves from that class of people born between 1910 and 1926. The total made available by such a measure would be at least 4,300,000 since such men could be taken from non-combat divisions which could be made up by older men. On the face of it such a proposal might seem disastrous to the armaments industry, but, in fact, the whole purpose of trying to convince Hitler of the necessity for such a plan was to safeguard the skilled workmen, most of whom would have been born before 1910, from the call-up. Furthermore, Speer tried to persuade Hitler to call-up the 1910–26 age group in three stages. The first stage would not touch people born before 1918. By sugaring the pill so that it appeared to be a proposal for making the Army more efficient Speer hoped to get Hitler to swallow it. But the

[1] Ibid., p. 5.

nasty medicine was too apparent and Hitler would not swallow it. He was not prepared to undertake so fundamental a re-organization. The plan failed and Speer was unable to prevent the formation of the Volkssturm and the consequently heavy call-up which finally meant the abandonment of the principle of qualitative superiority.[1]

These three problems, the insufficiency of certain steels, the structural weaknesses within the armaments industry, and the maldistribution of the labour force resulting in a shortage of skilled labour, were inherent in the German economy. They were enormously exacerbated by the external interference of the Allies in that economy. The development of the long-range bomber provided a means of economic warfare infinitely more effective than the traditional blockade. Not that the traditional processes of economic warfare were abandoned, or became any less useful. But the bomber offered a way of extending the pressure on raw materials supplies in a more positive fashion. And since many of the calculations on which the naval blockade had been based had been nullified by Germany's extension of her territorial area of control the bomber was all the more welcome. It effected a veritable revolution in economic warfare. Not all Allied bombing had a primary or even a secondary economic purpose. But even those parts of the Strategic Air Offensive which were not economic in their intentions presented Germany with a new range of economic problems. Many deeply-entrenched ideas on war economy were severely jolted and practices which had gradually become accepted had to be abandoned quickly. Although most German military strategists since 1918 had worked on the assumption that the domestic base of Germany's economy might be damaged by air attack few economists or administrators had foreseen the scale of the economic problems which such massive interference in the working of the economy would entail.

Speer gave his opinion that

The total damage suffered by the armament programmes as a result of air attack during the year 1943 was not considerable. With regard to the year 1944 on the other hand, it may be assumed that on the average there was a fall in production amounting to 30–40 per

[1] See Chapter VII.

cent for had it not been for the air attacks the projected output programme would certainly have been achieved.[1]

One of the main reasons for the relative lack of success of Allied bombing in 1943 was the fact that a convincing bombing strategy had not yet been worked out.[2] At the very outset of the year, at the Casablanca conference, the Allies had agreed on a combined bomber offensive which would prepare the way for the invasion of Germany. Having decided on this, they then found themselves, especially in the field, in disagreement as to the methods by which the air attack could best be directed to such an end. The dispute lay between 'general attack' and 'selective attack'. 'Selective attack' meant selecting certain weak links in the chain of German production, a concentrated attack on which would bring Germany to the point of economic collapse. Such a concept could also include area attacks on certain towns and cities which could be considered especially important economically. Area attack was frequently directed against the living quarters of the workers as a first priority. The advocates of 'general attack' argued that there were no weak links in the economy that could not be sufficiently strengthened once the direction of 'selective attack' was perceived by the enemy, that the expert assessments on which 'selective attacks' had to be based were impossible in wartime and that 'selective attack' was often not possible without greater technical development than the Allied air forces possessed in 1943. They believed more in spreading psychological dismay among the enemy population and in creating economic disruption by the destruction of essential services such as water and electricity. The compromise reached between these two points of view was no genuine compromise at all for some time, and it was the Allied failure to co-ordinate policy which enabled the German economy to behave with such buoyancy in 1943 in spite of the new problems which it faced.

The concept of 'general attack' was pursued in 1943 by the concentrated bombing of the Ruhr, Hamburg, and, in the

---

[1] Speer Report No. 26, p. 4.

[2] Sir C. Webster and N. Frankland, *The Strategic Air Offensive against Germany 1939–45*. I am indebted to these excellent volumes for much general information on Allied bombing strategy which it has not always been possible to acknowledge.

autumn, Berlin. Pre-war statesmen's fears about the impossibility of defence against the bomber seemed to be coming true at last when the fire-storm raised in Hamburg that Summer killed 50,000 people, but such destruction in such a short time was not to be repeated until the raids on Dresden in 1945. The autumn 'Battle of Berlin' was fought in weather which was often very cloudy. Considerable destruction was wreaked on Siemensstadt, the largest single electrical engineering complex in Germany, and on the Alkett tank factory, but whereas Berlin as a city was an easy target, the economically vital parts of it were more difficult to hit. Although 200,000 tons of bombs were dropped on Germany in 1943, 'general attack' had none of the psychological effects on the population which had been claimed for it. People proved able, physically and mentally, to withstand a far greater degree of bombing than had been anticipated. Although doubts about the efficacy of 'general attack' were growing at the end of 1943, 'selective attack' seemed to have little better to offer. For that year, it had been directed principally against air-frame manufacturing, and ball-bearing production. After heavy losses were incurred, and disappointing results obtained, in the October raids on Schweinfurt, the centre of the German ball-bearing industry, it even began to appear as though the strategic bombing offensive might be a total failure. Certainly the savage losses sustained in the protracted land battles on the Eastern front were more worrying to Hitler and his ministers in 1943 than the Allied air offensive.

From Spring 1944 until September a considerable amount of Allied bombing power had to be devoted to the attacks on communications which preceded and accompanied the Allied invasion of France. In fact these attacks on communications proved among the most troublesome of all forms of attack for the German economy to resist. However, although this necessarily proved the biggest part of Allied air force strategy, the original methods of attack were not abandoned but were pursued whenever possible. After September 1944 both 'selective attack' and 'general attack' were renewed on an even greater scale than before. On 12 May the Eighth Air Force opened what would prove to be the most vital part of the air offensive when it began the campaign against the German oil industry. The apparent superiority of Schweinfurt as a target when compared to the much more scattered oil manufacturing plant, and the operational difficulties of flights into Eastern Europe, had led to the rejection of the German oil industry as a target in 1943. In 1944 it proved to be the most vulnerable part of the German economy, at precisely the moment when the Allies were best equipped to attack it. The idea of 'general attack' had its greatest, and most ghastly, single success later with the utter destruction of large parts of the city of Dresden.[1] Economically, however, the destruction done in the Ruhr, which presented an excellent target for such an attack, was more significant.

Germany's chief response to this situation was to make every effort to step up the production of defensive aircraft, and improve air-raid precaution and anti-aircraft measures. In a situation where she had abandoned bomber production, and three of her opponents, in July 1944, had an available operational strength in Europe of 5,246 bombers, this was the only thing she could do.[2] In March 1945 Bomber Command and the Eighth Air Force dropped more than 130,000 tons of bombs on Germany, twice as much as they had dropped in 1942, and not far short of the 1943 total for Bomber Command. The effects of this increasing weight of explosives were felt most strongly in the final months of the war; but even while German armaments production was still rising serious difficulties began to appear because of Allied intervention.

Although it did not start until May the offensive against oil production proved right from its beginning to be the most dangerous single threat to Germany's economy. Germany had access to very few supplies of crude oil. Total production on the Hungarian oil fields and in Austria was relatively small; and a great deal had to be imported during the war from Roumania. Even in 1943 the Roumanian refineries at Ploesti had been shown to be in reach of enemy bombers. The attempts to strengthen Germany's domestic consumption which had been undertaken by the Four-Year-Plan were carried on with greater vigour during the war by the erection of Fischer-

---

[1] D. Irving, *The Destruction of Dresden*.
[2] Sir C. Webster and N. Frankland, III, 3.

Tropsch processing plant for the manufacture of synthetic oil, and also by the erection of Bergius hydrogenation plant. In all, the German oil industry presented about 100 separate targets, and the crude oil producers and refiners were easy to hide. But of these 100 targets, only a few were important. One-third of the production by the Bergius hydrogenation method was concentrated in two large works at Leuna and Pölitz. One-third more was in only five other plants. Much of the Fischer-Tropsch synthetic production was in the Ruhr. In addition 90 per cent of the production of aviation spirit came from the hydrogenation process, the rest from Roumanian crude oil.

The shock of the first blow in May reverberated through the Speer Ministry and urgent measures were taken to restore production. Geilenberg, former chairman of the main committee for munitions, was appointed General Commissioner for Special Measures to reconstruct the works in as short a time as possible.[1] Not only was one of the most able men in the Ministry taken from his own work and detailed for this emergency but he was allowed to operate without any of the usual restrictions. Speer's view was,

It is a question here of helping with everything that is necessary, and getting these works going again in the shortest time. Though otherwise we must be thrifty with the allocation of labour strength to building, here the opposite must apply. We must provide a surplus of building strength for these construction sites. We must, in contrast to the Building Chief's desires, insist that he has 30 to 40 per cent more strength, and the Building Chief is responsible for finding ways and means of employing these people adequately.[2]

Geilenberg was successful. But whether the Speer Ministry would have been able to maintain oil production had the attacks been more closely spaced is doubtful. Initially it was possible to get a hydrogenation plant at work again in six to eight weeks after air attack.[3] This was a much shorter interval than the Allies had expected. Speer had prophesied this caustically: 'We have a powerful ally in this matter, that is to say that the enemy has an Air Force general staff as well.'[4] By

[1] Speer Report No. 77, Part IV, p. 2. K. Weissenborn gives a most unflattering account of Geilenberg which is not substantiated elsewhere.
[2] FD 3353/45 vol. 88, 'Bautagung, Magdeburger Börde', p. 8 (incomplete doc.).
[3] Speer Report No. 26, p. 9.   [4] FD 3353/45 vol. 88, p. 9, Speech by Speer.

the time the follow-up attack was delivered on a hydrogenation plant, output equivalent to a fortnight's full production had been obtained.[1]

Several attacks on the same plant, however, would fundamentally weaken its structure and as the attacks were better timed later and coincided with the resumption of production, even the Geilenberg programme proved insufficient. In April 1944 Air Force consumption of aviation spirit had amounted to 165,000 tons; production had met this demand fairly comfortably. Also stocks of aviation spirit in May were 574,000 tons; stocks of all automotive fuels were 1,336,000 tons. From April onwards production failed to keep up with demand.

Production of aviation spirit[2]

April	1944	175,000 tons
May	1944	156,000 ,,
June	1944	53,000 ,,
July	1944	29,000 ,,

The average daily production of aviation spirit in April 1944 was 5,803 tons. The average daily production from 1 July to 18 July was 1,220 tons. On 17 July production topped the 2,000 tons mark for the first time that month. After that the crisis developed in earnest.

Daily production of aviation spirit
July 1944[3]

17 July	2,307 tons
18 July	1,378 ,,
19 July	856 ,,
20 July	970 ,,
21 July	120 ,,
22 July	140 ,,
23 July	140 ,,
24 July	600 ,,
25 July	417 ,,

[1] Speer Report No. 26, p. 3.
[2] FD 3353/45 vol. 92, Speer to Hitler, 28 July 1944, p. 2.
[3] Ibid., pp. 3–4.

The decline in aviation fuel production immobilized a greater number of fighter planes and made the defence of the hydrogenation and Fischer-Tropsch plants even more difficult. But the decline was not limited merely to aviation spirit.

Production of carburettor fuel[1]

April 1944	125,000 tons
May 1944	93,000 ,,
June 1944	76,000 ,,
July 1944	56,000 ,,

Production of diesel fuel[2]

April 1944	88,900 tons
May 1944	74,000 ,,
June 1944	66,000 ,,
July 1944	62,000 ,,

The production of gas-propellant, the most important fuel substitute on the domestic front was also declining over the same time from 37,600 tons to 5,000 tons.[3]

In fact the Speer Ministry survived this crisis thanks to energetic dispersal and reconstruction, but survival it was and no more. After June 1944 production of aviation fuel for the rest of the war was only 197,000 tons, not much more than one month's supply before the raids had started.[4] The effective use of the German Air Force, at a time when more planes were available than ever before, became impossible. Consumption cuts of two-thirds were ordered in aviation fuel. In spite of its energetic efforts the Speer Ministry was unable to reconstruct or disperse either hydrogenation or Fischer-Tropsch process plant before the decline in fuel production had become crippling to the German economy.[5]

The attacks on ball-bearing factories raised similar but not such comprehensive problems. Roughly one-half of German ball-bearing and roller-bearing manufacture took place at Schweinfurt in three large factories. The rest was mainly at Erkner (Berlin), at Cannstatt, and at Steyr, in Austria. About

[1] Ibid., p. 4.   [2] Ibid., p. 4.   [3] Ibid., p. 5.   [4] U.S.S.B.S., *Effects*, p. 81.
[5] See Chapter VII for a discussion of the situation after June 1944.

one-quarter of Germany's annual ball-bearing needs were supplied by imports. Of these imports about one-half came from Sweden, including mainly the more specialized types of bearing. The remainder came from France and Italy. Schweinfurt was a town of only 60,000 people, but, once it was located by the aircrews, it seemed to offer an ideal 'selective' target.

To deal with the threat caused by the first raids Speer appointed a special plenipotentiary, Philip Kessler, who turned out to have been an excellent choice. Kessler's primary task was reconstruction, and, when it proved feasible, the dispersal of the factories. Production was concentrated into the four main works, and the machine-tool industry was forced to manufacture certain categories of machine which had previously always been obtained from Sweden.[1] Sweden proved quite willing to change the structure of her export quota of bearings to Germany so that it consisted very largely of the scarcer kinds of bearing. Since Sweden owned a good deal of the capital in the German industry the Allied strategists might have foreseen this possibility more clearly than they did. Nor had the Allied strategists made sufficient allowances for the enormous quantities of bearings which German industry had stocked. A survey of stocks undertaken by the Speer Ministry revealed that most firms had from six to twelve months' supply of bearings in reserve. In such a situation Kessler had plenty of room for manoeuvre. To maintain deliveries he initiated a special delivery system. Transit times between factory and consumer were cut from a matter of months to a fortnight, or even a few days.[2] There is no indication that essential armament output was affected by the attacks on the ball-bearing plant. The first attack was in October 1943. The figures for roller-bearing production over the period of the offensive indicate a fall in production which was not severe enough to weaken the economy overall.

As with the hydrogenation plant, reconstruction was effected in an incredibly short time. Although production at the four main centres had come almost to a standstill by February 1944 this had been temporary. On 6 April Kessler reported that

Those works remaining intact had set to on the March production with the greatest willingness, and the heavily damaged works have

[1] FD 3353/45, vol. 92, op. cit., p. 7.   [2] Speer Report No. 26, p. 11.

exerted themselves enormously following my advice in repairing damage and in further dispersal. So, in spite of all interruptions, we have succeeded in getting a March output about 70 per cent of the average output of the second part of 1943.[1]

Speedy reconstruction alone would not have enabled the industry to meet all demands. Other measures were necessary. The urgent problem was not the total output of ball-bearings but the output of certain specialized types. Consequently all possible substitution of bearings was enforced as well as a saving of up to 60 per cent in the use of ball-bearings in some kinds of equipment.[2] Machine tools already ordered for new ball-bearing plant were used to replace those destroyed when machine shops were burned out in the early raids. Certain processes in machining were carried out by other industries, leaving only the final processing, hardening, grinding, and polishing to be done by the specialists.[3]

Production of roller-bearings[4]

	Oct. 1943	Jan. 1944	Feb. 1944	March 1944
Smallest bearings, including point and special bearings	3,593,853	3,247,360	2,944,982	2,787,258
Small bearings	3,055,235	2,820,999	2,412,261	1,848,090
Medium bearings	1,180,298	1,390,231	1,289,181	969,618
Large bearings	7,028	20,519	14,022	6,934
Chain track needle bearings	981,839	1,182,011	1,109,000	1,200,000
Total output	8,818,303	8,661,120	7,760,446	6,811,900

The bombing offensive against German aircraft production started in July 1943 when the offensive against submarine construction yards had been in progress for over six months. But this form of offensive was neither so concentrated nor so effective as that against tank production, the main reason being the scattered and well-defended nature of the targets. From August to October 1944 in a series of systematic attacks all tank assembly plant and several of the main engine factories were bombed.[5] This was a direct offensive on finished armaments

[1] FD 3353/45 vol. 86, Kessler to Speer, p. 4.   [2] Speer Report No. 26, p. 13.
[3] FD 3353/45 vol. 86, op. cit., p. 5.   [4] Ibid., p. 3.
[5] U.S.S.B.S., *Effects*, p. 147.

production rather than on a weak link in the production chain. Again it fell short of the results obtained by the attack on fuel production.

The Speer Ministry's counter was another 'special action'; this time it compelled machine-tool producers to concentrate their production on replacing damaged machine tools. Stocks of components were stored away from the factories, and all combustible matter was removed from stores and factories alike.[1] Each firm established between ten and twenty dumps for parts in a circle away from the factory. All this was highly inconvenient and definitely slowed down production. The loss and damage of machine tools and the concentration on their repair and replacement meant a loss of time in replacing and repairing machines elsewhere. Since stores in the factories were being deliberately kept at a low level the dispersal of parts in the neighbourhood proved a great hindrance and caused periods of idleness on the assembly lines. Special express transport facilities had to be created to get tank parts to the assembly lines.[2] The time taken over the assembly was drastically cut. Instead of the previous six weeks, only ten to twelve days were allowed between the arrival of the parts and the completion of the tank. Work had now to be pressed on as quickly as possible and by a constant series of improvisations demanding last minute alterations in the disposition of the workers and the arrangement of the production line. These difficulties were greatly increased by the tremendous strain put upon the workers by the nerve-racking experience of long hours and constant air-raid warnings.

In estimating the effect of bombing on the output of armoured fighting-vehicles it is difficult to decide whether production targets were not reached because of bombing or because of the shortage of special steels. Hulls, suspension gear, and other equipment were in short supply to the assembly plant because of raids on other factories. Speer's general conclusion that 'supplies of weapons and equipment were not substantially affected thanks to the decentralized organization of the subsidiary advance depots',[3] should perhaps be modified in the case of tank production. Wagenführ's index of tank production (January–February 1942 = 100) gives an almost constant rise

---

[1] Speer Report No. 65, p. 15.   [2] Ibid., p. 17.   [3] Speer Report No. 26, p. 14.

to a figure of 589 in July 1944. In August it falls to 527 and in October is 516, the first falling-away in production since 1941. Once the bad weather at the end of 1944 reduced the frequency of the raids production increased again very rapidly to its former level. The November index figure is 571, that for December 598. The whole problem was never so urgent as those raised by the attacks on oil or on ball-bearings. In its conception the tank offensive was skilful, but Germany's production of tanks was so high that she could take the setbacks of August, September, and October 1944 without flinching.

In any case by the autumn of 1944 it becomes somewhat pedantic to isolate the effects of bombing on any particular industry from the general economic situation. Increasing dislocation was caused by the raids on transport and communications. The area bombing in the Ruhr absorbed much of the Speer Ministry's efforts, although in Autumn 1944 it still had the situation under control. The damage to marshalling yards and railway signalling systems was often overcome by the use of fleets of motor lorries, for instance.

A quite new set of economic problems was raised by the Ministry of Armaments' attempts at avoiding the consequences of heavy air-raids by the policy of 'dispersal'. There were no previous plans in existence for such a policy which was an improvisation forced on the Speer Ministry by the circumstances of 1944. It is curious that the plans should have had to be formulated out of the blue since between the wars the vulnerability of the Ruhr to air attack had been a constant preoccupation of all German rearmament plans. In 1943 50 per cent of the Reich coal output came from the Ruhr, 67 per cent of the coke output, 42 per cent of Thomas steel production, 50 per cent of Siemens-Martin steel production, and 52 per cent of electro-steel production.[1] Those products, essential to the armaments industry, the manufacture of which was specifically dependent on gas supply, came to a great extent from the Ruhr, which accounted for 50 per cent of German gas production. By 1943 the bombing of the Ruhr had become severe enough to demonstrate the accuracy of many pre-war forebodings. In the light of the geographically uneven pattern of Germany's heavy

[1] FD 3353/45, Speer, 'Rede vor den Gauleitern', 21 June 1943, p. 1.

industry the policy of 'dispersal' was an interesting economic experiment.

Obviously any policy of large-scale dispersal of the armaments industry from the Ruhr was out of the question. The total industrial complex was too interdependent for many parts to be removed. Dispersal, as a policy, therefore had to be reserved for individual plants in a vulnerable spot producing goods in short supply, or for industries too heavily concentrated in one or two places. Speer's concern was to prevent dispersal from being undertaken except as an ultimate necessity. He was obliged to circumvent the Gauleiters' insisting on too many dispersals or even blithely evacuating factories of their own accord to the few sites which Speer had earmarked as 'safe' for more important industries.

Even if there were no plans prepared there were plenty of available factory buildings. Speer's efforts throughout 1943 and 1944 to close down German textile production entirely and rely on French output had met with partial success. Factories vacated by the textile industry in Lower Silesia were occupied by radar production units brought from Berlin.[1] It was easier to move this kind of precision engineering than larger tank or aircraft factories. The larger the plant the easier target it provided for air attack. Therefore before dispersal of armaments factories took place some system of protection in their new home had to be worked out. Theoretically responsible before the war had been the Reichs Aviation Ministry, but, according to Speer, their plans were unrealistic. They had worked out a system under which no factory vital to war production would be built within a circle of a certain radius drawn from another similar plant. So large were the circles that it would have been impossible in 1944 to have fitted all the necessary factories into Germany.[2] The tendency under the Speer Ministry, once the raids started, was to provide massive defensive protection for each large factory as a deterrent. Rather than move armaments assembly plant the Ministry preferred to redouble the defences of armament factories and leave them where they were.[3]

The hydrogenation plants were a different story. Geilenberg's reconstruction programme contained plans for re-erection in

---

[1] Speer Report No. 5, p. 2.   [2] Ibid., p. 3.   [3] Speer Report No. 79, p. 5.

underground sites.[1] Aircraft production also was undertaken underground, and some of the cave-space allocated for this purpose was transferred to hydrogenation plant when the fuel crisis was at its most desperate.[2] Geilenberg's estimate was that by November 1945 90,000 tons of aviation spirit and jet fuel would be able to be produced underground monthly.[3]

Hydrogenation plant could be constructed underground less easily than could ball-bearing factories. As soon as the Strategic Bombing Offensive against the latter began, plans were instituted to disperse the most vulnerable of the factories at Schweinfurt to four separate underground sites, Wellen, Neckarzimmern, Roigheim, and Seckach. The amount of space available in these underground areas was large, Neckarzimmern had a floor-space of 50,000 square metres, with a possibility of 100,000, Wellen had 40,000 square metres; the other areas were much smaller,[4] and would be used for the production of bearings for caterpillar tracks. In spite of the available space many valuable machines had to be stored in caves away from the factories. In April 1944, the official starting date for underground production, the caves were not yet ready. Therefore the Air Force gave up part of the floor-space of an aircraft munitions factory at Rottershausen, not far from Schweinfurt. Part of a similar factory making Army munitions at Bamberg was also surrendered, and in April 1944 one of the Schweinfurt ball-bearing factories was left to the bombers. By the same time the Cannstatt factory had already been partially dispersed above ground in the Württemberg area, waiting for underground projects to be completed.[5]

Dispersal was a response to an emergency rather than a coherent plan. The transport difficulties caused by bombing were aggravated by dispersal. So, also, was the problem of administration within the firm. There was not sufficient underground space available for the only really safe kind of dispersal, and some of what was available was used by the SS for 'Nordwerk' and 'Mittelwerk', their own private projects. Nevertheless more foresight earlier in the war might have enabled Germany to

[1] Speer Report No. 6, p. 3.
[2] FD 3353/45 vol. 216, Geilenberg to Speer.   [3] Ibid.
[4] FD 3353/45, vol. 86, Kessler to Speer, p. 3.   [5] Ibid., pp. 1–4.

maintain high levels of war production for longer than she was able.

The successes of German war production from 1942 to 1944 were due to inspired improvisation, to skilled administration, and to the undeniable threat to Germany, which gave a sense of urgency lacking in some quarters earlier. After the abandonment of Blitzkrieg economics the Ministry of Armaments had stuck to the general principle of qualitative superiority in the face of all difficulties and had at the same time managed to maintain a high overall level of armaments production. This policy, on which all hopes of victory were based, was practical only as long as the situation did not deteriorate to the point where any form of long-term planning would be fruitless because what was possible could no longer be precisely ascertained. Once it was no longer a question of deciding how much of the quantity of production could be sacrificed to maintain the quality of the armament being produced, but merely of whether it was possible to produce the armament on a level that was at all high enough, qualitative superiority ceased to be a principle which could hold out hopes of victory or even of avoiding defeat.

During a long illness of Speer's in Spring 1944 Hitler had had his own way more frequently over armaments. In April he published a decree the intention of which was to concentrate production effort on those weapons already in series production rather than on future developments. When Speer returned he felt convinced that Hitler's decision was a good one and that long-term planning for qualitative superiority was now no use. He therefore persuaded Hitler to publish an even stronger directive.[1] The Concentration Order[2] of 19 June 1944, which was partly thought of by Hitler as a response to the establishment of an Allied military front in France, marks a turning-point in Germany's war economy second only to the abandonment of the Blitzkrieg.

In order to promote the concentrated production of those weapons and the equipment of the armament industry, which, by their revolutionary new characteristics, are able to give us improtant advantages over the enemy, and, furthermore, in order to abolish

---

[1] Speer Report No. 27, p. 2.　　　　　　[2] 'Konzentrationserlass'.

the excessive number of modifications to those types whose development can be considered completed, I hereby order, . . .

1. (5) That modifications to those weapons and equipment, which are produced under conditions of mass manufacture, cause a disturbance in production which is generally out of proportion to the advantages obtained.[1]

The only development projects allowed to go forward were those that could be brought to a successful conclusion in six months, apart from certain more important armaments which needed a little longer. This meant that to all intents and purposes improvement of German armaments would come to a standstill in December 1944. Each production committee appointed a Concentration-Commissioner who would draw up the list of projects for improvement and development allowed to continue.

Doubtless the continual alterations to weapons and the constant modification of armament types had resulted in a lower rate of production. But this was Germany's one hope of superiority over her enemies. If the manpower released by this decree had been used in a last effort to increase armaments production Germany would have been engaging in that mass-production battle which she had always managed to avoid even after January 1942. But even this did not happen. On 18 October 1944, with the creation of the Volkssturm, civilian status within the Reich virtually disappeared.[2] All males between sixteen and sixty, except a handful of skilled workers in the armaments industry, came under the control of the Wehrmacht. The creation of the Volkssturm marked that point in the German war economy when manpower to hold weapons became more important than manpower to make them; an ironical sidelight on the Blitzkrieg.

In such a way between June and October 1944 did Hitler finally reject the general principle on which hopes of victory, however optimistically, had been built in 1942. 'Quality versus quantity' had been the slogan. This was now deliberately rejected in favour of a final death struggle in which Germany's

[1] Speer Report No. 50, Part IV, Appendix 1, FD 3533/45 'Nachrichten des Reichsministers für Rüstungs-und Kriegsproduktion, 3 Aug. 1944'.
[2] FD 1260/45, 'Der deutsche Volkssturm'.

chances of outproducing her opponents were not worth the calculation.

Hitler was a nostalgic man. Just as in the summer of 1942 he had cast a longing eye back at the Blitzkrieg so in the winter of 1944–5 he brooded over the idea of qualitative superiority,

> Now you can't say, 'I don't believe it', or, 'That doesn't interest me', or, 'I don't believe it can be produced in great quantities'. In that way I would not have brought into use the long 8·8 cm. The 7·5, and the short 8·8 were quite good enough for the familiar Panther. But at that time I had already said: you must make further provision. On top of that people still wanted to make difficulties with me over the Tiger. . . . However, in reality it must be a universal general technical consideration of all the wars known to us from ancient times to the present day. Then people would see with how slightly technically superior weapons wars were often decided, really very slight. If Hannibal, as we are told, instead of his seven or thirteen elephants, which he had altogether when he crossed the Alps, or instead of the eleven—you must know the exact number—had had fifty, or two hundred and fifty, then in the long run that would have been sufficient to have allowed him to capture Italy.[1]

[1] *Hitlers Lagebesprechungen*, op. cit., p. 817.

CHAPTER VI

The Effect of Political Pressures on German War Production

ISTORIANS of National Socialist Germany have often been puzzled to find where the exact responsibility for carrying out any line of policy lay. The impulses which Hitler sent through the machinery of administration grew weaker in the maze of administrative bodies. Add to this the fact that in many instances Hitler did not make the decisions but left them to others, and that often when he did make the decisions their implications had to be worked out by others, and it can readily be seen that the idea of National Socialist Germany as a monolithic dictatorship is quite false. This is particularly so in the field of economic policy and administration. There the National Socialist state is seen in its most bureaucratic and complex form.

Not that Speer was, in the ordinary sense, a bureaucrat. Both he and Todt had made their reputation as practical men who could avoid the red tape which clogged other ministries. But both Speer and Todt accepted the principles on which National Socialist bureaucracy operated. Tasks of special difficulty were performed by the creation on the spot of improvised administrative bodies under the control of one powerful man, who was given full powers to by-pass whatever departments would normally be responsible. Just as the National Socialist administration was fragmented into a series of 'personal' bureaucratic machines, of which the Speer Ministry was one, so the Speer Ministry itself was fragmented in the same way, for instance, by the appointment of Geilenberg to rebuild the synthetic oil plant, and of Kessler to disperse the ball-bearings industry. Of such a nature, finally, was the 'Fighter Staff'.[1]

[1] See below, p. 142.

The exact delimitation of the administrative boundaries of the Speer Ministry is difficult to establish. The process of deploying Germany's economic potential to the full needed a large degree of central control over different sectors of the economy not immediately engaged in war production. Therefore the importance, the influence, and the absolute power, of the Speer Ministry grew in ratio with the extent of Germany's economic commitment.

The task of mobilizing Germany's resources was a political one as well as economic. Each successive reform or adaptation of the cumbrous political machinery was likely to arouse a greater degree of opposition. The more Speer tried to 'simplify' matters by extending his control over different sectors of the economy the more political pressure he needed to exert. The Reichs Ministry for Armaments and Munitions, when first started under Todt on 17 March 1940, had been a typical National Socialist *ad hoc* committee, with a small staff and no tasks other than gingering up Army munitions production and trying to economize on copper. By 1945 it had evolved into one of the most important and one of the most complex ministries in the State. 'Why did it happen?' and 'How did it happen?' are the two questions which must be answered.

Such questions straight away involve consideration of the reasons why certain vital aspects of the war economy, such as finance or the procurement of raw materials, always remained separate from the Speer Ministry. Other aspects of war production, especially aircraft production, only came under the control of the Speer Ministry when it was too late. How did these vital omissions affect Germany's war production? To what extent was the economic task of fighting the war impeded by political pressures?

Speer himself drew up an account of the expansion of his Ministry as material for a speech to be made at Posen in June 1944.[1] He regarded Spring 1942 as being the time when long-term planning was really introduced. This was followed by the taking over in May 1942 of the Armaments office from OKW and the amalgamation of WiRüAmt with the Ministry. In June 1943 when Dönitz followed Raeder as Commander-in-Chief of

[1] FD 3353/45 vol. 78, 'Unterlagen Rede', photostat p. 3569.

the Navy, the direct control of all naval production was handed over to the Speer Ministry. On 2 September 1943 the responsibilities for war production still remaining with the Ministry of Economics were handed over to Speer.[1] This left Speer with effective direct control over a great deal of German heavy industry. Speer now took as his title Reichs Minister for Armaments and War Production. On 22 June 1944 the production of air armaments was taken over by the Speer Ministry. This was to be the key-stone of his Ministry.[2] The impression given in his speech was to be one of general understanding on the part of all others concerned. However, between Spring 1942 and June 1944, there was a great deal of active opposition to Speer and to his activities.

The first period of development ended in June 1942 with the WiRüAmt under Speer's control, a fairly reliable system of cooperation with the Navy and the Air Force, and an effective control over supplies of raw material throughout the economy. Between this time and June 1943 Speer had to meet considerable opposition from the vested interests he had ousted.

Relations between Todt and Göring had been bad. Göring's opposition to Central Planning had delayed its operations for at least a month. Even after Central Planning had begun to work, the powers which Speer exercised therein were nominally exercised by him as a deputy of Göring. This surrender of power by Göring had never been very clearly defined. Nor had the actual position of the Four-Year-Plan Office been very clearly defined. Some of Speer's functions were exercised 'within the Four-Year-Plan'. By October 1942 this failure to define properly relative spheres of authority led to quarrelling when Göring roused himself from his increasing physical and mental deterioration. He exercised few of his functions as Head of the Four-Year-Plan Authority, but he guarded the privileges fiercely. At the beginning of November 1942 he chose to make a stand on a decree having some bearing on the operation of the Four-Year-Plan but not signed by himself.[3] Speer tried to claim in answer that his powers were greater than they actually were.

[1] FD 3533/45, 'Erlass des Führers über die Konzentration der Kriegswirtschaft'.
[2] FD 3353/45 vol. 78, 'Unterlagen Rede', photostat p. 3570.
[3] FD 3353/45 vol. 79, Göring to Speer, 5 November 1942.

On 5 November he was smartly rapped over the knuckles by Göring who pointed out that the determining factor in whether matters debated in Central Planning should be referred to him was their importance. Speer had never been given charge of the whole of the industrial war economy, which he was now claiming. The Four-Year-Plan was by no means defunct.

I would like to lay it down here, for historical truth, that not for a moment have I let the most important aspects of the Four-Year-Plan out of my hands.[1]

Perhaps, suggested Göring, the quiet soundness and efficiency of the Four-Year-Plan had deceived Speer, used as he was to more strident methods.

So far I have avoided having photographic albums and graphic representations on the subject of present achievements made, as other departments are ever more rapidly having done.[2]

In fact so long as Göring chose to assert himself he could still impose limits on Speer's economic functions.

Similar problems persisted with regard to labour control and Sauckel's personal machine. Sauckel claimed control over the building labour employed by the *Organisation Todt*.[3] Speer for his part tried to exercise control over the use of foreign labour in industries situated outside the Reich but essential to the armaments industry. In May 1943 Speer had to seek special permission from Hitler to safeguard the labour supply of the Ukrainian iron-ore mines.

These objections to the expansion of the Speer Ministry were in part responsible for checking its evolution into an overall Ministry of War Production. It was not until a chance political event that further progress was made. This event was the appointment of Dönitz in place of Raeder as Commander-in-Chief of the Navy. Raeder, although seeing the advantages of co-operating with the Speer Ministry, had been determined to maintain the German Navy as a separate organization. Consequently he had kept a tight control over the naval dockyards. Dönitz, on the other hand, was a stronger adherent of the Nazi régime. In addition he wished to switch naval production

[1] Ibid.   [2] Ibid., p. 2.
[3] FD 3353/45 vol. 38, pp. 4/5, Führerkonferenz, 13/15 May 1943.

priorities towards submarine manufacture, where the technical capacity of the Speer Ministry had already proved successful. Furthermore, he and Speer had co-operated successfully in the construction of submarine pens in France in 1941, and their association had ripened into friendship.[1] The anonymous chronicler of the Speer Ministry noted that after Dönitz became Commander-in-Chief he was more often in the Speer Ministry than before.[2]

German naval production policy had been radically modified by Hitler's decision on 6 January 1943 to end all work on the construction and conversion of larger vessels and to decommission all battleships, pocket-battleships, and heavy and light cruisers except where needed for training.[3] The capital ships always had to be too heavily protected to be value for money in 1943. Dismantling them would spare aircraft normally used for their protection and would permit their heavy guns to be used in coastal batteries. The advantages of dismantling such expensive armaments were surely exaggerated by Hitler. The Quartermaster's Division of the Naval Staff calculated that only 125,000 tons of iron and steel would be obtained by scrapping the larger vessels.[4] It would certainly not be worth while to aggravate the labour shortage for such a result as that. Dönitz managed to mitigate Hitler's drastic decision; but he, himself, was primarily interested in U-boats. He had already decided to transfer submarine production to Speer, so that 'auxiliary vessels' over and above the current target of 30 submarines per month could be built.[5] On 31 May he persuaded the Führer to grant an official increase in production to 40 per month.[6] In these circumstances Dönitz decided to transfer control of naval shipyards to the Speer Ministry while retaining for the Naval High Command some of the repair functions in the dockyards and the control of naval arsenals. To meet these demands Speer transformed the scope and composition of the main committee for shipbuilding, and appointed a new chairman. On 28 May,

---

[1] Speer Report No. 1, p. 5.
[2] FD 3037/49, Section 1, Sc. 132. p. 38, 'Chronik der Dienststellen des Reichsministers Albert Speer'.
[3] *Führer Naval Conferences*, 6 January 1943.
[4] Ibid., 2 January 1943. [5] Ibid.
[6] Ibid., 31 May 1943. Also, A. Martienssen, *Hitler and his Admirals*, p. 177.

before Hitler actually sanctioned the increases, a joint conference attended by many economic advisers had been held by the
Ministry and the Navy.

This breakthrough by the Speer Ministry was followed the
same month, possibly on 8 June,[1] by an agreement between
Speer and Funk. The Ministry of Economics surrendered control of all those sectors of the civilian economy which it had previously directed except that of the distribution to civilians of all
goods other than foodstuffs. This agreement was made 'un-
willingly' on Funk's part.[2] In effect it ratified a state of affairs in
existence for some time past whereby Speer, in order to obtain
the desired armaments output, had been obliged to interfere in
these spheres of the civilian economy that were under the lax
control of the Ministry of Economics. Local chambers of commerce created, in an ill-defined way, after 1934, were now to
hand over such power as they possessed to the committees
of the Speer Ministry. They had never done much more than
meet but their removal meant that another trace of Germany's
civilian economy had been obliterated. Where the personnel
of the chambers was the same as that of the committees the
change was insignificant, but the industrialists' freedom to subordinate public to private interest was further curtailed.

However, even as late as Summer 1943, the Speer Ministry
still had to contend with Göring, with Sauckel, and with the
Air Force. As a Ministry of War Production it was up against
the problem that the most costly, complicated, vital, and
rapidly-developing branch of armaments, that of aircraft, was
out of its control. The production of aircraft can be seen as one
of the great overall failures of the German war economy. In
itself it was a microcosm of all those political and economic
pressures which clashed at different times and with differing
intensity in other branches of the economy. No other sector
illustrates more clearly how utterly unrevealing it is to attempt a
purely economic analysis of Germany's war economy. The problems of aircraft production were entwined in the very roots of
the National Socialist state.

Early programmes for expanding the size of the Air Force all
fell short of attainment. At the outbreak of war the intention

_____

[1] FD 3037/49, Section 1, Sc. 132, pp. 92/93.   [2] Ibid.

was to increase production to 2,000 planes a month by the end of 1940. In the course of 1940 this programme was twice revised upwards.[1] The actual number of aircraft produced in December 1940 was about 779.[2] Of the target total of 2,300 aircraft only 370 fighters were to be produced; the main effort was to be concentrated on bombers. So certain were the Air Staff and the High Command of victory that, after the French campaign, far more emphasis even than before was put on the production of existing types rather than on the development of new ones.[3] It was not expected that the Russian war would last long enough to outdate any of the German planes. Nor did the failure to attain production targets deter the High Command from continually revising them upwards. At the same time, and in conformity with the principles of the Blitzkrieg, modifications to the number of each type of plane to be produced were being made as the strategic situation changed. Unfortunately the economic principles underlying the Blitzkrieg continued to govern aircraft production when Germany switched in other sectors to full-scale war production.

By July 1943, the target stood at 3,000 aircraft a month. This target was no nearer being reached than the targets of three years before. In June 1943 2,316 aircraft were produced, a mere 300 above the target of December 1940.[4] The immediate response to the bombing of aircraft factories was to step up the production targets even more. November 1943 saw the publication of 'Programme No. 225'. Although the new sense of urgency was due to the air-raids the relative proportion of defensive aircraft produced did not increase. Göring would not abandon his dreams of retaliation against England. And since bombers were so much more complex than fighters the monthly totals of German plane production were kept low. Frydag, chairman of the main committee for the production of aircraft frames, explained this in terms of the bombing of the factories.[5] But this only worsened an already bad position for the German aircraft industry. The production of a particular type

[1] Speer Report No. 18 (Appendix 2), p. 2.
[2] Gen. Qu. 6 Abt.   [3] Speer Report No. 18 (Appendix 2), p. 2.
[4] Gen. Qu. 6. Abt., 'acceptance' not production figures.
[5] Speer Report No. 18, Appendix 2, passim.

could be severely set back by a successful raid. One such example was the raids on the component and assembly plants of the Me. 108 and Me. 109 at Les Mureaux on the Seine near Mantes. Production of the Arado 196 was abandoned because of the vast quantity of machine tools destroyed in the factory at St. Nazaire. Yet there were equally disastrous ways in which production could suffer through setbacks to one particular type, ways which had nothing to do with Allied bombing.

In the middle of 1942 it was decided to abandon the Me. 210, which had a production target of 500 a month set for July 1943. The gap was filled by reopening the series production of the Me. 110.[1] All factories producing the Me. 210 had to be re-tooled therefore to produce the Me. 110. Such an event was symptomatic of a much larger problem.

The separation of aircraft production from the production of other armaments had the unfortunate effect of inducing the Air Staff to believe that aircraft production was taking place in the midst of plenty. When the need to distribute raw materials arose they were not in the position of having to decide between different completed armaments. Nor, because of Göring's influence in the State, was their raw material situation as difficult as that of other people. Consequently, they found it easy to slip into a position where they demanded as many different types of operational aircraft as they felt to be theoretically desirable. In June 1943 thirty different types of plane were being produced. Apart from the continual development of new types, there was also a constant stream of modifications to existing types. The consequence was that the lapse of time between prototype and series-production was far too great.[2] The constant demand from the Air Staff for small improvements of detail caused the time spent between early models and the series production to be five or ten times greater than it need have been.[3] A longer time spent on development and experiment with a modified type would have been more valuable and would have eliminated those technical snags in series production which were still a

[1] Ibid., p. 3.

[2] FD 3210/45, Fiesler–Storch Papers, R. Lusser, 'Denkschrift über Entwicklung und Entwicklungsplanung in der deutschen Luftrüstung', pp. 5 ff.

[3] FD 4355/45, Messerschmitt Papers, vol. 5. Personal Correspondence between Messerschmitt and Udet, passim.

feature because of the constant last-minute alterations in detail. In their misguided policy the Air Staff were only encouraged by the conflicting interests of the producers, all of whom bid against each other to get their prototypes accepted for production. The Air Staff were often fatally tempted to effect a compromise between the vital interests of firms. As early as January 1942 there was a movement to place new developments of any required type of planes with only one or two firms who would then be forced to concentrate on the development of that particular requirement alone, but this was thwarted by the combined interests of the manufacturers.[1]

The methods of production of the manufacturers were often inefficient. There was not the same pressure on them as on other armaments manufacturers. The German aircraft industry, wandering in the maze of political intrigue which dictated air strategy, harassed by the minute and technically exacting demands of the Air Staff, and free from any controlling hand or supervising authority, was in danger of relapsing into an industry producing only prototypes.

The harmful effects of such a situation spread into the rest of the economy. The constant need for re-tooling factories aggravated the shortage of skilled workmen. In December 1943, when the Me. 262 and other types were put into production 3,000 tool-makers were suddenly needed. The only way to get such a number was to recall them from the Army. Consequently a special drive, to last four months, had to be begun to recall skilled men from the Army for Air Force production.[2] At the end of these four months some of these men were sent back to the Army.

There was no hope of altering the difficult situation without some kind of fundamental reorganization. In the last resort authority over the Air Force and the aircraft industry lay with Göring. As his idleness and taste for opulent living increased, so his active direction decreased. By 1943 he would occasionally rouse himself, collect the Air Staff and the manufacturers together, abuse them heartily, and invite them to dinner. Messerschmitt has left a record of one such gathering, a

[1] Ibid., p. 13.
[2] FD 3353/45 vol. 54, p. 2, Führerkonferenz, 16/17 December 1943.

meeting in March 1943 at Karinhall.[1] The meeting was opened with a speech, lasting an hour and a half, by Göring in which he divided the aircraft industry into several compartments and demonstrated to his own satisfaction the sheer incompetence of each compartment. In the first place their aircraft types were inferior to those of the Allies. The Me. 109 had become inferior to the Spitfire. Their engines were inferior to those produced abroad. Their guns were even more so. Germany had no four-engined bomber although the English daily flew unharmed in such planes all over Germany. He ordered the German aircraft industry to produce such a plane. The old dream of reprisal quite carried him away; what Germany really needed was a long-range bomber.

He scolded the aircraft industry in the sharpest words. They did not have the air of men to be taken seriously, but of jugglers and magicians, they seemed to him like a circus; for instance, two years ago in Augsburg the plans for a plane which could fly to the east coast of America and back had been laid before him. Now he was forced to recognize that such a task was technically not in the least capable of being achieved. Moreover, the aircraft would be especially useless for military purposes, since it would have 'a thickly-riveted, non-shot-proof fuel tank'.[2]

It must be conceded that German aircraft producers had no friends and many critics. Their own designers would have preferred a more rational system. Even Milch is on record as saying that the only way to get fighters was to buy Italian ones.[3] The defence of the industrialists was that they were short of labour; but it was their own policies which in part created this shortage. The Speer Ministry could perhaps have reorganized production on more rational lines; after all it had achieved this in many other fields. But the Air Staff and Göring would not consider this policy, the Air Staff because they wished to retain strategic and tactical independence which meant dictating plane types to the producers, Göring because he detested Speer and his Ministry. Only a position of acute danger could break such a deadlock.

[1] FD 4355/45 vol. 2, 'Industriebesprechung beim Reichsmarschall in Karinhall', 20 March 1943.
[2] Ibid., p. 2. [3] Ibid., p. 4.

The increasing ferocity of Allied raids on German aircraft factories rose to a climax in February 1944. By the end of that month three-quarters of the airframe component and assembly plants had received structural damage assessed at up to 75 per cent and damage to equipment and tools up to 30 per cent.[1] The effects of this were expected to cause a drastic fall, perhaps by as much as two-thirds, in the monthly output figures for March.[2] The chances of avoiding so great a fall were lessened by the beginning of the new tank-production programme, which would encroach upon the reserves of accessories and materials on which the aircraft manufacturers would need to draw. Factories making aero-engines would, even if there had been no bombing, have found themselves short of sparking plugs, injection pumps, and crank shafts. A further complication was the growing transport difficulty. Production could only be maintained, even at the lower level, with a greater degree of transport priority. The problem was doubly acute; how to maintain production of aircraft in the face of increasing Allied air attack and how to ensure that aircraft production, previously favoured, would not now suffer through competition with other branches of armaments production.

It was this second aspect of the problem which was the more important in causing the industry to turn to the Speer Ministry. As Speer came increasingly to control all economic activity in Germany, and as survival became a matter of production figures rather than new strategy, the favoured independence of the aircraft industry, hitherto an asset to the Air Staff, became, even in their eyes, a liability. Milch was already an important ally of Speer's in Central Planning, and the two had long co-operated successfully. Göring, in fact, blamed Milch for collaborating too much with Speer. To try to eliminate harmful competition Milch had arranged weekly meetings between his own staff and officials of the Speer Ministry. But the Speer Ministry still seemed to be favouring those branches of armaments production under its own control, to the detriment of the Air Force. Milch,

[1] Speer Report No. 18, Appendix 1, p. 2.
[2] Milch informed Speer that March production would be 30–40 per cent of that of February, Speer Report No. 1, p. 9. Saur's estimate was 60 per cent, Speer Report No. 18, Appendix 1, p. 2. Speer calls estimates of 60 per cent 'optimistic', Speer Report No. 1, p. 9.

therefore, decided to go the whole hog and merge his staff with Speer's. The miniature ministry thus formed was to be called the Fighter Staff, since its concern was to be solely to increase the output of fighters. This was an aim dearly cherished by Speer who thought the lack of defensive aircraft one of the greatest handicaps to a high level of armaments production in Germany.

The Fighter Staff was a replica of the Speer Ministry. Representatives from all departments of the Ministry were allocated to it and empowered to take independent decisions on a great many matters. Speer was its nominal head, Milch his deputy; but the question of who was actually to be chief executive was tricky. Milch wanted Speer's deputy, Saur, appointed. Speer was afraid of his pushing, ruthless, subordinate who had now reached the stage of sometimes conducting the Führer-Conferences in his place. Therefore he tried to get Gauleiter Hanke, whom he had previously tried to install as Plenipotentiary-General for Labour, appointed. But Hitler's preference was for Saur.

The Fighter Staff arose out of a private agreement between Speer and Milch. Göring and the manufacturers were not at first consulted. It came into existence on 1 March 1944, and on 5 March Hitler recognized the *fait accompli*. His only objection was to the title, firstly on the grounds that it revealed too much about the limitations of German aircraft production, secondly that people might mistake the title (*Jägerstab*) for a policy of state assistance to hunting and be driven furious.[1]

The Führer-Conference of 5 March sketched out general policy for the Fighter Staff. It was to launch a production drive greater than any yet undertaken. There would be extra social welfare services for all workers on the production lines. There would be much longer hours of work, with better conditions, more food, and more clothing as bonuses. Wherever the skilled labour was in sufficient supply a 72-hour working week was introduced. Each factory reported daily to the Fighter Staff which kept a strict check on production and efficiency. Each factory had a member of the Fighter Staff permanently attached to it, and each factory had one of its own staff on permanent

---

[1] FD 3353/45 vol. 57, p. 2, Führerkonferenz, 5 March 1944. This conference was attended by Saur, not Speer.

loan to the Fighter Staff. Special and drastic measures, of the same kind which Kessler was taking in the ball-bearing industry, were introduced to counteract the effects of bombing. A series of four special flying squads were held in reserve ready to go at once to any bombed factory, rally the staff, and supervise site-clearing, emergency rebuilding, and the restoration of essential services. These small squads of specialists at first would stop at the site for about two days but very soon the factory managers became accustomed to taking the necessary measures themselves. Dispersal of production would have meant temporary production losses which could not be afforded. Therefore the policy had to be one of continued production on the same site. A large part of the work of the Fighter Staff was accordingly concerned with trying to find specialized remedies to mitigate the effects of bomb-damage. Blast walls were built to protect valuable machines, wooden structures and inflammable materials were removed from the factory. New kinds of fire-proofing, some of them highly effective, were invented. Saur's midnight visits on the 'Saur Train', which would collect the managers for pep talks and later deposit them on remote railway platforms, saw to it that such measures were put into action vigorously![1]

As originally constituted the Fighter Staff had no part in planning production and worked within the framework of the Air Staff's 'Programme No. 225'. But maximum utilization of the industry's capacity could scarcely be achieved without a more rational approach to production planning such as had existed for over two years elsewhere in the armaments industry. On 8 July 1944, the Fighter Staff published 'Programme No. 226'. The new programme called for an output of all types reaching a peak of 6,400 planes a month; a total later increased to 7,400. To attain these figures the number of types and the extent of modifications allowed were drastically reduced. A final decision was taken to abandon altogether the production of bombers, including the He. 177 on which Göring had based such high hopes.

The introduction of the new programme in July led to some

---

[1] Speer Report No. 77, Part 1. The whole of Weissenborn's remarks are greatly exaggerated.

modifications in existing Fighter Staff practice. In face of re-peated heavy attacks it was found necessary to adapt a mild form of dispersal, called 'decentralization'. The number of main components being dealt with at any time in any single plant was limited according to the type of plane. This 'decen-tralization' moved slowly, however, and was eventually over-taken in the autumn by a different set of problems due to Allied invasion.

More important and significant were the underground air-craft factories which were started. Underground construction was one way of solving the Fighter Staff's main difficulty. Their plans for the end of 1945 provided for the occupation of 3,000,000 square metres of underground space. Even before 'Programme No. 226', as early as May 1944, production was started ten-tatively in 200,000 square metres of underground space.[1] Be-tween June and August this total was quintupled. But from August onwards the total shrank because space was evacuated in front of the invading armies. The idea of semi-underground factories (*Bunkerwerke*), had already commended itself, and con-struction of such works had been experimentally opened before the founding of the Fighter Staff. The whole process of under-ground or semi-underground production was looked upon by the Fighter Staff as an unfortunate necessity, arrangements for which would delay production of those planes necessary for Germany's survival. Hitler on the other hand, thought of it as a solution to all Germany's difficulties and wanted it to proceed at a much faster pace. On 5 March 1944 he tried to force the Fighter Staff to adapt underground construction as a universal panacea, not as a limited expedient.

The Führer commands that those measures which have been started must under no circumstances be carried out as though they were transitional measures, but must be the starting-point for a large-scale and conclusive underground dispersal for all German industrial works, as only in this way, in the long run, can plans be drawn up for the maintenance of manufacturing installations for war production.[2]

To obviate this order Milch and Saur decided to act as though this were, indeed, their own policy, but to make it appear much

[1] Speer Report No. 18, Appendix 1, passim.
[2] FD 3353/45 vol. 57, p. 3. Führerkonferenz, 5 March 1944.

more difficult to implement than it really was. In reporting on 6 April they indicated that limited surface dispersal, 'decentralization', would be completed by August. Work could then start on 'the second instalment'—underground dispersal.[1] The most important works, they told Hitler, would be underground by the end of the year. Sooner was impossible, Milch claimed, because of the tremendous pressure which such large-scale construction projects put on the economy. But Hitler insisted that two huge aircraft production plants of 600,000 square metres each, one of a special air-raid-proof concrete construction, and the other an extension of an underground factory should be built. The delaying tactics on the part of the industry led to Hitler's attempt to bring in Hungarian Jews to supply 100,000 extra men. Hitler's other idea was to institute a co-operative scheme between German and Hungarian industry to set up a completely self-contained fighter factory in 200,000 or 300,000 square metres of underground space in Hungary.[2] The consequent loss to Hungarian armaments production would be compensated by deliveries of arms from Germany.

Speer did his utmost to prevent these new grandiose schemes from being put into operation since he felt that in 1944 they were economically a bad proposition. But some aircraft parts were under the control of the SS. Therefore SS underground production of aircraft parts proceeded more rapidly than that of the Speer Ministry. Nordwerk and Mittelwerk, both SS factories, produced jet engines and undertook work for the V2 in the Harz mountains limestone caverns. Although Saur, in his capacity as Head of the Technical Department of the Speer Ministry exercised a nominal control, he was actually powerless. Labour for these works was drawn from the ready supply controlled in concentration camps by the SS. This would have been the problem of instituting similar production centres for the Speer Ministry. Large-scale release of labour was only available in 1944 by courtesy of the SS. Yet the SS plants do not seem to have been efficient even if they were bomb-proof. There is no escaping the conclusion that the extremely fragmented nature of the National Socialist State told against aircraft

[1] FD 3353/45 vol. 58, p. 5, Führerkonferenz, 9 April 1944.
[2] FD 3353/45 vol. 59, pp. 4–5, Führerkonferenz, 1 May 1944.

production even after the Fighter Staff had apparently solved this problem.

What were the results achieved by the Fighter Staff? A tremendous increase in the output of day and night fighters flowed from the production lines between March and August 1944 and continued after the Fighter Staff had been merged into the Speer Ministry, although, of course, the fuel shortage prevented their all being effectively deployed.

Fighter plane production[1]

(Speer Ministry figures)

Date	New production	Repaired	Total
1943			
July–Dec. $\left(\begin{smallmatrix}\text{monthly}\\\text{average}\end{smallmatrix}\right)$	1,369	521	1,890
1944			
January	1,340	419	1,759
February	1,323	430	1,753
March	1,830	546	2,376
April	2,034	669	2,703
May	2,377	647	3,024
June	2,760	834	3,594
July	3,115	935	4,050
August	3,051	922	3,973
September	3,538	776	4,314

These figures are the Speer Ministry's own figures for production. Delivery and acceptance was not their responsibility but that of the Air Force itself. The 'acceptance' figures by the Air Force reveal considerable disparities which cannot be accounted for entirely either by the lack of coincidence between the production month and the acceptance month of any particular plane, or by the admittedly very large number of planes destroyed on the ground.[2] The following two production tables, the first the Speer Ministry's figures, the second the Quartermaster-General's Department of the Air Force's figures, show how wide the discrepancies can be. The second table includes certain

---

[1] FD 3353/45 vol. 78, 18 October 1944, photostat page no. 3534, 'Ausstoss–Übersicht Waffen und Geräte'.

[2] For instance the Air Force acceptance figure for March 1944 is 1667, Speer Report No. 18, Appendix 1, p. 6.

categories of repair as new planes, the first is only new planes; this accounts for the frequency of larger totals in the second table. Both serve to show the dramatic impact of the Fighter Staff on aircraft production.

New production of specific plane types[1]

(Speer Ministry figures)

Type	Monthly Av. July–Dec. 1943	Output Jan. 1944	Output Feb. 1944	Output March 1944	Output April 1944	Output May 1944
Bf. 109	625	645	715	827	806	999
Fw. 190	289	293	301	543	615	723
Me. 262	—	—	—	1	3	7
Bf. 110	146	107	44	75	197	157
Me. 410	58	70	33	99	64	108
He. 219	7	10	—	14	15	16
Ju. 88[2]	42	49	79	86	159	208

Quartermaster-General's estimates for the same period[3]

Type	Monthly Av. July–Dec. 1943	Jan. 1944	Feb. 1944	March 1944	April 1944	May 1944
Bf. 109	548	921	674	726	757	1,055
Fw. 190	296	404	269	616	646	769
Me. 262	—	—	1	—	—	8
Bf. 110	146	156	45	74	198	180
Me. 410	40	36	50	100	95	119
He. 219	—	11	5	11	25	14
Ju. 88[4]	83	34	98	82	165	229

The figures are indicative of the extreme efforts made by the Fighter Staff. Output figures such as these being obtained in the face of difficulties which were so much greater than anything previously faced by the industry show how very efficient the Speer Ministry was and how even constant bombing can be disregarded by the application of resource and determination. But some limitations must be admitted to this rosy picture.

[1] FD 3353/45 vol. 78, photostat page no. 3565.
[2] Part of the large discrepancy in the numbers of Ju. 88 recorded here and in the following table may be due to the inclusion of more operational types in the second table. The figures for Ju. 88 in this table do not include 'Kampfflugzeuge'.
[3] Gen. Qu. 6. Abt.   [4] See n.2.

The Quartermaster-General's department had not had the special facilities for increasing production which the Speer Ministry gave to the Fighter Staff. The food and clothing allocated as bonuses for a 72-hour week required special planning, unthinkable while aircraft production was independent from the Armaments Ministry. After the formation of the Fighter Staff the Air Force blamed the Speer Ministry for the low levels of aircraft output before 1944.[1] Speer had opposed the originally proposed target of 5,000 planes a month in 'Programme No. 224'. On 27 November 1943, they claimed, Speer had written off as unobtainable any increase over 'Programme No. 224'. However, when the Fighter Staff had been established Speer had readily made available the raw material supplies for the more difficult 'Programme No. 225'.[2]

Before the creation of the Fighter Staff, tank production had always had priority over any part of Air Force production. The 'Defence of the Fatherland' programme of 3 August 1943 had not been allocated top priority by Speer in spite of Air Force requests. Components factories supplying parts for tanks had been ordered on top priority to supply aircraft parts in March 1944. Between 1 September 1939 and 31 December 1943 the financial allocation for constructional works in the aircraft industry had fallen from an average of 92,000,000 reichsmarks a month to 22,100,000 reichsmarks a month. This latter figure was operative for the whole year 1 January to 31 December 1943. The creation of the Fighter Staff had caused the average allowance for the year 1 January to 31 December 1944 to be increased to 42,900,000 reichsmarks,[3] per month. In a similar way the allocation of iron for constructional purposes had increased; so had the reserves of machine tools which Saur had diverted from other sources. If the Air Force had had the resources of the Speer Ministry or even its full backing their earlier programmes would have come nearer to completion.

Of course, the Fighter Staff was formed precisely to enable such a special drive to take place, and to eliminate those faults in aircraft production due to its isolation from the rest of the

[1] FD 4439/45, Reichsluftfahrtministerium. 'Über die Gründe der erhöhten Lieferungen im Rahmen des Luftwaffenprogrammes vom März bis Juni 1944.'
[2] Ibid., p. 4.   [3] Ibid., p. 16.

economy. Nevertheless Speer was only prepared to throw everything into aircraft production once it was under his control; until then through Central Planning he kept a tight rein on the allocation of raw materials. Also there was a great deal of slack in the aircraft industry which was taken up by the Fighter Staff. The policy of continually changing the types of plane produced meant that many factories had had long periods without working at full capacity. It proved fairly simple in many cases for the Fighter Staff to utilize such capacity fully. In 1942 Speer had completed in six months the construction of the Ostmark aircraft engine works. This factory did not produce a single engine until mid-1944. It had been three times assigned to three different types of engine.[1]

The process was helped enormously by the decision to stop altogether the production of bombers. On Saur's estimate five fighters could be produced for every He.177 that came off the assembly lines. The very high production figures for September 1944 when, including repaired aircraft, the number of planes delivered to the Air Force amounted to 5,200,[2] are doubtless partly due to the fact that a gross imbalance was being created in the Air Force and it was only necessary to produce the smaller types of plane. The dribble of bombers of early 1944, irrespective of whether they were worth the production effort or not, certainly played its part in keeping production figures down. The Fighter Staff was increasingly selective in the types of plane it produced in large numbers. While this redounded to the credit of the Speer Ministry it made overall totals of planes produced easier to increase.

The creation of the Fighter Staff and the policies by which it attained its objectives correspond to the fundamental change which took place at the same time in other spheres of war production. Just as in rifles and tanks, quality was being discarded for quantity. Victory through qualitative superiority was being discarded in favour of survival at any cost.

The Fighter Staff's success was political as well as economic. It was another administrative triumph for Speer's policy of creating one all-powerful Ministry of War Economy. But theoretically he was still responsible only for fighter production.

[1] Speer Report No. 18, Appendix 1, p. 6.   [2] Gen. Qu. 6. Abt.

His aim was to control all Air Force production including the production of general equipment. But Göring had regarded the Fighter Staff as being at best a temporary measure, at worst a compromise which could go no further on the part of the Air Force. In June 1944, three months after the foundation of the Fighter Staff, Speer tried his strength with Göring again.

It was easy enough to take over the production of bomber planes, since the quantity produced was no longer significant, and after July none at all were built. This much Göring could concede willingly and it was done in June by agreement between Milch and Speer. Göring was not willing to allow general equipment production to be taken over; in his view, the only reason for the relatively low level of production was that Speer had deliberately sacrificed Air Force equipment for Army equipment which was under his control. Speer argued before Hitler that fighter production had been 'doubled' under the Fighter Staff, not by bringing in facilities from other spheres of production, but merely by using reserves available in the aircraft industry. Milch was in favour of turning all Air Force production over to the Ministry, but Speer wanted the initiative to come from Göring, so that he could later claim that he had not deliberately annexed others' responsibilities. The argument from the success of the Fighter Staff was irresistible:

I asked the Führer so to use his influence with the Reichsmarschall that there should be a possibility of the Reichsmarschall coming to *us* with the suggestion that Air Force armament should be incorporated in the Ministry. The Führer declared with unusual sharpness that Air Force armaments must be incorporated into the Ministry at the present moment and that he would express his opinion on this to the Reichsmarschall.[1]

The Fighter Staff continued to operate until 1 August 1944. Then, in accordance with the Führer's decision in June, it was dissolved and all Air Force production was directed through the newly-formed Armaments Staff. A main committee for aircraft production was formed with the usual apparatus of subcommittees.

The failure of the German economy to produce enough aircraft was very largely a political one. The conflicting and com-

[1] FD 3353/45 vol. 63, pp. 5/6, Führerkonferenz, 8 June 1944.

peting interests within the industry itself needed a strong control from the central authority. Such control was never imposed because of the nature of the Nazi State. Hitler abhorred strength at the centre which might limit his own field of decision. Bormann's great influence went hand in hand with his acquiescence in Hitler's policies. Speer was a man of a more independent stamp. His strength was in his indispensability. The longer the war continued the more vital economic issues became, and the more the logic of events showed the need for an all-powerful Ministry of War Production. But even so the whole failure or success of the Ministry depended on the personal situation of the Minister.

Speer's position can be looked at from several different points of view. Most vital was his relationship and personal standing with Hitler. This varied considerably during the history of the Ministry. Of less importance, but almost as vital for the German war economy, was his relationship with other leading Nazis. The profound implications of the rivalry and dislike existing between Speer and Göring have already been explored. The personal rivalry between Bormann, in reality a much more powerful man than Göring, and Speer proved even more harmful to the institution in Germany of a thoroughgoing war economy. This rivalry of Bormann and Speer was the surface reflection of sharply contrasted views about the nature of the German war economy. Bormann and the Gauleiters, the inner caucus of the Nazi party, carried on a quite uncompromising opposition to the idea of 'total war', and were only converted when it was too late to matter. At the same time the local Party organizations feared the increasing strength on the district level of the Speer Ministry. From another area too, from the SS, Speer's methods and ideas met constant opposition.

Speer's relations with Hitler were never better than when he was first appointed Minister of Armaments and Munitions. From that time onwards it is almost true to say that their relationship constantly deteriorated. At first he always had access to Hitler and the Führer-Conferences took place at fairly regular intervals. Gradually Saur began to play his part in these conferences; he was an able man and his knowledge of specific questions of armaments (Hitler's favourite topic of discussion) was better than Speer's. The minutes of these meetings were always signed by Speer to give them more authority,[1] but sometimes important decisions could be taken between Hitler and Saur, as in the Conference of 7 June 1944.[2] Speer's long illness in Spring 1944 furthered this development. Dorsch, head of the Building Department of the Ministry, began a long intrigue against his Minister.[3] And in Autumn 1944 Speer found that for the first time he was unable to protect a subordinate, Schieber, against Hitler's anger. Yet his original friendship with Hitler survived his influence. At the end he was able to tell Hitler to his face that the war was lost and still retain his position. But since, from 1943 onwards, his personal influence with Hitler was on the decline he was often forced to abandon policies on which he had previously determined. This was particularly the case as Bormann's influence rose and with it the strength of the opposition to any further 'totality' in the war effort.

In Spring 1943 Speer tried to get Göring to reassert his influence and become an actual, rather than a nominal, head of the Party. The method would be to start regular meetings of the Reichs Defence Council.[4] The Council would be streamlined and Speer and Goebbels would become members under Göring's chairmanship. But a series of conferences between Goebbels, Göring, and Speer failed to induce the Reichsmarschall to abandon the pleasantly drifting pattern of his existence. Even more, they failed to restore Hitler's faith in Göring; indeed, on some days Hitler would hear no talk of him at all. In any case the differences between Speer and Göring were deep enough for Göring to have no wish to reactivate the Reichs Defence Council as a vehicle for Speer and Goebbels to pursue their policy of total war.

In such circumstances Speer was obliged to play the political game by the same rules as his competitors. He decided to trade on his prewar membership of Hitler's private circle of friends. Hitler had a surgeon, Dr. Brandt, who always travelled with

[1] Speer Report No. 1.
[2] FD 3353/45 vol. 64, Führerkonferenz, 8 June 1944.
[3] Speer describes him as a 'reprehensible character, ruthless', Speer Report No. 13.
[4] Speer Report No. 19, Part 1, p. 5.

him. Brandt had also been a member of the group of Hitler's personal friends at the Berghof. Speer therefore chose him as his agent at court, and he acted in this capacity, none too successfully. Hitler, with his immense working day, was of course abnormally dependent on doctors of all kinds. Bormann conducted a long campaign to get Brandt removed from his post. The chance came in late 1944 when Brandt and his deputy, von Hasselbach, tried, for purely medical reasons, to influence Hitler against taking the pills of Dr. Morrell. Morrell was more powerful and Bormann used the opportunity to get Brandt dismissed. This behind-the-scenes defeat coincided with the removal of Schieber from the Speer Ministry. Shortly before the occupation of Berlin Brandt was sentenced to death on a trumped-up charge but was taken prisoner before the sentence could be executed.[1]

In such battles Speer could normally count on the support of Goebbels. Goebbels, like many of the 'intellectual' wing of the Party, was in favour of total war. Of course as head of the Ministry of Propaganda he did not meet the same practical objections to it as did Bormann and his Gauleiters. After the defeat at Stalingrad Goebbels made an all-out effort to secure a complete shut-down of production for civilian purposes. In the disputes over control and distribution of the labour force in Summer 1943 Speer used Goebbels as a support against Sauckel.

What Speer reported from the Obersalzberg was encouraging. Führer is more convinced than ever that total war is our salvation. He won't let anybody push him off the course on which he has started.[2]

This was the obverse of the attitude of the Gauleiters. Each Gauleiter was Reichs Defence Commissioner for his own district, an office which gave him supervisory powers over quite a number of economic matters. The Speer Ministry could in part get round this by using the Armaments Inspectors, but this could only be done in the teeth of strong local opposition. Anything which the Speer Ministry needed the Gauleiters to perform, and which did not suit the Gauleiters, would be met by blank inertia. The Gauleiter was always interested in

[1] Speer Report No. 1. H. R. Trevor-Roper, op. cit., p. 74.
[2] *The Goebbels Diaries*, p. 202, 24 April 1943.

keeping the economy of his Gau intact, in some cases with a view to making the Gau independent of fiscal control after the war.[1] With such political backing at the centre as Bormann provided, local potentates like this could do a great deal to prevent the closing down of consumer goods industries in their area. The failure to reduce civilian consumption in Germany to a level consonant with what was needed can certainly be partly blamed on the weakness of Speer's position against Bormann at Hitler's headquarters, and the political opposition on a local level to the activities of the Speer Ministry.

To attempt to allay the antagonism of the local Party officials Speer would occasionally make ill-received speeches on confidential matters to meetings of the Gauleiters. On 21 June 1943 Speer defended his policy on 'dispersal' and on the defence of the Ruhr before the Gauleiters in Berlin. They were demanding a large say in the resiting of industry and were incensed at the apparent lack of air-defence in many areas.[2] On 6 October, in Posen, he explained his decision to make a more severe attack on the production of consumer goods and tried to make his audience see the need for such restriction. In Spring 1944 a speech on the same subject was badly received and Speer was obliged to exculpate himself before the Führer.

> Drew the Führer's attention to the fact that, according to my information, the speech to the Gauleiters in Posen, caused offence to several Gauleiters. I offered to read the manuscript of the speech to him.
>
> The Führer is satisfied with my statement that, although I spoke 'sharply', I had in no way attacked the Gauleiters and that, in a conversation with me following the speech, Reichsleiter Bormann had likewise remarked that the speech had not been too aggressive. The Führer said that he had indeed received complaints from a few Gauleiters, but as far as he was concerned the matter was closed.[3]

During the operations of Geilenberg to reconstruct the synthetic fuel-producing plant the matter became more acute. Bormann regarded such reconstruction on the site as being quite worthless and allowed the Gauleiter to place certain re-

---

[1] Speer Report No. 19, Part 1, pp. 22–24.
[2] FD 3353/45, vol. 88. Speech by Speer.
[3] FD 3353/45 vol. 61, Führerkonferenz, 26 May 1944.

strictions on the special labour force involved. Speer wrote to Bormann on 16 September 1944 expressing the view that the effective continuation of the war depended entirely on the successful rebuilding of fuel plant.[1]

But bulletins, speeches, and appeals were all fruitless and the wearisome administrative struggle to effect total mobilization of the economy always failed when faced with the determined refusal on the part of the National Socialist Party to accept the facts of Germany's economic situation. On 17 January 1944 the Speer Ministry determined not to increase its timber allocation and building allowance to the Party for the purpose of building extra barracks. The consequences of increasing air-raids were great increases in the necessary allocations of timber to factory and house construction. It was 'impossible to contemplate' even a small increase in the allocation to the Party, which, for the first and second quarters of the year, would be 8,000 cubic metres.[2] In addition the Ministry appealed to the Party Building Administration to cut down its heavy demands because of the mounting volume of bomb damage. The reply was that while making every allowance for the serious situation and the needs of the armament industry the Party Building Administration could be content 'with nothing less than their full demand, which was 137,000 cubic metres of sawn coniferous timber'. In any case there was an important matter of principle at stake. 'The clearly defined constitutional sovereignty of the Party must find its expression in the economic control of building activities.'[3]

The struggle between the Speer Ministry and the local officials of the National Socialist Party was a prolongation of the earlier controversy between the advocates of 'armament in depth' and those of the Blitzkrieg. But there was an equally determined struggle, involving different questions of principle, between the Speer Ministry and the *élite* of the National Socialist movement, the SS.

The SS formed a state and a society of its own within the framework of the National Socialist state. It controlled the most

---

[1] FD 2690/45 vol. 3, Speer to Bormann, 16 September 1944.
[2] FD 3353/45 vol. 83, Speer to Schwarz, 17 January 1944.
[3] Ibid.

important police functions through the Gestapo;[1] it had its own secret service, the SD;[2] it controlled the concentration camps; it had considerable power in the administration of the occupied territories in the East: and it had its own fighting troops, the Waffen-SS, whose number by the end of the war had risen to almost 600,000. To sustain this organization the SS had its own separate legal organization, its own bureaucracy, medical services and schools. Furthermore it had its own economic empire which by the end of the war consisted of over forty different undertakings with about 150 different firms.[3] The activities of these firms ranged from quarrying and mining, through the production of foodstuffs and mineral waters, to the manufacture of armaments and textiles. The whole empire was under the control of *SS-Obergruppenführer* Pohl, chief of the Head Office for SS Economic Administration.[4] Most of the firms were organized in limited companies, and in 1940 they were pulled together into one large trust, the 'Deutsche Wirtschaftsbetriebe G.m.b.H.' (DWB).

To maintain itself as a 'state within a state' the SS had needed from its beginnings some manufacturing capacity. But the development of this economic empire into the size it had attained by the end of the war was more particularly based on the control of labour in concentration camps. As these camps became less necessary for purely political reasons Himmler found a new reason for their existence as economic undertakings. In this way emerged the biggest of all the SS firms, the German Earth and Stone Works (DEST).[5] Ironically enough this organization, which was later to give the Speer Ministry so much trouble, had been founded in Spring 1938 in connection with Speer's rebuilding activities as official architect to the Third Reich.[6]

In the later years of the war some of the firms under the control of DEST were converted to armaments manufacture. Their co-operation with Messerschmitt was of special importance. After the bombing of the Messerschmitt works at

[1] Geheime Staatspolizei.   [2] Sicherheitsdienst des Reichsführers-SS.
[3] E. Georg, *Die Wirtschaftlichen Unternehmungen der SS*. The first thorough examination of the extent of the SS economic operations.
[4] SS Wirtschafts-Verwaltungshauptamtes (WVHA).
[5] Deutsche Erd- und Steinwerke G.m.b.H.   [6] E. Georg, op. cit., p. 42.

Regensburg the SS provided the floor space and the labour for the manufacture, first of aeroplane components, and later of whole aeroplanes, at their works at Flossenburg and Mauthausen.[1] By the beginning of 1944 the SS controlled in this way the underground factory at St. Georgen, near Mauthausen, where the Me. 262 jet fighter was being assembled. 35 per cent of the total output of the Messerschmitt firm was by that time under the control of the SS in their role of provider of labour. The same SS combine, DEST, turned out enormous quantities of grenades and small-arms ammunition, which were not reserved entirely for the Waffen-SS. The rather inaptly named German Earth and Stone Works had become one of the biggest armament concerns in Germany by the end of the war.

The German Equipment Works (DAW),[2] on the other hand, produced mainly consumer goods of all kinds until 1942. As early as 1941 it had become a giant concern with branches spreading into nearly all the concentration camps. In 1943 it employed 15,000 prisoners and 500 civilians; the civilians being usually the skilled workers. Like many of the SS firms it was switched over to armaments manufacture in 1942–3, and eventually 90 per cent of its activities were concentrated on a rather slovenly and inefficient rifle and cartridge manufacture in many concentration camps. It produced 2,950,000 cartridge cases in 1943.

The Speer Ministry could interfere very little in this range of economic activity. Central Planning was responsible for allocating raw materials to the SS. However the SS could obtain certain raw materials independently in occupied territories where its influence was strong, and also the political pressure which it could exert to obtain larger supplies through Central Planning was great. The SS controlled great reserves of labour in the economy and deployed them just as it wished. When the shortage of labour was so acute, the Speer Ministry found it particularly irksome to see such a potential source of labour kept firmly out of its reach. To make things worse the SS used its labour with gross inefficiency. Productivity was very low and management very poor. Therefore Speer struggled constantly to get some powers of control over the SS economic activities.

[1] Ibid., p. 57.   [2] Deutsche Ausrüstungswerke G.m.b.H.

Saur had theoretical powers over the technical aspects of construction in the underground aeroplane factories but he was obliged to tread very softly. Sometimes Speer did win administrative victories, however, as in the case of the shale-oil production which the SS tried to start in Württemberg. Geilenberg, the Speer Ministry's Special Commissioner for the reconstruction of synthetic oil works, managed to secure overriding powers. Since he had at his disposal a team of experts who had mastered all kinds of new construction techniques this was an eminently logical decision. The labour was provided by the SS who had set up labour camps near the site with the intention of undertaking the whole job themselves. But Geilenberg contrived to get this labour force put temporarily under the *Organisation Todt*.

In 1944 Germany was more in need of oil than of any other raw material and Speer was thus able to fight the battle over the Württemberg shale-oil works on particularly favourable ground. Usually the situation was not so favourable. Outside the frontiers of Germany proper the SS was stronger. In the occupied territories, especially in the General-Government of Poland, the SS had control of all the Jewish labour force. In the Lublin district in 1943 the SS disposed of 45,000 prisoners for war production in its widest sense.[1] After a Führer-Command on 13 October 1942 even those work camps which had been set up by the civil administration near to the existing armaments factories had to be transferred to the SS. Agitation by the Speer Ministry against this state of affairs produced a Führer-Command on 3 November 1943 which withdrew Jewish labour from 'Eastern Industry',[2] a large SS concern mainly based in the Eastern territories. That particular company had to be liquidated since sufficient civilian labour was not forthcoming after the withdrawal of the Jews. But although 'Eastern Industry' was closed down the much larger combine of German Armament Works was able to survive. Its interests in the Lublin and Lemberg areas were mainly textiles, shoe-making, and printing. Although it lost control of 8,000 Jews it was able to replace the most important part of its labour force, the skilled workmen,

---

[1] E. Georg, op. cit., pp. 91–92.
[2] Ibid., p. 77.

by drafts from Dachau, Buchenwald, and Sachsenhausen concentration camps. It was precisely these skilled workmen whose deployment was so essential to the German war economy. In February 1944 the SS was still largely employing people in consumer goods production in the General-Government.

In fact the more the development of a war economy put emphasis on the employment of prisoners for war production the greater the economic influence in the hands of the SS. In occupied territories consumer goods production remained at levels higher than the Ministry of Armaments thought desirable. In Sudetenland and in the Protectorate of Bohemia and Moravia the SS manufactured a wide variety of goods such as furniture, pottery and mineral waters. In fact by maintaining its mineral water production when that in Germany was being reduced drastically it was able to gain a near monopoly of the German market. It also controlled the distribution of consumer goods among the population as a whole in the areas where it manufactured them, and its methods of allocation certainly differed from those preferred by the Speer Ministry.[1]

The lack of proper production figures for SS firms makes any accurate judgement of the extent to which they impeded the development of a full war economy difficult. After 1942 the SS turned its productive capacity increasingly towards armaments and in this capacity it did more damage than as a producer of consumer goods. Indeed by 1944 its consumer goods output was often reserved for the SS or for the concentration camps. But the worst aspect of this rivalry as far as the Minister of Armaments was concerned was that whereas his power increased at the expense of his other rivals as the war situation became more menacing that was not true of the rivalry between himself and the SS. While Speer was introducing greater rationality everywhere in the German economy he was coming to have less and less control over the economic undertakings of the SS.

The attitude of Himmler to the national economy is well summed up in a letter he wrote to Pohl, after Pohl had first made the suggestion that the SS should organize its own shale-oil production in Württemberg.

[1] There was a rebate of 40 per cent for personal staff of the Reichsführer-SS.

Dear Pohl,

Thank you for your letter of 11.11.43. I am entirely in agreement with you, and I also think that it is necessary to make ourselves fully independent. We must buy, or have ceded to us, an appropriate area in which shale-oils are to be found. I am really not at all in favour of surrendering labour strength to other sectors, since in that way we shall not get the oil for ourselves.[1]

The SS was concerned only with its own economic system. In this system there were strong elements of anti-capitalism. It was a system which came into conflict with what the SS called the 'private economy'. There is some evidence that the SS had long-term plans for spreading its system throughout the economy as a whole and destroying capitalism in Germany. It was perhaps obliged to postpone these long-term aims because of the war. But even in the war it was not prepared to allow any relaxation of control over its own sector in favour of Speer, whom it regarded as the representative of private capitalistic interest.

The SS was the only economic organization which grew more powerful in the teeth of Speer's opposition. Elsewhere the pressure of the war on the economy tended to make economic decisions more and more fundamental to Germany's survival and thus to make Speer's role more and more important in that survival. This can be clearly seen in the relationship between Speer and the Army. By 1944 the dispute about control over the economy between civilians and soldiers seemed very remote. The Speer Ministry by reasonably accurate calculations of economic possibilities could show that these possibilities were now the determining factor in strategic choices. In fact it was becoming rather arbitrary to distinguish between strategic and economic possibilities.

Nowhere is this better demonstrated than in the dispute over whether Germany should retreat behind the *Nibelungen* line to conduct a last desperate defence. Such a policy had come to be favoured on military grounds even by generals as experienced as Guderian. Guderian was rapidly disabused by Speer who pointed out that no war economy could be carried on behind the *Nibelungen* line; therefore as a strategic concept it was unten-

[1] Quoted by E. Georg, op. cit., p. 104. N.D., NI-15 588.

able. 'The retreat would therefore be synonymous with the extinction of the fighting capacity of the troops only a few weeks later.'[1] Nothing could better demonstrate than this incident the growth in importance of the Ministry of Armaments and Munitions.

Had Speer had greater political control of the economy earlier, had he ever achieved a situation in which decisions relative to the economy as a whole could have been executed without political opposition, Germany would have been able to prolong the struggle longer than she did. But Speer's rise to power was a product of the fundamental change in German strategy in January 1942. And the degree of his power was limited by the singular political structure of the National Socialist State. In these circumstances it was no historical accident that political opposition of various kinds should limit the extent to which Germany after January 1942 could be mobilized for war.

[1] FD 3353/45 vol. 218, Speer to Guderian, p. 3.

CHAPTER VII

The Collapse of the German Economy

IN a collapse such as that suffered by the Third Reich it would be foolish to look for one particular cause. But the military conquest and occupation of Germany was accompanied by a disintegration of economic unity, by a collapse of the economic capacity necessary to fight the war. This so-called 'breakdown of the German economy' was not due entirely to the occupation by the enemy of the territorial area of Germany. Rather the failure of the German economy was responsible to some extent, to an extent that is very difficult to estimate, for the military and social collapse. Germany had been socially and economically geared to a continually increasing rate of war production, and once the rate started to drop the enemy found his task increasingly easy and the administrative structure of the German economy came apart at the seams. By the summer of 1944 the German economy had been turned into a vehicle capable of travelling in only one direction. When the obstacles put in its way became insurmountable it dashed itself against them again and again, until it broke to pieces. By April 1945 Germany no longer had a central unified economic organization.

Why did the work of Todt and Speer prove so ephemeral? What did the 'breakdown of the German economy' constitute? And why did it happen? Is it possible, in the *débris* of 1945, to isolate any particular phenomena responsible for the failure to maintain production?

Thanks to the copious documentary evidence it is possible to observe the Speer Ministry from July 1944 almost until the end. It can be studied in its failures to discover expedients, finding itself no longer able to manipulate the economy by increased pressure on one sector, by released pressure on another, and finally realizing that the task of merely maintaining existing levels of production was too difficult.

Yet, even here, it is necessary to tread carefully. The blanket generalization 'breakdown of the economy' does more to conceal fact than reveal it. The 'breakdown' did not occur at the same time everywhere. The economy did not snap, like an overstrained plank of wood, suddenly and irreparably. Each sector performed differently under the strain. Some branches of German production did not decline. Tank production targets were achieved almost until the bitter end. Munitions production, on the other hand, began to decline in September 1944, and in January 1945 sank to the level of November and December 1942. Even at this level it was more than twice as high as it had been throughout 1941. The production of weapons generally did not begin its overall decline until December. But its collapse was terribly sudden. The production of many types of weapons was halved between December 1944 and January 1945. Nevertheless it remained much higher than it had been in the period of Germany's greatest successes. The important fact is not the severity of decline but the fact that there was a decline at all. Germany's only hope was a continual expansion of production. It was possible to hope while war production climbed. But in Autumn 1944, to all but fanatics, the war was economically lost.

The problem of examining the ultimate failure of Germany's war effort has been confused further by the arguments as to the relative merits of different bombing tactics. There can be no doubt that active interference of this nature in the work of the German economy hastened the decline in production. But the overall importance of bombing, as well as the importance of particular aspects of the offensive, has been exaggerated, often for the purpose of demonstrating the success of different kinds of bombing policy. Webster and Frankland have shown that the differences between the American bombing offensive and the English bombing offensive were not so great as has often been stated.[1] It also emerges clearly from their work how comple-

[1] Sir C. Webster and N. Frankland, op. cit.

mentary the two attacks, by day and night, could often be. But generally, although not exclusively, American strategy favoured the bombing of selected industries or supplies.[1] A weak link in the chain of production would be singled out, and the bombing offensive would be concentrated on this. Bomber Command preferred the night area bombing of large industrial concentrations like the Ruhr or Hamburg, and Harris, its chief, was scathingly sceptical about 'panacea' targets.[2] The argument was resolved, not ineffectively, by regarding both policies as complementary.

When the war was over both sides took more extreme positions than they had during it, and hastened to justify their respective policies. Consequently a large amount of the material on the later years of the German war economy has become involved with this controversy. Relevant though it is this has meant that the final stages of Germany's collapse have too often been looked at from a non-German viewpoint. This has even biased the documentary evidence. Too many of the interrogations of leading German industrialists were devoted to long analyses of the effects of bombing, when they could have been devoted to some problem on which the man interrogated was more knowledgeable. Faced with a barrage of questions on something on which he was not an expert, and to which answers could be given only in the most general terms, the 'prisoner' naturally tried to please his captors by his evidence. This, an intrinsic weakness of all evidence obtained by interrogation, was exaggerated by the habit of asking leading questions. For example, 'What caused the decline in production in Autumn 1944? If bombing was a cause, then what aspect of Allied bombing was concerned?' is a question begging the real issue for the historian.[3]

The United States Strategic Bombing Survey collected invaluable quantities of material on the war economy. But, with every priority, it was still limited by its terms of reference to a study of the effect of strategic bombing on the German economy. Consequently, as a picture of the working of the

---

[1] C. Spaatz, 'Strategic Air Power, Fulfilment of a Concept', in *Foreign Affairs*, No. 24, 1945–46.
[2] Sir C. Harris, *Bomber Offensive*.   [3] Speer Report No. 67, p. 1.

German economy, it is very sketchy between 1939 and 1942. Again, the documentary evidence published by Webster and Frankland is very much concerned with the effect of bombing alone on the German economy.

Speer thought that had it not been for the bombing attacks, German war production would ultimately have been limited by the shortages of raw materials which would have flattened out the production curve.[1] But this is a very theoretical argument and in 1944 the German war economy was not operating under text-book conditions. Germany had circumvented her raw material shortages very shrewdly throughout the war, by conquest and by substitution, although in theory they were her greatest weakness. Germany only momentarily came up against this limit to production, to see it recede again into the future. The failure to reach it, however, was not due solely to bombing, but to a complexity of different factors of which bombing was only one.

Certain acute shortages in the German economy were the direct result of Allied bombing. Particularly, the shortage of fuel oil should be singled out; but the shortage of steel in certain forms was equally attributable to this cause. In another field bombing savagely accentuated what was an inherent problem in the economy. The massive concentration of Germany's capital goods industries in the Ruhr, and, to a lesser degree, in Silesia was a problem of geography. But the effect of heavy bombing of means of communication was to bring this fundamental geographical problem into the foreground once more. The fears of pre-war economic planners and military strategists that Germany's productive capacity was too maldistributed to withstand the bomber were abundantly justified in the long run. This can best be seen in the quite artificial coal shortage which air attack and invasion combined to produce. In fact the coal shortage was not entirely the result of intervention by enemy powers in the German economy; but their intervention made it intolerable and insuperable.

Speer and his colleagues have been inclined to suggest that their economic edifice would never have fallen down had the Allies not first bombed the roof off and then occupied the rooms,

[1] Speer Report No. 31.

one by one. Yet the shortages of fuel oil, of steels, and of coal, were not the sole reasons for this destruction. The complexity of the economy of so highly-industrialized a country as Germany proved greater than the plans for strategic air warfare allowed. The breakdown of this economy can be seen in the more rapid succession of economic crises in late 1944 and in 1945. These crises can be brought into focus, but it is still difficult to discover the causes of the final crisis. However, it can be said that of an equal importance with the results of bombing were the chronic labour shortage, and the decline in vital raw material supplies as the Allies physically reoccupied territories on which Germany had depended. And, certainly not to be placed after these in order of importance, was the stark fact that the economic administration, which had sustained Germany in the face of all probability in 1944, was no longer in 1945 loyal to the economic policy of the régime. Speer, in fact, began to act quite independently because he reached the conclusion that Hitler's policy was a disaster. Thereafter a considerable part of the central economic organization of the state was concerned with actively frustrating the central political organization.

The crisis caused by the shortage of fuel oil was basically a continuation of the same crisis, due to the same causes, of Summer 1944. In May 1944 production of aviation spirit had fallen, for the first time, below Air Force consumption. Air Force consumption in April 1944 had been 165,000 tons. In May production had been only 156,000 tons.[1] On 30 June Speer told Hitler that production of aviation spirit for that month would be a mere 53,000 tons,[2] although the May production forecast for June had been 126,000 tons. Worse than this, the production for the second half of June was only equivalent to a monthly production of 42,000 tons. The May production of carburettor fuel had been 93,000 tons; the production estimate for June was now 70,400 tons. May production of diesel fuel had been 74,000 tons; June production was 66,300. Even if the potential imports of diesel fuel were added, this meant that only 94,000 tons would be available, whereas April

---

[1] FD 3353/45 vol. 92, p. 2.
[2] FD 3353/45 vol. 216, Speer to Hitler, p. 5; Quoted by Webster and Frankland, iv, 324.

consumption had been 194,000 tons. The production of the most important substitute for these fuels, propellant gas (*Treibgas*) had sunk from 37,600 tons in April to 10,400 in June. Of all these, decline in the output of aviation spirit was the most dangerous, since the figure was now so low that imports could make little difference. In any case the continued production of other synthetic fuels depended on keeping the Air Force supplied with fuel. The fact that output for the second part of June fell, compared to output for the first part, indicated that the July production would be even lower. Estimating the time necessary for the reconstruction of a hydrogenation plant to be between six and eight weeks, should air attacks continue at the same level, the low level of production in July and August would mean that by the end of August all available reserves of aviation spirit would have been used up. Unless something could be done to arrest this the Geilenberg reconstruction programme was a useless undertaking by itself.

Inevitably by September this year the supply of the amounts necessary to cover the most urgent requirements of the Wehrmacht will no longer be assured; i.e. from this moment on an impossible situation will arise which must lead to tragic results.[1]

Speer's plan to avoid this situation was to petition for increased air defence. But the difficulties of increasing the air defences of the Reich were obviously aggravated by the fall in output of aviation fuel. The increasing output of fighters by the Fighter Staff meant that, to economize on fuel, every flight must be cut down to the minimum, and all wastage of fuel by the Air Force must be stopped. The Wehrmacht must also work out a strategy involving the minimum possible amounts of diesel fuel. But, above all, the flak, fighter, camouflage, and smoke screen defences of hydrogenation plants had to be given first priority.

Hitler never liked reading of disasters. The report of 30 June proved strong meat. Yet its forecasts were only too accurate. A month later, on 28 July, Speer again reported on the situation.[2] Production of aviation spirit had been almost halved,

[1] FD 3353/45 vol. 216, Speer to Hitler, p. 8.
[2] FD 3353/45 vol. 92, Webster and Frankland, iv, 326.

reaching only 29,000 tons. The gap between the restoration of production and the next raid had now been almost eliminated by the Allies. Reconstruction work had, earlier, been responsible for the over-optimistic production forecast of 43,000 tons output of aviation spirit in August and 69,000 tons in September, but the heavy attacks on the Leuna works at the end of July now indicated an August production figure of a mere 15,000 tons. By 15 June daily production had reached 2,307 tons, the highest figure since 11 June.[1] But hope had been shattered by a series of heavy attacks. The attacks on Wehlheim and Brüx on 21 July had caused the daily production figures to drop below the previous nadir of 632 tons on 22 June. Production on 21 July was 120 tons, on 22 July and 23 July, 140 tons. It remained below the 600 tons mark for the rest of July. Production of carburettor fuel had fallen between June and July from 76,000 tons to 56,000 tons; production of diesel fuel from 66,000 tons to 62,000 tons; and production of propellant gas from 10,400 tons to 5,000 tons. The best the Air Force could now hope for in August or September was 10,000 to 20,000 tons of aviation spirit.

If . . . further attacks are made on the synthetic oil plants, and the enemy succeeds in throttling the aviation spirit production as hitherto, then a planned use of the Air Force in September or October will be impossible.[2]

The programme of underground dispersal had been supplemented by converting breweries and similar installations into primitive fuel-producing plants.[3] These primitive plants were widely scattered and relatively immune to air attack. The fact that they were needed now, in July, did not mean that the programme of underground dispersal was being carried out unsuccessfully, but that it had started too late, and no amount of acceleration could adequately close the gap between the tremendous drop in output due to bombing and the expected increase when the underground plant got into production. If the underground dispersals went according to plan, they should be able to guarantee, in December, 90,000 tons of aviation spirit and jet fuel. The labour force employed in the rebuilding

[1] FD 3353/45 vol. 216, p. 4.   [2] FD 3353/45 vol. 92, p. 5.   [3] Ibid., p. 12.

of damaged synthetic oil plant was as high as 150,000. It seemed, in July, as though the whole future working of the German war economy depended on the production of synthetic fuel, and that, to achieve this, September and October would be the decisive months.

In August the production of propellant gas fell to 3,000 tons, 2,000 tons below the July achievement.[1] Diesel fuel production remained steady at the low level of July, as did carburettor fuel production. But the indications for September were that carburettor fuel production probably would decline to 40,000 tons. Of course, the decisive factor would be aviation spirit. The gloomy forecast of July had proved a just one. Production had been more than halved, only 12,000 tons were produced in August, and the Leuna, Brüx and Pölitz hydrogenation plants had again been brought to a standstill for several weeks. The September production forecast was still between 10,000 and 15,000 tons. It was not merely the Air Force situation that was now perilous, the whole mobility of the Army was bound to be affected by the widespread shortage of diesel and carburettor fuel. The flow of fuel, on this basis, would cease altogether in October, and the Armed Forces would grind to a stop. Germany had one chance, and one only. Should the bomber attacks be split up by a better deployment of the fighter arm and should bad weather set in early in autumn, Germany might just survive.

The early days of September saw a great improvement in the situation. By 10 September the forecast figures had been reached and there seemed some chance of their being exceeded. It was a false dawn. Between 11 September and 19 September the Allies succeeded in stopping completely all aviation spirit production in Germany, except for one day.[2] The total September production was 9,400 tons; worse than the most pessimistic estimate. This could be only slightly offset by the increases in the supply of carburettor fuel (48,400 tons) and diesel fuel (77,300 tons). Repeated air attacks could be expected in October.

Had the weather not deteriorated so rapidly in October, and

[1] FD 3353/45 vol. 216, p. 5.
[2] FD 3353/45 vol. 99, Speer to Hitler, p. 1. Webster and Frankland, iv, 333.

had the Geilenberg programme not persevered in the teeth of the most overwhelming adversity, there would be no need to inquire further into the collapse of the German economy. But the almost total production stoppage of 11–19 September proved the worst moment. The October production of aviation spirit reached 20,000 tons, in November it was 49,000 tons, and in December 26,000 tons.[1] During the winter Pölitz could not be reached by enemy bombers, and substantial production took place there. Had the Allies managed to drive the October output below that of September the German war economy would probably have ceased to function; but, by the narrowest of margins, the strategic air offensive failed to smash Germany's economy by this one method of attack.

Nevertheless output of fuel remained too low for the Armed Forces to function efficiently. The following table sets overall consumption requirements against estimated output.

January 1945 estimates of future fuel consumption and production[2]

(in tons)

	Estimated production	Estimated consumption
Aviation Spirit		
January	12,000	45,000
February	9,000	40,000
March	12,000[3]	45,000
April	12,000	45,000
Carburettor Fuel		
January	60,000	63,000
February	53,000	57,000
March	50,000	61,000
April	50,000	60,000
Diesel Fuel		
January	65,000	84,000
February	66,000	83,000
March	68,000	90,000
April	68,000	95,000

[1] U.S.S.B.S., *Effects*, op. cit., p. 80. The original sources differ slightly in their estimates. Therefore Webster and Frankland, iv, 337 also give a difference here.
[2] Webster and Frankland, iv, 337.
[3] The moment when underground production was expected to become effective.

Bad though the situation was, in January 1945 it would still have been possible to cover the Air Force's requirements from April onwards if everything went according to plan and if sacrifices were made in other fields. In fact the January estimate of output of aviation spirit proved too high by 1,000 tons. The February production seems to have been even further below the estimates made for it in January, although statistical information is lacking for these last months. After January the planned use either of the Air Force or of the motorized sections of the German Army became impossible.[1] In such circumstances it was all too easy for the Allies to destroy completely the major oil-producing works and even to turn their attention to the minor ones. Germany now found that she had more tanks and planes than she could possibly use. The failure to press home the Ardennes counter-offensive, as at Bastogne for instance, or the failure to prevent the Russian break-out of the Baranov bridgehead and their subsequent capture of Silesia have both been attributed to the lack of fuel. But equally important was the breakdown of Germany's remaining air defences. Attacks such as that on Dresden were carried out with hardly any opposition from German fighters because they were grounded through lack of fuel.[2] The strategic air attacks on synthetic oil production must therefore be rated as one of the most important factors in the ultimate collapse of the German economy.

Such a verdict cannot be reached in the case of the similar attacks on synthetic rubber works. Except for the infrequent blockade runner from Japanese-occupied territory Germany had been almost completely dependent on synthetic rubber since the end of 1940. In spite of the great success of the attack on the Hüls plant in June 1943 the policy of bombing the synthetic rubber factories was never pursued so consistently as that of bombing the synthetic oil works.[3] The factory at Ludwigshafen, which started production in March 1943, maintained its

---

[1] Sir C. Webster and N. Frankland, iii, 234.
[2] D. Irving, *The Destruction of Dresden*, passim.
[3] But the two industries were closely connected. The hydrogen and gas necessary for the synthetic rubber industry were supplied by the Bergius hydrogenation plants. An attack on hydrogenation plant was indirectly an attack on the *buna* producing industry.

production figures without too much difficulty. The other two major factories, Hüls and Schkopau, were both severely damaged on only one occasion. To meet the bombing attacks an underground factory at Mühlsdorf, originally intended for bomber production, was constructed as a synthetic rubber factory, but it was not completed before the end of the war. Speer and Kehrl both believed that rubber scarcity had no effect on the mobility of the Wehrmacht or on the conduct of Wehrmacht operations, and their conclusions are supported by the evidence.[1] Only in December 1944 did synthetic rubber production fall really low.

In the case of the bombing attacks on manufactured component parts and completed armaments, estimates are more difficult to make than in the case of attacks on raw materials. It is hard to discover the precise degree by which supplies were reduced, and it is even harder to discover what effect this reduction had. The success of the 'special action' by Kessler in reconstructing the damaged ball-bearing factories has already been cited. The massive production of tanks was sustained until the end, in spite of the bombing attacks on tank-engine factories, and was one of the great successes of German war production. Certainly, in ultimate effectiveness, these extensions of the strategic bombing policy fell a long way short of what was achieved by the attacks on fuel production.

It would be a mistake to suppose, however, that of the bombing attacks only those on fuel plant hastened the collapse. Whereas most civilian economists before the war had prophesied that ultimate collapse would come because of Germany's serious shortages of essential raw materials, military economists had been mostly concerned with the grave dependence of Germany on the Ruhr industrial district and with the extremely vulnerable position of this district. When the constant Allied attacks on means of communication began, the problem of the Ruhr was seen from a different aspect, and its geographically perilous situation was stressed. Until November 1944 most attacks on German transport had been tactical in character, although the argument that Germany's means of communication were the most vulnerable of all her strategic targets had

[1] Speer Report No. 44.

often been advanced. As greater emphasis was placed on the paralysing of the railway and inland waterway systems, it became obvious that the problem of the Ruhr was not only its excessive vulnerability to air attack and invasion, but the fact that industrial production elsewhere in Germany depended to an alarming extent on raw materials and manufactured goods which had to be transported from the Ruhr.

Coal was the one raw material in which Germany was clearly self-sufficient. The coal industry was able, in spite of labour problems due to the size of the Armed Forces, to produce sufficient quantities throughout the war to sustain easily Germany's power stations and railways. But 80 per cent of this coal was mined in the Ruhr,[1] and although large quantities were consumed in that area, even larger quantities were sent out of it. It is ironical that of all Germany's raw materials the one in which she was best supplied should have been so responsible for the final collapse. The problem was one of transportation. For this reason it would distort the image too much to analyse separately the bombing of communications and the bombing of the Ruhr; from Germany's point of view they were different aspects of the same problem.

Coal was one of the few raw materials almost entirely dependent on the railways. Massive concentrations of lorry transport were prohibited by severe shortages of diesel fuel, nearly all of which had to be set aside for military purposes. In any case, no matter how massive a concentration of lorry transport could be organized, coal was a too bulky and a too heavily-used commodity to be adequately transported in such a way. Lorry transport could be used to avoid minor bottlenecks, caused, perhaps, by the destruction of single factory sidings, and it was so used.[2] But the effect of the wholesale destruction of marshalling yards and sorting-sidings, and the general breakdown of the signalling system, could not be overcome by motor transport. Nor could the breakdown of the inland waterways system by which one-third of the Ruhr's coal exports had previously arrived in the rest of Germany.

The normal transportation rate of coal out of the Ruhr was 22,000 railway wagons a day.[3] When coal movement first fell

---

[1] Excluding brown coal.   [2] Speer Report No. 26, p. 11.   [3] Ibid., p. 12.

below this rate, the effects were not felt, since the reduction in deliveries could be confined to those intended exclusively for winter stockpiling in large factories, power stations, and gasworks. But bad weather, the better planning of the Allied attack on communications, and the continuation of the attacks on the Ruhr area brought a violent crisis in November 1944.

The Speer Ministry met this crisis with its usual methods. A plenipotentiary-general was appointed and a Ruhr Staff, modelled on the Fighter Staff, was created. Dr. Lamertz, a railway executive, became plenipotentiary-general with authority over railways, canals, and inland shipping. The Ruhr Staff worked entirely in the Ruhr, an indication of the increasing difficulty of communication with the capital. This was one of the first symptoms of the dissolution of the Reich as a unitary state and a single economic unit.

On 11 November Speer reported to Hitler on the Ruhr situation.[1] The extreme gravity of the problem was reflected in the decision to release 30,000 workers from the armaments industry to help in the reconstruction of buildings and the transport system. If this proved insufficient, 10 per cent of Germany's mine workers would be withdrawn to help. Similar energetic measures were being taken to keep the canals in working order, since, with the partial destruction of the railway system, they had assumed a vital importance.

Judging by the report which *Reichsvereinigung Kohle* made to Central Planning on 8.11.1944, it must be stated that we stand at the beginning of the gravest coal production crisis since the start of the war.[2]

On 10 September the railways had nineteen days' supply of coal in hand. On 5 November they had less than eleven days in hand and had still to feel the worst effects of the crisis. Their stocks were decreasing by about 40,000 tons a day. All coal suitable and available for railway use was being supplied to them immediately without consideration for any other claimants. Before November began winter stocks in hand at power

[1] FD 2690/45 vol. 21, Speer to Hitler, 11 November 1944, p. 3. Webster and Frankland, iv, 349.
[2] FD 2690/45 vol. 21, p. 6.

stations had dropped to two-and-a-half weeks. This was an average figure; several power stations were on the point of complete closure. Many local gasworks in the west had ceased to operate for lack of coal. Important armament works and large steelworks were coming to a standstill. 'The Miag.' plant at Brunswick had already stopped production. Since armaments stocks in hand would cover a few weeks, the worst effects of these stoppages would be felt in December. Yet even by the end of November munitions output would be reduced by 25–30 per cent. Of the 22,000 wagons of coal which should daily have left the Ruhr, only 5,000 were now leaving.[1] A position of total isolation was being approached rapidly. Such an isolation would be utterly irremediable.

It is clear from Germany's overall economic structure that in the long run the loss of the industrial area of Rhineland-Westphalia would be a mortal blow to the German economy and to the conduct of the war.[2]

The slackening of Allied attacks due to bad weather only prolonged the crisis. In February 1945 the daily rate of coal wagons leaving the Ruhr had risen to 8,100, but this was only slightly more than a third of the rate necessary. As winter ended the air attack intensified again, and the problem was made more acute by artillery fire which could now reach the Ruhr. On 15 March Speer reported to Hitler that only 2,000 to 3,000 trucks were leaving daily.[3] Since coal deliveries from Silesia had now been reduced by the same amount, the situation was infinitely graver than before. But the problem was now of such a nature that, even if a respite were given in which to restore communications, resources in themselves would not be sufficient. Actual resources after the loss of Upper Silesia, the Saar and Lorraine would amount to a potential delivery capacity of 12,100,000 tons per month, 51·7 per cent of the capacity of January 1944. But this was almost a meaningless figure since the transport problem meant that the Ruhr coal delivery capacity could in fact only be exploited to the extent of 5,500,000 tons per month, 26 per cent of the figure for January, 1944.[4] This was a grossly

[1] FD 2690/45 vol. 21, p. 16.　　　　　　　[2] Ibid., pp. 18–19.
[3] FD 2690/45 vol. 6, Speer to Hitler, 15 March 1945, 'Wirtschaftslage März–April 1945 und Folgerungen'.　　　　　[4] Ibid., p. 2.

optimistic forecast and the Ruhr situation was almost bound to deteriorate to such an extent that even this figure could not be approached. Gasworks and power stations were being allocated only 33 per cent of their previous year's coal supplies. Whether they would ever receive their allocation was not known. Allocations to bakeries, dairies, hospitals, and other users were down to 25 per cent of the 1944 allocation.[1]

The bombing of the Ruhr and the shutting-off of coal supplies produced, by March, a severe crisis in the steel industry. After the destruction of the August Thyssen Hütte the steel capacity of the Ruhr was only 300,000 tons per month. In theory, the monthly capacity of the remaining areas was 410,000 tons per month, the total being 710,000 tons per month. A much more realistic estimate was that the rest of the Reich would produce only 150,000 tons per month. The effect of the concentration decrees had been to permit the construction of armaments from all stocks without any further development. Therefore this total quantity of 450,000 tons of steel per month could be almost entirely devoted to armaments construction. The irreducible minimum to maintain munitions production was 350,000 tons per month, which should provide an output of 175,000 tons of ammunition. This would leave a possible 100,000 tons of raw steel per month for all other purposes, including weapons, armour plate, U-boats, ships, and motor vehicles. The conclusion from such figures was inescapable.

In the long run it is impossible to maintain Germany's economic life for any length of time with the amount of hard-coal still available and the raw steel production capacity.

The German economy, to remain capable of life, needs, apart from armaments, at least a few hundred thousand tons of raw steel per month, which, under the present circumstances, is no longer forthcoming.

It is possible to delay this threatening collapse of the German economy for several months.

300–400,000 tons of raw steel per month is 10 per cent of the raw steel production available in spring 1944. The output which could still be achieved in January, February, and March was considerably higher than absolutely necessary given the limitations of this raw

[1] Ibid., p. 3.

steel output. So, therefore, armaments production in January, February and March was solely *the continuation* of a final process of manufacture of an earlier output on a higher basis.

The actual production figures corresponding to the present raw steel output will only amount to a fraction of the January output.

After the loss of Upper Silesia German armament *will no longer be even remotely in a position to meet the requirements of the front and the demands for new lists of equipment. The material superiority of the enemy can therefore no longer be balanced by the bravery of our soldiers.*[1]

Speer had said that the battle for the Ruhr was a battle for the existence of the Reich.[2] This proved to be no exaggeration. Even though the coal-supply crisis of November was partly circumvented, the problem returned in a worse form in March. There is no doubt that the failure of German coal supplies caused by bombing and the failure of steel production, in part a result of the breakdown in coal supplies, were primary factors in Germany's defeat.

Bombing contributed to a minor extent also in Germany's failure to solve her manpower difficulties. But basically this was a problem which had persisted in various guises throughout the years of the German war economy. It played a large part in the ultimate collapse.

The solution of the problem of manpower utilization was one of the greatest achievements of the British war economy.[3] It is only by such standards that Germany can be judged. But the question is not merely what percentage of the available labour force was employed and how long it was employed for; it was a question of how efficiently this labour force was deployed throughout the economy. The female labour force was never successfully utilized, because of Hitler's views on this matter, and because of pre-war National Socialist propaganda. Against this must be set the huge quantities of foreign labour at Germany's disposal.

Apart from periodic crises due to the shortage of skilled labour, the manpower requirements of the economy were met

[1] Ibid., pp. 8–10, Speer's italics.
[2] FD 3353/45 vol. 100, Meeting of Central Planning, p. 4.
[3] C. T. Saunders, 'Manpower Distribution, 1939–45', in *The Manchester School of Economic and Social Studies*. H. M. D. Parker, *Manpower*.

by the enforced draft of foreign labourers, by longer hours of working, by greatly increased productivity and efficiency, and by a redistribution of the available labour supply. By Autumn 1944 these expedients could no longer clothe the naked truth that Germany was engaged in a struggle which, in terms of manpower, was hopelessly unequal. The constant expansion of the Armed Forces, to cope with the huge American and Russian armies directly threatening German soil, made demands on the labour force of the armaments industries which could not be met if production was to be maintained at the necessary level.

By May 1944 12,385,000 men had been drafted into the Armed Forces.[1] Of these, 3,285,000 had been lost or discharged. With the appointment of Goebbels in July 1944 as Plenipotentiary-General for Total War a new drive to mobilize all available manpower began. The monthly series of 'actions' to replace the losses of the fighting services started to impinge on armaments production. Production began to fall more rapidly from July 1944 as withdrawals of labour increased. Speer responded with plans for the better distribution of civilian and military manpower. But it was probably too late to achieve anything like this. A properly planned use of manpower was now unobtainable. Bombing, and shortages generally, were bound to create spasmodic pockets of unemployment, even in industries which had not been directly hit. Transport difficulties impeded the mobility of labour. On 12 July 1944 Speer advocated releasing between 100,000 and 150,000 soldiers from the Wehrmacht to the armaments industry.[2] On 20 July detailed plans to effect such a changeover were published by the Ministry.[3] But Hitler refused to take the bait, and Goebbel's demands went unchecked.

On 25 July the call-up of 200,000 men from war industry began. In September Goebbels decided to take another 100,000. By September the gaps in war industry left by the original July draft would still take another three or four weeks to fill.[4] Even the Gauleiters believed that by 5 October only a very small

[1] U.S.S.B.S. *Effects*, p. 35.   [2] FD 2690/45 vol. 5, Speer to Hitler, 12 July 1941.
[3] FD 2690/45 vol. 5, Speer to Hitler, 20 July 1944, p. 5.
[4] FD 2690/45 vol. 5, Speer to Hitler, 26 September, 1944, p. 5.

number could be called up, and by 25 October perhaps 401,000 in all. The Speer Ministry felt that even this was too high. Time was needed to train replacements for skilled and semi-skilled workmen. Speer wrote to Hitler

Armaments and war production can release some 60,000 men for call-up up by 25.10.1944, of which 5,000 students and 16,000 'ticket-of-leave' men can come under the call-up some 14 days earlier. Up to 15 November 1944 a further 40,000 UK-graded men can be drafted.

A call-up of 100,000 KV-graded men from the armaments industry in the next few days is, even in the opinion of the Gauleiters, impossible without a severe interruption of production.[1]

Having made his protest, Speer set off on an inspection tour of the bombed areas of the Ruhr and Rhineland. He returned seven days later to find that Hitler, while he had modified Goebbels' demands, had persisted in his policy. The draft had been ordered for 14 October, eleven days earlier than Speer's estimate of the earliest possible date. The numbers had been lowered from 100,000 to 60,000, but Speer was not to be allowed to include in the quota either technical students or ticket-of-leave men. On 2 October he wrote to Bormann to say that the compromise was useless since it would still incapacitate the armaments industry.[2] If the ticket-of-leave men were to be recalled at the same time as the new quota was drafted, this would mean a double loss of skilled labour, since most of the ticket-of-leave men were skilled workmen employed in aircraft factories. The following day Speer lodged a more formal protest with Hitler.

As the Minister responsible for armaments and war production I must, after having consulted my departmental heads, and according to my duty, make it quite clear that a break will occur in weapons production for the front because of this draft, and, at the same time, the programme increases which have been forecast will be impossible.[3]

The armaments industry was running at its full production capacity and any further large-scale disturbance would inevitably bend the production-curve downwards. The 30,000 UK-graded men from the Reichs railways, whom Speer had hoped to

[1] Ibid., p. 2.   [2] FD 2690/45 vol. 5, Speer to Bormann, 2 October 1944.
[3] FD 2690/45 vol. 5, Speer to Hitler, 3 October 1944, p. 2.

secure as replacements for the men he was losing, were also to be called up. This would be bound to cause serious transport difficulties anyway. Speer repeated his original recommendations on overall manpower distribution and reduced the situation to its simplest terms by asking Hitler to decide whether the production of weapons or the number of soldiers was the most important need at that moment. But the indisputable fact was that Germany must now choose. There was no time to recover from earlier mistakes. It was no longer possible to increase the size of the Armed Forces and increase weapons production at the same time.

Between February 1942 and January 1945, 687,000 UK-graded men were taken out of the armaments industry and other essential war industries by special drafts. 254,000 of these were drafted after 1 August 1944.[1] During this same period one and a half million apprentices, who, having completed their term of apprenticeship, would have become skilled workmen, were lost to industry because of the draft. By November 1944 the reserves available for draft, at no matter what sacrifice, were tiny. On 1 November there were 448,000 UK-graded men within the age limits of military service.[2] Some of these were not under Speer's jurisdiction. Some were in occupations exempted by special decree, front-line members of the *Organisation Todt*, or dock-workers. 130,000 were considered too essential to draft even by Hitler. Speer suggested a further solution in November whereby whenever momentary pockets of unemployment occurred due to bombing the workmen involved would be drafted on a sort of reversed ticket-of-leave system, until production was ready to start again. Such periods of service could be as short as a fortnight. Such a plan is a remarkable testimony to the manpower difficulties facing the Reich!

Before November the case had already been decided against the Ministry of Armaments and Munitions. By October Hitler had become convinced that guns were now less important than that every man should fight for his country. On 18 October the announcement establishing the Volkssturm was promulgated.[3] This virtually marked the end of civilian status in the Reich.

[1] FD 2690/45 vol. 5, Speer to Hitler, 6 December 1944, p. 1.
[2] Ibid., p. 2.   [3] FD 1260/45, 'Der deutsche Volkssturm', passim.

All males between sixteen and sixty would now become soldiers. Every man was put under military law. Every able man was now liable to, and obliged to undergo, some form of military training.

The levies would be led on the district level by the Party, but in action would come under the Wehrmacht. The only large class of people exempted were those already in the Armed Forces, but a very small number of people in vital war work would receive a Z-card.[1] Such a card, issued from their place of work and approved by the district Armaments Inspectorate, indicated the extent of their availability for Volkssturm service. But it never carried exemption from training, only some form of mitigation of the most arduous and distant duties. The situation was made worse by the fact that eligibility for Z-cards was decided in the first instance by the Gauleiters,[2] who thus could decide the total number of armaments workers to receive partial exemption.

The effect of such wholesale disturbance on the labour force was disastrous. Labour mobility, never more necessary, was drastically restricted. Factories did not know how many of their skilled workmen would be free to report at any particular time. The Gauleiters screwed down the allocation of Z-cards as tightly as possible.[3] Manpower for the Armed Forces had become the sole criterion. In such circumstances it could only be expected that armaments production would fall continuously, as indeed it did until the final surrender.

If the manpower problem was as potent a cause of Germany's failure as Allied bombing, the effect of territorial losses should also be reckoned on the same level of importance. The Reich had followed a policy of, as far as possible, keeping the essential war production within the frontiers of Germany proper. This had made German industry very heavily dependent on imports of labour and raw materials, and, to a lesser extent, consumer goods and foodstuffs. The process of adjustment as these territories were lost was a painful one.[4] Nor was the problem solely one of physical reconquest by the Allies. As it became

[1] Zuteilungskarte.   [2] Ibid., pp. 15–17.   [3] Ibid., p. 13.
[4] *Hitlers Lagebesprechungen*, p. 231, 20 May 1943, 'The retention of the Balkans is truly decisive for us, etc.' See also p. 122, 1 February 1943.

clear that Germany was losing the war, the reluctance of neutrals to supply her increased correspondingly.

In particular this was the case with the 10,000,000 tons of iron ore which Germany imported from Sweden. Such a quantity could not be foregone. Even in 1943 when Sweden had expressed its willingness to continue the supply of iron ore to Germany in 1944 Speer was not convinced that Germany would be able to obtain the full ten million tons. The chief worries were the low phosphoric value of the German ores and the necessity to adjust German industry so that a sudden alteration or cessation of supply would not cause too big a drop in production.[1] The Swedish ores were much richer in phosphorus content than the native German or Lorraine ores and therefore very important for armaments steel manufacture. If imports in 1944 were unattainable, or could only be obtained in return for quantities of war equipment too great for Germany to export, the decrease in overall steel production would be severe. But in particular this would be the case with Thomas steel and Siemens-Martin steel, the twin bases of all armaments output.

This impending fear was present behind all discussions of armaments increases in 1944. On 1 May 1944, after the decree establishing top priority for tanks had been decided on, the Führer gave voice to this fear, and tried to start the development of uneconomical German ores to replace Swedish imports.

Since, in that respect, it must be taken into account that iron ore supplies from abroad may presently decrease or even stop altogether, the Führer desires that an extensive special action, taking effect immediately should be instituted to increase iron production at the Erzberg.[2]

The Thomas steel production of greater Germany and the occupied territories was 1,290,000 tons monthly. Once supplies from the Lorraine *minette* ore field had ceased, together with

---

[1] FD 3353/45 vol. 215, Speer Ministry, 'Die Bedeutung der Zufuhr an schwedischen und norwegischen Eisenerzen', 11 November 1943. (The document is incomplete, as also is the copy in FD 2690/45 vol. 13, which has been 'edited' by the addition of some information from FD 3353/45 vol. 220, a quite different document of the same date.)

[2] FD 3353/45 vol. 59, pp. 3/4, Führerkonferenz, 30 April 1944.

Scandinavian supplies, and production in the Saar and Luxembourg had been lost to Germany, the maximum possible output of Thomas steel would be 450,000 tons monthly.[1] This figure allowed for maximum production in the Ruhr, Central Germany, Silesia, the Protectorate, and the Ostmark. In these areas the remaining stocks would be enough theoretically to sustain production until April 1946 at the same level. In fact this level, although it could, in theory, be sustained for so long, was so low as drastically to reduce the output of certain specialized armaments steels. Once Silesia and the Ruhr were lost no amount of stocks of iron ore could prevent a production collapse.

An examination of the picture with regard to Siemens-Martin steel confirms the picture. Stocks of low-phosphorus-content ore were 1,900,000 tons in September 1944; in the Ruhr, Central Germany, Silesia, and the Protectorate 1,500,000 tons of Siemens-Martin steel and electro-steel could be manufactured from these stocks.[2] This was a drop of 120,000 tons monthly in the output of the most specialized steels, compared to the former production of Greater Germany and the occupied territories. But once the Ruhr and Silesia were eliminated a 35 per cent fall in the output of these steels, which had not been expected until September 1945, set in much earlier. The special measures ordered at the Erzberg could produce only 16,500 tons daily.[3]

From Autumn 1944 onwards Germany was able to use only the smallest fraction of the low-phosphorus-content Lorraine ore while, at the same time, deliveries of high-phosphorus-content Swedish ores fell steadily behind. In 1945 Germany was unable to manufacture steel at all from Swedish ore. The fall in German steel production was most severe in open-hearth and Thomas steels because of the failure of the raw material supply. Her Bessemer steel output fell less drastically, but it was of less use to the war economy.

Stocks of non-ferrous metals were generally sufficient at the end of the war to have sustained German armaments production for several months further. There is one exception, and it is an

[1] FD 3353/45 vol. 211, Speer to Hitler, 5 September 1944, p. 12.
[2] Ibid., p. 13.   [3] Ibid., p. 14.

important one, to this generalization. Stocks of chrome were chronically short. Principally this was because they were dangerously situated, many being held at the mining source in the Balkans. The largest stocks were in Albania, rivalled closely by the undelivered chrome accumulating in Turkish ports.[1] Armour-plate production was dependent on chrome. It was the base of all alloy-steels for armament. Without it no highly-developed armaments industry could function. Withdrawal from the Balkans left Germany with five and a half months' stocks in November 1943.[2] These were supplemented by later rescues of large stockpiles in Macedonia and Albania. But the abandonment of the Balkans meant an overwhelming loss in new production. The decrease of Germany's chromium supply could not be described as being an important cause of her economic collapse. But it illustrates how the loss of her territorial area limited her possibilities. The accumulation of such minor shortages meant that Germany's situation became increasingly hopeless.

The last general survey of the German economy made during the war was that made in January 1945, a survey of production for 1944. This dramatically reveals how little the German economy could bear the loss of the western industrial areas.[3] Steel production plans had envisaged an output of 37,200,000 tons of crude steel in 1944. The output of the first quarter had almost reached target.[4] In the last quarter it was 3,960,000 tons. The loss of the Ruhr made the catastrophe complete.

One cause remains to be considered for Germany's economic breakdown, the opposition which sprang up on policy between Hitler and Speer. Hitler seems to have believed that if his Reich were to be borne to defeat, then Germany itself should be obliterated. Germany was no longer worthy of the Führer. If it were no longer possible to halt the enemy advance Germany should be devastated before the oncoming troops. The instru-

---

[1] FD 3353/45 vol. 221, 12 November 1943, 'Die Legierungsmetalle in der Rüstung und die Bedeutung der Chrom-Zufuhren aus dem Balkan und der Türkei'.
[2] Ibid., p. 7.
[3] FD 3353/45 vol. 212, 27 January 1945.
[4] It was 9,180,000 tons, ibid., p. 2.

ment of this destruction would be the Speer Ministry. Speer, however, convinced that the war was lost, decided that the best possible arrangements should be made for the future. At the very least the basic economic services and supplies, on which the lives of the German people depended, must not be destroyed, but preserved to make the peace more bearable.

Consequently, by acting through the trustworthy people in his Ministry he tried to modify the proposed scorched earth (*Zerstörung*) policy to one of paralysis (*Lähmung*). Scorched earth involved the complete destruction of factories and power plant; paralysis involved taking away and burying certain vital parts. In favour of the modified policy it could be argued to Hitler that if the territory were reconquered from the Allies, the economic life of the area could be started again more efficiently.[1] This argument proved momentarily successful and on 18 August Hitler gave it his consent.[2]

By September the atmosphere in Berlin had changed. On returning from a tour of inspection on 14 September, Speer found that his Ministry had been issued with instructions on a scorched earth policy, instructions which it was to transmit to all its agencies, although the actual work of destruction was to be carried out by the Gauleiters. The following day Speer drew up a telegram to all the western Gauleiters and sent it to Bormann with a request that it be forwarded. The telegram explained that the areas must eventually be reoccupied, therefore it was necessary to avoid all far-reaching acts of destruction and evacuation. Indeed, no factory evacuation would be countenanced unless the output of the factory was more than 50 per cent of the entire national output of its product. Transport facilities were scarcely available for evacuation. Nor were there sufficient sites elsewhere in Germany. It would be more advantageous to continue production on the same site until the last possible moment. In general the principle to be followed should be that of carefully labelling and removing essential electrical parts and either burying them or taking them to another part of the Reich.[3] Bormann could hardly refuse to

[1] Speer Report No. 7, p. 4.
[2] FD 3353/45 vol. 69, p. 3, Führerkonferenz, 21 August 1944.
[3] FD 4734/45, Speer, 'Verbrannte Erde', p. 2.

transmit such a telegram, but it is significant that Hitler altered the wording of the first sentence. It read in the original,

The Führer has laid it down that he can effect within a short time the recovery of the territories at present lost.[1]

Amended by Hitler it read,

The recovery of part of the territories which have been lost for the time being in the West is no longer out of the question.[2]

On 19 September Speer informed industrialists that if paralysis were carried out prematurely, those concerned would be blamed, but they would not be blamed if they gave their orders too late and no paralysis was effected.[3] From September 1944 until March 1945 the Speer Ministry devoted a great deal of administrative energy to frustrating Hitler's ends.

Speer was privately convinced that the war was lost. To make his opinions public was a different matter, and it was not until 30 January 1945 that he put them before Hitler.

Therefore it is a matter of estimating with certainty the final collapse of the German economy in four to eight weeks. . . . After this collapse the war can no longer be pursued militarily.[4]

Whatever Hitler's private opinion the only effect of Speer's memorandum was to weaken his position still further. On 15 March Speer submitted a memorandum in the same vein; its implication was that the war was over. The immediate result was a violent quarrel between Speer and Hitler on 18 March. It may well be that only their long-buried personal friendship saved Speer from an equally immediate punishment.

Once he believed the situation to be hopeless Hitler could not be restrained from the complete destruction of what was left of the German economy. The Führer-Command of 19 March ordered the total destruction of all aspects of German economic life. Hitler had said to Speer, in their quarrel, that

---

[1] Ibid., p. 9.
[2] Ibid., p. 11.
[3] Speer Ministry circular, ibid., p. 13, 19 September 1944.
[4] FD 2690/45 vol. 6, 'Zur Rüstungslage Februar–März 1945', 30 January 1945.

if the war was lost the people would be lost as well. It was not necessary even to consider the fundamentals necessary for life to be continued on its most primitive level. It was better to destroy even these things.[1]

From the promulgation of this decree Speer abandoned all pretence of carrying out directives from the centre and set himself to preserve as much as possible of German economic life. Tommy-guns and pistols were distributed to the managerial staff of the most important works threatened with destruction. Under the pretence of increasing the amount of explosive available for ammunition a complete ban was put on the production of all explosive which might possibly get into 'civilian' use. Engineers in charge of power stations were issued with weapons. It was not possible to carry on such activities for long without repercussions.

On 28 March Speer was summoned to Führer Headquarters. Hitler accused him of defeatism and recommended that he should leave his post. For the events of that day and the following we have largely to rely on Speer's own evidence. This, briefly, is that he refused to resign, again told Hitler that the war was lost, was given twenty-four hours to change his mind, but refused to retract. The upshot is more certain, and perhaps throws some doubt on Speer's version of the events of March 28–29. On 30 March detailed instructions were given for the implementation of the Führer-Command of 19 March, and execution of the work of destruction was transferred from the Gauleiters to the Speer Ministry.

Whatever passed in those two days Speer's policy had not changed. The scorched earth orders were thus transmitted from the Speer Ministry with a series of detailed instructions modifying them so far that they were in fact Speer's original policy of paralysis. That the Speer Ministry's modifications to the decree found favour with manufacturers can scarcely be questioned. The decree of 30 March can be found with the instructions from the Speer Ministry on the same date, attached to a report by a works manager of Eugen Grill G.m.b.H. to the directors. The manager's report shows that even the Speer

---

[1] FD 4734/45, loc. cit., p. 46. This collection should be used with care. Speer may have adapted many of the original documents to help his defence.

Ministry's instructions had been watered down, so that the whole plant was preserved virtually intact.[1]

What effect did this period of disagreement have? Speer calculated that between January and May 1945 he committed about sixty separate acts of high treason.[2] The main concern of the Speer Ministry eventually was to thwart Hitler's policy. This collapse of the centralized economic machinery was all the more severe because of the position of Speer himself. The Speer Ministry deserved its title for it was dependent on the personality and capability of the Minister. It was the impulse which Speer continually gave to the machinery which was responsible for so many of its most remarkable achievements. It was that lack of impulse which at the end made itself felt. Even by 30 January Speer had publicly stated that he believed the war lost. Privately he was convinced before this date. It is difficult to believe this did not also play its part in Germany's collapse. Certainly, in the geographical fragmentation of the Third Reich, this breakdown of unified control, in what had hitherto been the most powerful central Ministry, must have had great influence.

So complex was the working of the German economy that its collapse was equally complex. From July 1944 to May 1945 the German economy was tried with so many stresses applied from different directions that it is impossible to say which was the heaviest stress and which caused the final break. Nor is it entirely reasonable to separate the causes of this collapse from each other. The supply of labour, for instance, has been considered separately from the effects of bombing; yet great numbers of men were needed to clear away rubble left by air-raids, men who would otherwise have been employed in industry. But to the question, 'What caused the collapse of the German economy?' an answer in very general terms can be attempted.

Firstly the direct interference of the Allies in the working of the German economy was very important. Although certain aspects of the strategic air offensive were not as successful as the

---

[1] FD 3138/45, Eugen Gill G.m.b.H., letter from works manager to proprietor, 4 April, 1945.

[2] Speer Report No. 7, p. 11. W. Baumbach, *Zu Spät?*, pp. 264 ff., purports to give a curious example.

Allies hoped, the attacks on synthetic oil supplies and on transport facilities drastically reduced supplies of oil, coal, and steel to the economy. The effect of bombing means of communication was to emphasize the inherent weakness of Germany's heavy dependence on the Ruhr area. By Autumn 1944 the insufficiency of German manpower in a war where she was heavily outnumbered became very evident. Nor was the labour force mobilized to the best advantage. After Autumn 1944 Germany was involved in a perpetual manpower crisis; there could be no longer any compromise between the needs of the Armed Forces and the needs of the armaments industry. These problems were all aggravated by the constant loss of territory, firstly of occupied territories, and secondly of territory within the Reich frontiers. The loss of the European *Wirtschaftsraum* which Hitler had originally aimed for was a grievous blow. Once the Ruhr and Silesia had been lost no proper war economy was possible. To all these causes must be added the final change of mind of Speer himself. The Speer Ministry had controlled the German war economy with increasing authority and increasing efficiency for almost three years; its abdication from this position gave the final push to a tottering system.

AFTERMATH AND CONCLUSION

At the trials of the Nazi War Criminals in Nürnberg Albert Speer was acquitted of complicity in the organization of slave labour. He was found guilty of helping to wage aggressive war against other powers and was sentenced to twenty years imprisonment. At the trial he gave evidence which helped to condemn other leading figures in the régime. He was frank about his own motives, and tried earnestly to convince the other prisoners that their defence should be contrition. He brought into captivity with him many of the most valuable documentary records we now have relating to wartime Germany. He showed no indication of retaining any of his former National Socialist views. He is still in Spandau prison.

The separation of duties between the Speer Ministry and the Office of the Plenipotentiary-General for Labour meant that Sauckel was responsible for drawing the reserves of foreign labour into Germany. Sauckel was sentenced to death and executed for this offence 'against humanity'. Since his incarceration Speer has shown no inclination to comment further on his wartime role. It is possible that after his release from Spandau further light may be shed on some of the more puzzling events of his period of office. But twenty years in gaol may have changed the man and the picture.

There are three roughly-defined stages in the history of German war production. The first, continuing from peacetime to the winter of 1941–2, is the period of Blitzkrieg economics. Germany's economy was geared for small-scale quick wars which would not unduly disturb her civilian standard of life. This phase was ended by the Führer-Command, *Rüstung 1942* of 10 January 1942. From that point onwards, Germany tried to avoid the logical consequences of a war against powers economically stronger than herself by pinning her faith in qualitative superiority. This second phase where Germany was trying to combat her opponents' mass-production resources by the superior quality of her armaments, was closed by the *Konzentrationserlass* of 19 June 1944. From that point onwards Germany pinned her hopes on mass-production of the weapons she already had, and in an inflated Army, in the hope of making one last throw for survival.

This last phase quickly became coincident with declining overall levels of production and an economic collapse which speeded the end of the war.

Within this general framework it can be said with certainty that Germany's prolonged resistance was partly due to the great ability of Todt and Speer. On the most basic economic level the war was lost for Germany once Russia and the United States would only accept 'unconditional surrender'. It is within this framework that the work of Speer must be viewed.

APPENDICES

1. Wagenführ's Index of Armaments Production[1]

Time	Total prod.	Weapons	Tanks	Motor vehicles	Aeroplanes	Ships	Munitions	Powder	Explosive
1941	98	106	81	—	97	110	102	96	103
1942	142	137	130	120	133	142	166	129	132
1943	222	234	330	138	216	182	247	200	191
1944	277	348	536	110	277	157	306	212	226
1942									
Jan.	103	98	93	108	112	90	98	103	101
Feb.	97	102	107	93	88	111	102	97	99
March	129	111	80	129	151	109	115	111	123
April	133	122	129	123	135	162	124	108	125
May	135	150	152	125	133	113	144	116	141
June	144	125	122	137	131	165	173	129	149
July	153	148	122	131	145	113	177	132	138
Aug.	153	135	134	123	140	136	201	134	122
Sept.	155	149	131	105	142	133	202	160	131
Oct.	154	150	144	116	133	134	209	151	147
Nov.	165	155	146	109	134	202	222	148	153
Dec.	181	195	199	135	155	187	229	153	150
1943									
Jan.	182	169	154	128	172	190	215	168	176
Feb.	207	185	169	132	227	164	230	184	169
March	216	216	210	168	205	233	239	185	200
April	215	212	289	145	216	185	229	194	169
May	232	235	465	144	211	207	245	205	191
June	226	238	340	161	233	208	230	200	199
July	229	238	367	146	236	163	238	214	192
Aug.	224	240	328	129	228	158	245	200	189
Sept.	234	260	405	128	222	191	259	201	194
Oct.	242	269	454	133	237	171	265	216	206
Nov.	231	264	364	122	216	168	282	219	211
Dec.	222	280	415	116	186	140	288	208	198

[1] *Die Deutsche Industrie im Kriege 1939–45*, pp. 178–81. Planungsamt: Indexziffern der Deutschen Rüstungsendfertigung.

Time	Total prod.	Weapons	Tanks	Motor vehicles	Aeroplanes	Ships	Munitions	Powder	Explosive
1944									
Jan.	241	274	438	142	232	140	281	204	208
Feb.	231	284	460	122	186	170	303	219	234
March	270	301	498	133	262	153	314	226	263
April	274	320	527	121	285	127	302	230	254
May	285	337	567	126	295	152	301	242	276
June	297	361	580	133	321	107	—	223	276
July	322	384	589	117	367	139	319	209	267
Aug.	297	382	558	116	308	141	323	224	182
Sept.	301	377	527	84	310	184	335	219	175
Oct.	273	372	516	79	255	217	321	205	205
Nov.	268	375	571	78	274	124	307	173	201
Dec.	263	408	598	63	224	233	263	166	178
1945									
Jan.	227	284	557	60	231	164	226	162	128

January–February 1942 = 100.

2. Indices of weapons and ammunition production, monthly, September 1939–December 1941[1]

Time	Weapons	Ammunition
1939		
September		90
October		58
November	quarterly average 63	83
December		82
1940		
January		74
February	quarterly average 68	86
March		86
April		106
May	quarterly average 79	120
June		149
July		178
August	quarterly average 83	127
September		112
October		103
November	quarterly average 86	105
December		98
1941		
January	88	99
February	120	112
March	114	105
April	117	108
May	114	104
June	123	107
July	126	99
August	114	109
September	88	91
October	95	93
November	91	100
December	83	92

January–February 1942 = 100.

[1] Planungsamt: Indexziffern der Deutschen Rüstungsendfertigung, U.S.S.B.S., *Effects of Strategic Bombing on the German War Economy*, p. 283.

BIBLIOGRAPHY

1. Primary Sources

This book is based mostly on unpublished documentary evidence which is at present in the archives of the Air Historical Branch of the Air Ministry in London. A lot of the material is available for consultation in the National Archives at Alexandria, Virginia, U.S.A. The Committee for the Study of War Documents of the American Historical Association is preparing catalogues of some of this material, which are published by the General Services Administration of The National Archives and Records Service. I have chosen to refer to my sources by the system of reference in use in the hand catalogue of the Air Historical Branch, where they can all be found by their 'FD' numbers.

The most important of the Air Ministry collections is, perhaps, that known collectively as the 'Speer Documents'. These comprise a large part of the records of the *Reichsministerium für Bewaffnung und Munition*. Their origins are interesting. When the Minister, Albert Speer, surrendered to the Allies at Flensburg he brought into captivity with him a 'bulging briefcase' containing a large collection of valuable documentary evidence on the last few months of the German war economy. This collection has become known as the 'Flensburg Documents'.

Two other collections are also included in the Speer Documents. These are the 'Hamburg Documents' and the 'Herford Documents'.

Generally the Flensburg series is concerned with the overall work of the Speer Ministry but it has a particularly valuable reference to the closing months of Germany's war effort. The Hamburg series is much larger and equally valuable. It is distinguished among the captured archives in its information on the actual making of top-level planning. The whole series of conferences between Speer, from the moment he became Armaments Minister, and the Führer is contained in the Hamburg series. The reports of the Führer-Conferences were intended for Speer's own use after the event. For 1945 the Conferences are less valuable because less frequent, and they are to some extent replaced as a guide to top-level decisions by the aide-memoires contained in the Flensburg series. Apart from the *Führer-Konferenzen* the Hamburg Documents contain the minutes of *Zentrale Planung*. The rest of the collection is very miscellaneous.

The Herford Documents, also available in the Air Ministry, are a large collection of a much more heterogeneous nature than the Flensburg or Hamburg Documents. Among their more valuable features are all the routine administrative circulars of the Ministry and all the decrees issued by the Minister himself. There is, besides, a curious day-to-day chronicle of the working of the Ministry for 1943. Most, but not all, of the correspondence of the Ministry of Armaments comes in the Herford Documents. Some can be found in the other two series. Where I have referred to the Herford Documents I have tried to give as full details as possible of the reference.

These three series of Documents by no means exhaust all the material relating to the *Reichsministerium für Bewaffnung und Munition*. Some of the most valuable evidence can be found in the 'Saur Documents'. Otto Saur was Speer's Deputy as Minister of Armaments and War Production, and the collection is named after the reports which Saur drew up later and which are included therein. One of the weaknesses of the records of the *Reichsministerium für Bewaffnung und Munition* is the scattered and incomplete nature of some of the statistical evidence. Apart from this they are among the most revealing of the captured archives.

Second in order of importance are the documents emanating from *Wirtschafts- und Rüstungsamt* of *Oberkommando der Wehrmacht*. These are the principal source of information on German economic strategy in the years before the *Reichsministerium für Bewaffnung und Munition* became important. They do not have the top-level value of the Speer Documents, but they contain a great deal of valuable statistical material, and correspondence.

With the papers of the *Wirtschafts- und Rüstungsamt* should be put the personal correspondence of General Georg Thomas, and also his memoranda of conversations. In this collection too is the manuscript of Thomas's book, 'Gründlage für eine Geschichte der deutschen Wehr- und Rüstungswirtschaft', much used by the Bombing Survey.

Much less complete, and not so valuable, are the papers and correspondence emanating from the *Reichswirtschaftsministerium*. There is information on other subjects to be found there however.

Of considerable value for this book were the papers of certain private firms. The Messerschmitt Papers are the most revealing of these, but the Gerhard Fiesler Werke papers are also of great interest in the history of German aircraft production.

Finally there is a certain amount of information on the operations of the *Vierjahresplan*, but not much of any new significance.

To supplement this documentary evidence I have drawn on the interrogations of captured prisoners after the War which are also available in the Air Ministry. Such interrogations have been referred to individually. The best, and best-known, of these Interrogation Reports are those of Albert Speer. But I have also used the interrogations of many of the officials of the Speer Ministry and of those industrialists who were interrogated. The interrogations were made under the auspices of the Field Information Agency, Technical Branch, of the Army of Occupation. At first they were general and exploratory. When it was realized that certain prisoners had invaluable personal experiences and records the general interrogations gave place to detailed studies and reports written by the prisoners and based on questions submitted by various agencies. Unfortunately in the competition to extract information from the prisoners, too much time was given to those with influence rather than those with something useful to ask. Consequently it is important to use the interrogation evidence with care. It is not too difficult to identify the interrogators who persisted in asking leading questions and to disregard the results obtained in that way. The written reports are much more valuable than the interrogations. And some of the interrogations are better not used at all.

Apart from these unpublished sources, all of which are available in the Air Ministry archives, certain published sources have obvious value for the economic history of the War. Much the most comprehensive is the not very widely obtainable work of the United States Strategic Bombing Survey. There are 208 volumes of their work for the European Theatre, and of these Nos. 4, 60, 64, 93, 95–99, 134b–199 (except 138, 139 and 188) are classified as secret. In the Pacific Theatre, Nos. 78, 91, 94, 95, 98–105 and 108 are classified. The manuscript of the book *Aufstieg und Niedergang der Deutschen Rüstung* written by R. Wagenführ, Head of Planungsamt in the Speer Ministry during the War, also practically qualifies as an original source. It has since been published by Deutsches Institut für Wirtschaftsforschung as *Die Deutsche Industrie im Kriege 1939–1945* (Berlin, 1954). Other sources of especial value are:

Trial of the Major War Criminals before the International Military Tribunal (Nürnberg, 1947–1948—*Documents in Evidence*).
Führer Conferences on Naval Affairs, 1939–1945. Also published in 'Brassey's Naval Annual', 1948.

Documents on German Foreign Policy 1918–1945, Series D (London, H.M.S.O.).
Geschichte des zweiten Weltkrieges in Dokumenten, edited by M. Freund (Freiburg and München, 1955–).
Hitlers Lagebesprechungen, edited by H. Heiber (Stuttgart, 1962).
Kriegstagebuch des Oberkommandos der Wehrmacht 1940–1945, edited by H. Greiner, P. E. Schramm (Frankfurt-am-Main, 1963–).
The Goebbels Diaries, edited by L. Lochner (New York, 1948).
Hitler's Secret Conversations (New York, 1953).

2. Secondary Sources

(Many of the secondary sources on the subject of German economic activity and strategy in the Second World War contain documentary material not otherwise available.)

Bibliographical Works

Bibliothek für Zeitgeschichte, Bücherschau der Weltkriegsbücherei.
F. Herre and H. Auerbach, Bibliographie zur Zeitgeschichte und zum zweiten Weltkrieg für die Jahre 1945–1950. Institut für Zeitgeschichte (München, 1955).
Vierteljahrshefte für Zeitgeschichte, bibliographical supplements.

Periodicals

A certain amount of not very reliable information can be gleaned from periodicals published in Germany in wartime. Most importantly,

Mitteilungsblatt der Gesellschaft für europäische Wirtschaftsplanung und Grossraumwirtschaft.
Der Vierjahresplan-Zeitschrift für nationalsozialistische Wirtschaftspolitik.
Die Deutsche Volkswirtschaft, nationalsozialistischer Wirtschaftsdienst.

A summary of the material appearing in German periodicals in war time can be found in the series published regularly from 1939 to 1945 in The Economic Journal, 'The German War Economy in the Light of Economic Periodicals'. It is, as might be suspected, very slight and often the information is misleading.

General

ANDIC, S. P. and VEVERKA, J., 'The Growth of Government Expenditure in Germany since the Unification', Finanzarchiv, vol. 23, 1964.
ARNTZ, H., 'Die Menschenverluste im zweiten Weltkrieg', Bilanz des zweiten Weltkrieges (Oldenburg and Hamburg, 1953).
— 'Die Menschenverluste der beiden Weltkriege' Universitas, vol. 8, 1953.

BIBLIOGRAPHY

ARON, R., *Histoire de Vichy 1940–1944* (Paris, 1954).

ASSMANN, K., *Deutsche Schicksalsjahre* (Wiesbaden, 1950).

— *Deutsche Seestrategie in zwei Weltkriegen* (Heidelberg, 1957).

BACKE, H., *Um die Nahrungsfreiheit Europas, Weltwirtschaft oder Grossraum* (Leipzig, 1942).

BALOGH, T., 'The Economic Background to Germany', *International Affairs*, vol. 18, no. 2, 1939.

BAUDHUIN, F., *L'Economie belge sous l'occupation, 1940–1944* (Brussels, 1945).

BAUDIN, L., *Esquisse de l'économie française sous l'occupation allemande* (Paris, 1945).

BAUMBACH, W., *Zu spät? Aufstieg und Untergang der deutschen Luftwaffe* (München, 1949).

BECK, E. R., *Verdict on Schacht*, Florida State University Studies, 20 (Tallahassee, 1955).

BENSEL, R., *Die deutsche Flottenpolitik von 1933 bis 1939*, Beiheft 3, *Marine-Rundschau*, 1958.

BETTELHEIM, C., *L'Economie allemande sous le Nazisme* (Paris, 1946).

BIDWELL, P. W., 'Our Economic Warfare', *Foreign Affairs*, April, 1942.

BILLIG, J., 'Le rôle des prisonniers de guerre dans l'économie du troisième Reich', *Revue de l'histoire de la deuxième guerre mondiale*, vol. 10, 1960.

BIRKENFELD, W., *Der synthetische Treibstoff 1933–1945* (Göttingen, 1963).

BLEICHER, A., *Elsass und Lothringen wirtschaftlich gesehen* (Berlin, 1942).

BRACHER, K. D., SAUER, W. and SCHULTZ, G., *Die Nationalsozialistische Machtergreifung* (Köln, 1960).

BRANDT, K., *The German Fat Plan and its Economic Setting*, Stanford University Food Research Institute, Fats and Oils Studies, no. 6 (Palo Alto, 1938).

BRANDT, K. et al., *The Management of Agriculture and Food in Fortress-Europe*, Stanford University Food Research Institute (Stanford, California, 1953).

BRÄUTIGAM, H., *Wirtschaftssystem des Nationalsozialismus* (Berlin, 1932).

BREDOW, W., *Alfred Krupp und sein Geschlecht. Die Familie Krupp und ihr Werk 1787–1940* (Berlin, 1943).

BREGEAULT, G., *Le deuxième conflit mondial*, 2 vols (Paris, 1946–1947).

BROSZAT, M., *Der Nationalsozialismus* (Stuttgart, 1960).

— *Nationalsozialistische Polenpolitik 1939–1945*, Schriftenreihe der Vierteljahrshefte für Zeitgeschichte, 2 (Stuttgart, 1961).

BROWN, A. J., *Applied Economics* (London, 1947).

BRY, G., *Wages in Germany 1871–1945* (Princeton U.P., 1960).

BUCHHEIM, H., 'Die SS in der Verfassung des dritten Reiches', *Vierteljahrshefte für Zeitgeschichte*, vol. 2, 1955.

— *Das dritte Reich, Grundlagen und politische Entwicklung* (München, 1958).

BULLOCK, A., *Hitler, A Study in Tyranny* (London, 1952).

BURNHAM, J., *Total War* (Boston, 1943).

BUTLER, E. and YOUNG, G., *Marshal Without Glory* (London, 1951).

BUTLER, J. R. M., *Grand Strategy, vol. 2*, Official History of the Second World War, Military Series (London, H.M.S.O., 1957).

BIBLIOGRAPHY

BUTLER. R., *The Roots of National Socialism, 1783–1933* (London, 1941).

CALVOCORESSI, P., *Nuremberg* (London, 1947).

CAMPBELL, P. F., *A History of Basic Metals Price Control in World War Two* (London, 1948).

CASTELLAN, C. G., *Le réarmement clandestin du Reich, 1930–1935, vu par le 2e. Bureau de l'Etat Major Français* (Paris, 1954).

— *Choix de documents sur le Konzern Krupp et le réarmement de l'Allemagne 1918–1943* (Paris, Faculté des Lettres, thèse, March 1952).

— 'Aspect militaire de l'Anschluss', *Revue d'Histoire Moderne et Contemporaine*, vol. 1, 1954.

— 'Reichswehr et Armée Rouge, 1920–1939', J. B. DUROSELLE, *Les relations germano-soviétiques, 1933–1939* (Paris, 1954).

CÉRÉ, R., *La seconde guerre mondiale*, 1939–1945 (Paris 1947).

CHARDONNET, J., *Les conséquences économiques de la guerre 1939–1946* (Paris, 1947).

— *Une force à détruire: l'économie allemande* (Paris, 1945).

— 'L'industrie de l'essence synthétique en Allemagne durant la guerre', *Annales de Géographie*, 1947.

CHURCHILL, SIR W. S., *The Second World War*, 6 vols (London, 1948–1954).

CIANO, G., *Diario, 1939–1943*, 2 vols (Milano, 1948), trans. *Ciano's Diplomatic Diaries, 1939–1943*, ed. by H. Gibson (New York, 1946).

COLLIER, B., *The Defence of the United Kingdom*, Official History of the Second World War, Military Series (London, H.M.S.O., 1957).

COOPER, R. W., *The Nuremberg Trial* (London, 1947).

CRAVEN, W. F. and CATE, J. L., *The Army Air Forces in World War II*, 3 vols., prepared by the Office of Air History, United States Air Force (Chicago 1948–1951).

DAESCHNER, L., *Die deutsche Arbeitsfront* (München, 1934).

DAHMS, H. G., *Der zweite Weltkrieg* (Tübingen, 1960).

DALLIN, A., *German Rule in Russia, 1941–1945* (London, 1957).

DALTON, H., *Memoirs*, vol. 2, *The Fateful Years* (London, 1957).

DALUCES, G., *Le troisième Reich*, Bibliothèque Générale d'Economie Politique (Paris, 1950).

DAVIN, L., *Les finances de 1939–1945. L'Allemagne* (Paris, 1949).

DEUTSCHE BANK, *Das Sudetenland im deutschen Wirtschaftsraum* (Berlin, 1938).

DEUTSCHES INSTITUT FÜR WIRTSCHAFTSFORSCHUNG, *Die deutsche Industrie im Kriege 1939–1945* (Berlin, 1954). A published edition of the manuscript *Aufstieg und Niedergang der deutschen Wirtschaft*, written by R. WAGENFÜHR, head of Planungsamt in the Speer Ministry. The manuscript fell into the hands of the Allies at the end of the war. It was later found in the Library of Congress and edited by the Deutsches Institut für Wirtschaftsforschung. But the credit for the work goes to Wagenführ. The book is in reality a primary source compiled at the time by a civil servant.

DICKENS, G., *Bombing and Strategy. The Fallacy of Total War* (London, 1947).

DIEBEN, W., 'Die innere Reichsschuld seit 1933', *Finanzarchiv*, vol. 2, 1948–1949.

BIBLIOGRAPHY

DOMARUS, M., *Hitler. Reden und Proklamationen 1932–45*, 2 vols (Neustadt a.d. Aisch, 1962).

DÖNITZ, K. *Zehn Jahre und zwanzig Tage* (Bonn, 1958).

DORMAN, J. R., 'Hitler's Economic Mobilization', *Military Review*, no. 33, 1953–1954.

DUBAIL, R., *Une expérience d'économie dirigée. L'Allemagne nationale-socialiste* (Paris, 1961).

DUCROCQ, A., *Les armes secrètes allemandes* (Paris, 1948).

DUTTWYLER, R. E., *Der Seekrieg und die Wirtschaftspolitik des neutralen Staates* (Zürich, 1945).

EARLE, E. M., ed., *Makers of Modern Strategy; Military Thought from Macchiavelli to Hitler* (Princeton U.P., 1944).

EHRMAN, J., *Cabinet Government and War, 1890–1940* (Cambridge, 1958).

— *Grand Strategy*, vols 5 and 6, Official History of the Second World War, Military Series (London, H.M.S.O., 1956).

EINZIG, P., *Hitler's New Order in Europe* (London, 1941).

— *Economic Warfare* (London, 1940).

— *Economic Warfare 1939–1940* (London, 1941).

— 'Hitler's "New Order" in Theory and Practice', *The Economic Journal*, vol. 51, 1941.

EMESSEN, T. R., ed., *Aus Görings Schreibtisch. Ein Dokumentenfund* (Berlin, 1947).

EMMENDORFER, H., *Die geschäftliche Beziehungen der deutschen Eisen- und Stahlindustrie zur eisenschaffenden Industrie besetzter Gebiete 1939–1945* (Dissertation, University of Cologne, 1955).

ERBE, R., *Die nationalsozialistische Wirtschaftspolitik 1933–39 im Lichte der modernen Theorie* (Zürich, 1958).

ERFURTH, W., *Die Geschichte des deutschen Generalstabes von 1918 bis 1945*, Studien zur Geschichte des zweiten Weltkrieges, Arbeitskreis für Wehrforschung in Frankfurt-am-Main (Göttingen, 1957).

FACIUS, F., *Wirtschaft und Staat. Die Entwicklung der staatlichen Wirtschaftsverwaltung in Deutschland vom 17. Jahrhundert bis 1945*. Schriften des Bundesarchivs, 6 (Boppard-am-Rhein, 1959).

FISCHER, W., *Die Wirtschaftspolitik des Nationalsozialismus* (Lüneburg, 1961).

FREDE, G. and SCHUDDEKOPF, O. E., *Wehrmacht und Politik, 1933–1945*, Beiträge zum Geschichtsunterricht, vol. 29 (Braunschweig, 1953).

FREUND, M., *Der zweite Weltkrieg* (Gütersloh, 1962).

FREY, R., *Die theoretischen Grundlagen der deutschen Währungspolitik unter dem Nationalsozialismus* (Bern, 1948).

FRIEDENSBURG, F., *Die Rohstoffe und Energiequellen im neuen Europa* (Oldenburg, 1943).

FULLER, J. F. C., *The Second World War* (London, 1948).

GAFENCU, G., *Prelude to the Russian Campaign* (London, 1948).

GALLAND, A., *Die Ersten und die Letzten* (Darmstadt, 1953).

GANTENBEIN, J. W., *The Documentary Background of World War II, 1931–1941* (New York, 1948).

201

BIBLIOGRAPHY

GEORG, E., *Die wirtschaftlichen Unternehmungen der SS*, Schriftenreihe der Vierteljahrshefte für Zeitgeschichte, 7 (Stuttgart, 1962).

'GERMANICUS', *Germany, The Last Four Years* (New York, 1937).

GIESE, F. E., *Die deutsche Marine 1920 bis 1945* (Frankfurt-am-Main, 1956).

GILBERT, G. M., *Nuremberg Diary* (London, 1948).

GORDON, D. L. and DANGERFIELD, B., *The Hidden Weapon* (New York, 1947).

GÖRLITZ, W., *Der zweite Weltkrieg*, 2 vols (Stuttgart, 1951–1952).

— and QUINT, H. A., *Adolf Hitler-eine Biographie* (Stuttgart, 1952).

GREINER, H., *Die oberste Wehrmachtführung, 1939–1943* (Wiesbaden, 1951).

GRUCHMANN, L., *Nationalsozialistische Grossraumordnung*, Schriftenreihe der Vierteljahrshefte für Zeitgeschichte, 4 (Stuttgart, 1962).

GUDERIAN, H., *Errinerungen eines Soldaten* (Heidelberg, 1951).

— *Panzer-Marsch* (München, 1956).

GUILLAUME, H., *La guerre germano-soviétique 1941–1945* (Paris, 1949).

GUILLEBAUD, C. W., *The Economic Recovery of Germany* (London, 1939).

— *The Social Policy of Nazi Germany* (London, 1941).

— 'Hitler's New Economic Order for Europe', *The Economic Journal*, vol. 50, 1940.

GUNTHER, A. E., *The German War for Crude Oil in Europe 1934–1945*. Control Commission for Germany, British Section, British Oilfield Investigations, 912 Military Government (Celle, 1947), mimeographed.

GUTH, K., *Die Reichsgruppe Industrie* (Berlin, 1941).

HAGGLOF, G., *Svensk Krigshandelspolitik under andra Världskriget* (Stockholm, 1958).

HALDER, F., *Hitler als Feldherr* (München, 1949).

HALE, O. J., 'Adolf Hitler als Feldherr', *Virginia Quarterly Review*, no. 24, 1948.

HALLGARTEN, G., 'Adolf Hitler and German Heavy Industry 1931–1933', *Journal of Economic History*, no. 12, 1952.

HANCOCK, W. K. and GOWING, M. M., *The British War Economy*, Official History of the Second World War, Civil Series (London, H.M.S.O., 1949).

HANCOCK, W. K., ed., *History of the Second World War, A Statistical Digest*, Official History of the Second World War, Civil Series (London, H.M.S.O., 1951).

HARRIS, SIR A., *Bomber Offensive* (London, 1947).

LIDDELL HART, B. H., *The Other Side of the Hill* (London, 1951).

HASLUCK, E. L., *The Second World War* (London, 1948).

HEBERLE, R., *Landbevölkerung und Nationalsozialismus*, Schriftenreihe der Vierteljahrshefte für Zeitgeschichte, 6 (Stuttgart, 1963).

HEINCKEL, E., *Stürmisches Leben*, edited J. Thorwald (Stuttgart, 1953).

HILLGRUBER, A., *Hitler, König Carol und Marschall Antonescu: die deutsch-rumänischen Beziehungen, 1938–1944*, Veröffentlichungen des Instituts für europäische Geschichte (Mainz, 1949).

HINSLEY, F. H., *Hitler's Strategy* (London, 1951).

HITLER, A., *Mein Kampf*, English trans. J. Murphy (London, 1939).

— *Hitlers zweites Buch*. Ein Dokument aus dem Jahr 1928, G. L. Weinberg, Quellen und Darstellungen zur Zeitgeschichte, 7 (Stuttgart, 1961).

HOFER, W., 'Die Diktatur Hitlers bis zum Beginn des zweiten Weltkrieges', Brandt-Meyer-Just; *Handbuch der deutschen Geschichte*, vol. 4, section 4 (Konstanz, 1959).

HOOVER INSTITUTE, *French Life Under the Occupation 1940–1944*, 3 vols, Hoover Institute, Stanford University (Stanford, Cal., 1957).

HÖPKER-ASCHOFF, H., 'Währungsmanipulationen seit 1914', *Finanzarchiv*, vol. 2, 1948–1949.

HUBATSCH, W., 'Zur deutschen militärischen Memoirenliteratur des zweiten Weltkrieges', *Historische Zeitschrift*, vol. 171, 1951.

— ed., 'Das dienstliche Tagebuch des Chefs des Wehrmachtführungsamtes im OKW, Generalmajor Jodl, für den Zeitraum 13. Okt. 1939 bis zum 30. Jan. 1940', *Welt als Geschichte*, vol. 12, 1952.

— *Die deutsche Besetzung von Dänemark und Norwegen 1940*, Göttinger Beiträge für Gegenwartsfragen (Göttingen, 1952).

— *Hitlers Weisungen für die Kriegsführung* (Frankfurt-am-Main, 1962).

INSTITUT FÜR KONJUNKTURFORSCHUNG, *Rohstoffbilanz der europäischen Länder* (Berlin, 1940).

INTERNATIONAL COUNCIL FOR PHILOSOPHY AND HUMANISTIC STUDIES, *The Third Reich* (London, 1955).

INTERNATIONAL LABOUR OFFICE, *The Exploitation of Foreign Labour by Germany*, prepared by J. H. E. Fried (Montreal, 1945).

— *The Displacement of Population in Europe* (Montreal, 1943).

IRVING, D., *The Destruction of Dresden* (London, 1963).

JACK, D. J., *Studies in Economic Warfare* (London, 1940).

JACOBSEN, H.-A., *1939–45. Der zweite Weltkrieg in Chronik und Dokumenten* (Darmstadt, 1959–).

JARMAN, T. L., *The Rise and Fall of Nazi Germany* (London 1955).

KALDOR, N., 'The German War Economy', *The Review of Economic Studies*, vol. 13, 1945–1946.

KERSTEN, F., *Hitlers Krankengeschichte* (Hannover, 1947).

KESSELRING, A., *Soldat bis zum letzten Tag* (Bonn, 1953). *A Soldier's Record* (New York, 1954).

KISSEL, H., 'Der deutsche Volkssturm 1944–45', *Wehrwissenschaftliche Rundschau*, vol. 10, 1960.

KLASS, G. VON, *Die drei Ringe. Lebensgeschichte eines Industrieunternehmens* (Tübingen, 1953).

KLEIN, B. H., 'Germany's Preparation for War, a Re-examination', *American Economic Review*, 1948.

— *Germany's Economic Preparations for War* (Harvard U.P., Cambridge, Mass., 1959).

KOGON, E., *Der SS-Staat. Das System der deutschen Konzentrationslager* (5th ed., Frankfurt-am-Main, 1959).

KOLLER, K., *Der letzte Monat. Die Tagebuchaufzeichnungen des ehemaligen Generalstabschefs der deutschen Luftwaffe* (Mannheim, 1949).

KORDT, E., *Nicht aus den Akten* (Stuttgart, 1950).

KUCZYNSKI, J. and WITT, M., *The Economics of Barbarism; Hitler's new Economic Order in Europe* (London, 1942).

BIBLIOGRAPHY

— *Die Wirtschaft des deutschen Faschismus* (Paris, 1938).

— *Germany's Economic Position*, Germany To-day Special, no. 1 (London, 1939).

— *Economic Conditions under Fascism* (New York, 1945).

— *Die Bewegung der deutschen Wirtschaft von 1800 bis 1946* (Mannheim, 1948).

KUMPF, W., *Die Organization Todt im Kriege* (Oldenburg, 1953).

LAJOS, I., *Germany's War Chances as Pictured in German Official Publications* (London, 1939).

LANGE, E., *Der Reichsmarschall im Kriege* (Stuttgart, 1950).

LANTER, M., *Die Finanzierung des Krieges. Quellen, Methoden, und Lösungen seit dem Mittelalter bis Ende des zweiten Weltkrieges, 1939–1945* (Luzern, 1950).

LAUTERBACH, A. T., *Economics in Uniform* (Princeton U.P., 1943).

LEAGUE OF NATIONS, *World Economic Survey, Eleventh Year, 1942–1944* (Geneva, 1944).

LEE, A., *The German Air Force* (London, 1946).

LEEB, E., *Aus der Rüstung des Dritten Reiches. Das Heereswaffenamt, 1938–1945* Wehrtechnische Monatshefte, Beiheft 4 (Frankfurt-am-Main, 1958).

LE MASSON, H., 'Les constructions navales allemandes pendant la guerre de 1939 à 1945', *Revue Maritime*, vol. 27, July, 1948.

LENZ, F., *Zauber um Dr. Schacht* (Heidelberg, 1954).

LICHTENBERGER, H., *L'Allemagne nouvelle* (Paris, 1938).

LIESBACH, I., *Der Wandel der politischen Führungsschicht der deutschen Industrie von 1918 bis 1945* (Hannover, 1957).

LINDHOLM, R. W., 'German Finance in World War II', *The American Economic Review*, no. 37, 1947.

LÜBKE, A., *Das deutsche Rohstoffwunder* (Stuttgart, 1940).

LUDDE-NEURATH, W., *Regierung Dönitz*, Academia Georgia Augusta, Institut für Völkerrecht an der Universität Göttingen (Göttingen, 1950).

LURIE, S., *Private Investment in a Controlled Economy, Germany, 1933–1939* (New York, 1947).

LUSAR, R., *Die deutschen Waffen und Geheimwaffen des zweiten Weltkrieges und ihre Weiterentwicklung* (München, 1956).

LÜTGE, F., 'Die deutsche Kriegsfinanzierung im ersten und zweiten Weltkrieg', Beiträge zur Finanzwissenschaft und zur Geldtheorie, Festschrift für Rudolf Stucken (Göttingen, 1953).

MARTIENSSEN, A., *Hitler and his Admirals* (London, 1948).

MAU, H. and KRAUSNICK, H., *Deutsche Geschichte der jüngsten Vergangenheit, 1933–1945* (Tübingen, 1956).

MEDLICOTT, W. N., *The Economic Blockade*, 2 vols, Official History of the Second World War, Civil Series (London, H.M.S.O., 1952, 1959).

MEER, F. TER, *Die I. G. Farben Aktiengesellschaft* (Düsseldorf, 1953).

MEINCK, G., *Hitler und die deutsche Aufrüstung, 1933–1937* (Wiesbaden, 1959).

MENDELLSSOHN, P. DE, *The Nuremberg Documents* (London, 1946).

MICHAUX, T., 'Rohstoffe aus Ostasien', *Wehrwissenschaftliche Rundschau*, 1955.

MOLTMANN, G., 'Goebbels Rede zum totalen Krieg', *Vierteljahrshefte für Zeitgeschichte*, vol. 12, 1964.

MÜHLEN, N., *Die Krupps* (Frankfurt-am-Main, 1960).

MÜLLER-HILLEBRAND, B., *Das Heer 1933–1945. Entwicklung des organisatorischen Aufbaues*, vol. 1 (Darmstadt, 1954).

— 'Das Heer zwischen Westfeldzug 1940 und Feldzug gegen die Sowjetunion 1941', *Wehrwissenschaftliche Rundschau*, vol. 6, 1956.

NATHAN, O., *Nazi War Finance and Banking* (New York, 1944).

— *The Nazi Economic System. Germany's Mobilisation for War* (Duke University, N. Carolina, 1944).

NATIONAL INSTITUTE OF ECONOMIC AND SOCIAL RESEARCH, *Lessons of the British War Economy*, Economic and Social Studies, no. x (Cambridge, 1951).

NECKER, W., *Nazi Germany can't win* (London, 1939).

OXFORD UNIVERSITY INSTITUTE OF STATISTICS, *Studies in War Economics* (Oxford, 1947).

PARKER, H. M. D., *Manpower*, Official History of the Second World War, Civil Series (London, H.M.S.O., 1957).

PETERSON, E. N., *Hjalmar Schacht. For and Against Hitler. A Political-Economic Study of Germany 1923–1945* (Boston, 1954).

PLETTENBERG, M., *Guderian—Hintergründe des deutschen Schicksals 1918–1945* (Düsseldorf, 1950).

POSTAN, M. M., *British War Production*, Official History of The Second World War, Civil Series (London, H.M.S.O., 1952).

QUINT, H. A., *Die Wendepunkte des Krieges* (Stuttgart, 1950).

RADANDT, H., *Kriegsverbrecherkonzern Mansfeld. Die Rolle des Mansfeld-Konzerns bei der Vorbereitung und während des zweiten Weltkrieges* (Berlin, 1957).

RAEDER, E., *Mein Leben*, 2 vols (Tübingen, 1956–1957).

RAUSCHNING, H., *Die Revolution des Nihilismus* (Zürich, 1938).

REITLINGER, G., *The Final Solution* (London, 1953).

— *The SS: Alibi of a Nation* (London, 1956).

RIECKHOFF, H. J., *Trumpf oder Bluff? 12 Jahre deutscher Luftwaffe* (Geneva, 1945).

RITTERHAUSEN, H., 'Die deutsche Aussenhandelspolitik von 1879–1948. Eine Auseinandersetzung zwischen monopolistischen Interessen und sich anbahnender Wettbewerbsordnung in der Welt.' *Zeitschrift für die Gesamte Staatswissenschafts*, vol. 105, 1948.

ROBERTSON, E. M., *Hitler's Pre-War Policy and Military Plans, 1933–1939* (London, 1963).

ROSEN, S. M., *The Combined Boards of the Second World War. An Experiment in International Administration* (New York, 1951).

ROSSI, A., *Deux ans d'alliance germano-soviétique* (Paris, 1949).

ROUSSY de SALES, R. de, ed., *My New Order* (New York, 1941).

ROYAL INSTITUTE OF INTERNATIONAL AFFAIRS, *The World in March 1939*, Survey of International Affairs 1939–1946 (London, 1952).

— *The Economic Structure of Hitler's Europe*, Survey of International Affairs, 1939–1946 (London, 1954).

RUMPF, H., 'Die Industrie im Bombenkrieg', *Wehrwissenschaftliche Rundschau*, vol. 3, 1953.

BIBLIOGRAPHY

— *Das war der Bombenkrieg. Deutsche Städte im Feuersturm. Ein Dokumentarbericht* (Oldenburg and Hamburg, 1961).

SANT, P. T. and VICKERY, R. E., 'The food and agricultural statistics of the Reich Food Administration', *Agricultural History*, vol. 21, 1947.

SASULY, R., *I. G. Farben* (New York, 1947).

SAUNDERS, C. T., 'Manpower Distribution 1939–1945', *The Manchester School of Economic and Social Studies*, vol. XIV, no. 2, 1946.

SCHACHT, H., *Abrechnung mit Hitler* (Hamburg and Stuttgart, 1948).

— *76 Jahre meines Lebens* (Bad Wörrishofen, 1953).

SCHECHTMAN, J. B., *European Population Transfers 1939-1945* (New York, 1946).

SCHIEDER, T., 'Die Ostvertreibung als wissenschaftliches Problem', *Vierteljahrshefte für Zeitgeschichte*, vol. 8, 1960.

SCHNEIDER, E., 'Technik und Waffenentwicklung im Kriege', *Bilanz des zweiten Weltkrieges* (Oldenburg and Hamburg, 1953).

SCHÖNLEBEN, E., *Fritz Todt* (Oldenburg, 1943).

SCHRAMM, P. E., 'Die Treibstoff-Frage vom Herbst 1943 bis Juni 1944 nach dem Kriegstagebuch des Wehrmachtführungsstabes', *Mensch und Staat in Recht und Geschichte, Festschrift für K. Kraus* (Kitzingen-am-Main, 1954).

SCHULER, F., *Das Handwerk im Dritten Reich. Die Gleichschaltung und was danach folgte*, Schriften des Handwerks, no. 10 (Bad-Wörrishofen, 1951).

SCHULTZ, J., *Die letzten dreissig Tage. Aus dem Kriegstagebuch des OKW* (Stuttgart, 1951).

SCHUMACHER, E., *Geschichte des zweiten Weltkriegs* (Zürich, 1945).

SCHWADTKE, K. H., *Die deutsche Handelsflotte 1939 und ihr Schicksal* (Hamburg 1953).

SCHWEITZER, A., 'Die wirtschaftliche Wiederaufrüstung Deutschlands von 1934 bis 1936', *Zeitschrift für die gesamte Staatswissenschaft*, vol. 114, 1958.

VON KROSIGK, SCHWERIN, *Es geschah in Deutschland* (Tübingen, 1952).

— 'Wie wurde der zweite Weltkrieg finanziert?' *Bilanz des zweiten Weltkrieges* (Oldenburg and Hamburg, 1953).

SIMPSON, A. E., 'The struggle for control of the German Economy 1936–1937', *Journal of Modern History*, vol. 21, 1959.

SLESSOR, SIR J., *The Central Blue* (London, 1956).

SONNEMANN, T., *Die Wirtschaft als Kriegswaffe* (Berlin, 1941).

SPAATZ, C., 'Strategic Air Power—Fulfilment of a Concept', *Foreign Affairs*, no. 24, 1945–1946.

SPIEGEL, H. W., *The Economics of Total War* (New York, 1942).

STALEY, E., *Raw Materials in Peace and War* (New York, 1937).

STERNBERG, F., *Die deutsche Kriegsstärke* (Paris, 1938).

STOLPER, G., *German Economy, 1870–1940* (New York, 1940).

STUCKEN, R., *Deutsche Geld- und Kreditpolitik 1914–1952* (Tübingen, 1952).

STUEBEL, H., 'Die Finanzierung der Aufrüstung im Dritten Reich', *Europa-Archiv*, 6, 1951.

SWEEZY, M., *The Structure of the Nazi Economy* (Cambridge, 1951).

SYRUP, F., *Hundert Jahre staatliche Sozialpolitik 1839–1939*, edited by J. Scheuble (Stuttgart, 1957).

TAYLOR, A. J. P., *The Origins of the Second World War* (London, 1961, 1963).

TEDDER, LORD, *Air Power in War*, The Lees-Knowles Lecture (Cambridge, 1947).

THYSSEN, F., *I Paid Hitler* (New York, 1941).

TIPPELSKIRSCH, K. VON, *Geschichte des zweiten Weltkriegs* (Bonn, 1951).

TREUE, W., 'Politische Kohle im ersten und zweiten Weltkrieg', *Welt als Geschichte*, 1951.

— *Wirtschaft und Politik, 1933–1945* (Braunschweig, 1953).

— ed., 'Hitlers Denkschrift zum Vierjahresplan', *Vierteljahrshefte für Zeitgeschichte*, 1955.

— *Gummi in Deutschland. Die deutsche Kautschuksversorgung und Gummi-Industrie im Rahmen weltwirtschaftlicher Entwicklungen* (München, 1955).

— 'Gummi in Deutschland zwischen 1933 und 1945', *Wehrwissenschaftliche Rundschau*, vol. 5, 1955.

TREVOR-ROPER, H. R., *The Last Days of Hitler*, 3rd ed. (London, 1956).

— 'The Responsibility for Germany's Defeat', *The Wiener Library Bulletin*, no. 3, 1949.

— ed., *The Bormann Letters* (London, 1954).

— 'Hitlers Kriegsziele', *Vierteljahrshefte für Zeitgeschichte*, vol. 8, 1960.

— 'Hitlers Testament. Die letzten Gespräche mit Bormann (Februar 1945)', *Monat*, vol. 14, 1961.

UDET, E., *Ein Fliegerleben*, ed. J. Thorwald (Berlin, 1954).

UNITED STATES BUREAU OF THE BUDGET, *The United States at War. Development and Administration of the War Program by the Federal Government* (Washington D.C., 1946).

UNITED STATES, DEPARTMENT OF WAR, INTELLIGENCE DIV., *German Army Mobilisation* (Washington, D.C., 1946).

UNITED STATES, OFFICE OF STRATEGIC SERVICES, RESEARCH AND ANALYSIS BRANCH, Civil Affairs Handbook, Germany, Section 27, Government and Administration, *Economic Control in Nazi Germany* (Washington D.C. 1946).

VERMEIL, E., *Doctrinaires de la révolution allemande 1919–1938* (Paris, 1939).

— *L'Allemagne contemporaine, sociale, politique et culturelle, 1890–1950*, 2 vols (Paris, 1953).

— 'Réflexions sur les mémoires du Dr. Schacht', *Politique étrangère*, vol. 15, 1950.

VIERTELJAHRSHEFTE FÜR ZEITGESCHICHTE, 'Der Generalplan Ost', *Vierteljahrshefte für Zeitgeschichte*, 1958.

VULLIEZ, A., *Analyse des conférences navales du Führer* (Paris, 1949).

WEBSTER, SIR C. and FRANKLAND, N., *The Strategic Air Offensive Against Germany, 1939–1945*, 4 vols., History of the Second World War, United Kingdom, Military Series (London, H.M.S.O., 1961).

WEHRWISSENSCHAFTLICHE RUNDSCHAU, 'Verluste der deutschen Wehrmacht (Heer, Kriegsmarine, Luftwaffe) vom 1.9.1939 bis 31.1.1945', vol. 12, 1962.

BIBLIOGRAPHY

WEINBERG, G., *Germany and the Soviet Union, 1939–1941*, Studien zur Geschichte Osteuropas, vol. 1 (London, 1954).

WELTER, E., *Der Weg der deutschen Industrie* (Frankfurt-am-Main, 1943).

— *Falsch und richtig Planen. Eine kritische Studie über die deutsche Wirtschaftslenkung im zweiten Weltkrieg*, Veröffentlichungen des Forschungsinstituts für Wirtschaftspolitik an der Universität Mainz, no. 1 (Heidelberg, 1954).

WHEATLEY, R., *Operation Sea-Lion* (Oxford, 1958).

WILMOT, C., *The Struggle for Europe* (London, 1952).

WITTEKIND, K., 'Aus 20 Jahren deutscher Wehrwirtschaft', *Wehrkunde*, vol. 6, 1957.

WOLFE, M., 'The development of Nazi monetary policy', in *Journal of Economic History*, vol. 15, 1955.

WOREMANN, E., *Schaubilder zur deutschen und europäischen Ernährungswirtschaft* (Berlin, 1944).

ZIEGELMAYER, W., *Rohstofffragen der deutschen Volksernährung* (Dresden and Leipzig, 1941).

ZIMMERMANN, W., *Deutschland und der Norden* (Lübeck and Berlin, 1941).

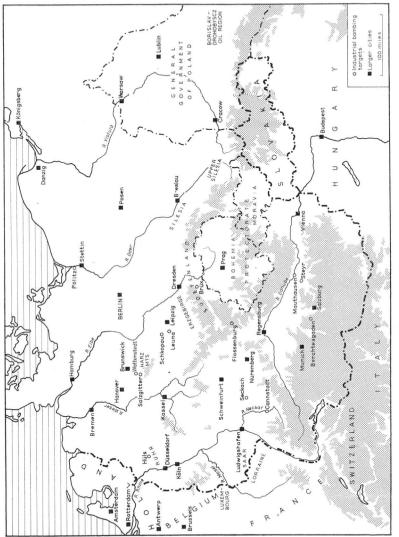

Germany in 1939–45

INDEX